# Inhabitants of Frederick County Maryland

## Volume 1
## 1750-1790

### Stefanie R. Shaffer

HERITAGE BOOKS
2006

# HERITAGE BOOKS

*AN IMPRINT OF HERITAGE BOOKS, INC.*

## Books, CDs, and more—Worldwide

For our listing of thousands of titles see our website
at
www.HeritageBooks.com

Published 2006 by
HERITAGE BOOKS, INC.
Publishing Division
65 East Main Street
Westminster, Maryland 21157-5026

Other books by the author:

*Inhabitants of Frederick County, Maryland, Volume 2: 1749-1800*

International Standard Book Number: 978-1-888265-84-1

# CONTENTS

# INTRODUCTION

The main purpose of this book is to aid in the location of an ancestor in respect to time and place. The following lists contain the names of several thousand Frederick Countians who lived in the county during the period, 1750-1790. The author has included a wide range of records held by the Maryland State Archives. The identifying Archives Accession Numbers are included with each list.

Most of the lists are self explanatory. A few words need to be said regarding the following lists:

**1761 Tax List** - In using the 1761 Tax List for Old Town and Sugarland Hundreds note that the tax act of 1712 stated that all male persons and all female slaves of the age of 16 or above shall be accounted taxable except clergymen and such poor people as receive alms from the county and all such slaves as adjudged to be past labour. Although excluded as a non-taxable, the name of a white woman may appear on these lists, in which case we would assume her to be the owner.

**Estrays** - The list of estrays refers to persons who have in their custody stray animals (horses, cows, pigs, sheep, etc.). The law required individuals to report this fact shortly after the animal strayed onto the farm.

**Levy lists** - This list refers to payments made by the county court. The actual amount of the payment has been omitted in these abstracts. At certain periods a bounty was paid to persons for the killing of wolves, squirrels, bears, crows and other animals. Many persons who did not own property and would otherwise not appear public records may appear on these lists.

There is a great wealth of genealogy to be found in court records beyond that covered here. Occasionally a relationship is revealed, a date of death or other bits of information not found elsewhere. The author plans to continue her exploitation of these records in future volumes with a second volume for Frederick County planned for the immediate future.

F. Edward Wright
Westminster, Maryland
1998

# PETITION FOR A ROAD

*From the Judgements Records of 1749, Frederick County:*
"Sundry of the Inhabitants of Linganore and Sams Creeks preferr to ... necessity of a road to be cleared from the Chaple which the sd Inhabitants is now building between the Drafts of Linganore and the Drafts of Sams Creek to the main Waggon Road from Annapolis to Fredk Town and to fall in to sd road neer Mr. Edward and Willm. Bettys... Signed: John Phillips, Joseph Wood, John Carmack, Jno. Howard son of Gideon, Phillip Howard Juner, Stephen Richard, Pattrick Holligan (his mark), Daniel Sings, Daniel Ryan, Darby Ryan, William Carmack, John Justice Junr., Thos. Wiles, Rubin Phillips, John Williams, Jacob Nicholas, John Willes, Arch'l Cambill, John Justis Senior, Mounst Justice, James Brown, Mathyas Stallcup, Robert Burchfield, Solomon Sparks, James Mackdanl, William Lacefield, Charles Wood, John Brightwell, Richard Combs Senr., Richard Combs Junr., Denis Ensey."

This petition was granted. Major Henry Munday and Captain John Middagh were appointed to "view the places and lay out the roads."

# FREDERICK COUNTY COURT RECORDS 1750

*Maryland Archives C 773-1 1/41/6/39 and C 773-2 1/41/6/40*

Province vs. Anne Welles. Welles described as a widow "late of Frederick County". Sheriff George Gordon to bring her to March Court 1751 if she is to be found.

William Munfoord, farmer of Frederick Co. to appear in March Court 1750 to answer to the complaint of George Gordon, Esq.

William Munfoord, farmer of Frederick Co. to appear in March Court 1750 to answer to the complaint of Robert Dunlop and Thomas Dunlop.

William Leakey, planter of Frederick Co. to appear in March Court 1750 to answer to the complaint of John Ross, gentleman of the City of Annapolis, to whom Leakey owed money.

Thomas Douthit, farmer of Frederick Co. to appear in March Court 1750 to answer to the complaint of Abraham Miller.

Neal Ogullion, farmer of Frederick Co. to appear March Court 1750 to answer to the complaint of Francis Porter.

Owen McDonald, farmer of Frederick Co. to appear in March Court 1750 to answer to the complaint of Richard Smith.

Edward Wyatt, taylor of Frederick Co. to appear in March Court 1750 to answer to the complaint of Aaron Price.

Abraham Miller, farmer of Frederick Co. to appear in March Court 1750 to answer to the complaint of Thomas Douthit.

John Hopkins, Senr., planter of Frederick Co. to appear in March Court 1750 to answer to the complaint of Humprey Batts.

Lockland Winters, planter of Frederick Co. to appear in March Court 1750 to answer to the complaint of Richard Snowden, to whom Winters owed money.

Francis Spicer, planter of Frederick Co., previously of Prince Georges Co., to appear in March Court 1750 to answer to the complaint of Richard Snowden, to whom Spicer owed money.

Thomas Anderson, blacksmith of Frederick Co., otherwise called Thomas Anderson of Anteatum in Prince Georges Co., to appear in March Court 1750 to answer to the complaint of Richard Snowden, to whom Anderson owed money.

Peter Bumgardner, planter of Frederick Co. to appear in March Court 1750 to answer to the complaint of Richard Snowden, to whom Bumgardner owed money.

Darby Ryan, farmer of Frederick Co. to appear in March Court 1750 to answer to the complaint of Richard Snowden.

Evan Shelby, farmer of Frederick Co. to appear in March Court 1750 to answer to the complaint of Nathan Wells.

Evan Shelby, Senr., farmer of Frederick Co. to appear in March Court 1750 to answer to the complaint of William Beall.

John Bell, farmer of Frederick Co. to appear in March Court 1750 to answer to the complaint of Philip Kence, to whom Bell owed money.

Edward Sprigg, Junr., planter of Frederick Co., to appear in March Court 1750 to answer to the complaint of Samuel Duvall and Garah Davis. Sprigg assaulted Duvall and Davis in Frederick Co.

Patrick Halligan, farmer of Frederick Co. to appear in March Court 1750 to answer to the complaint of Abraham Miller.

George Scott, plaintiff vs. Thomas Hunt. James Dickson, William Wilburn and Eleazor Hunt to appear in March Court 1750 to testify for Scott.

Henry Wades, plaintiff vs. Michael Hodgkis. Unckle Unckles to appear in March Court 1751 to testify for Wades.

Thomas Cresap, Admin. of Wm. Griffith, plaintiff vs. George Croghan. Edward Wyat and Elizabeth Mitchel to appear in March Court 1751 to testify for Cresap.

George Gordon, plaintiff vs. Thomas Willet. Archebald More to appear in March Court 1751 to testify for Willet.

Martin Adams, plaintiff vs. Thomas Kelly. Joseph Robonet, John Land, John

McFadden and Kennedy Farrell to appear in March Court 1751 to testify for Kelly.

James Gore, plaintiff vs. Wodsworth Wilson. Mary Gallon, Jane Gore and Mary Allison to appear in March Court 1751 to testify for Gore.

Thomas Conn, plaintiff vs. Jno. Tenny and Henry Poulson. William Beall, Senr., John Ramsey and John Johnson to appear in March Court 1751 to testify for the plaintiff.

William Williams, plaintiff vs. James Fowler. John McFadden and Rachel Vandevour to appear in March Court 1751 to testify for Fowler.

William House, plaintiff vs. Henry Touchstone. Richard Touchstone to appear in March Court 1751 to testify for the defendant.

Garah Davis, plaintiff vs. Edward Sprigg, Junr. William Luckett, John Norris the third, and Samuel Duvall to appear in March Court 1750 to testify for Davis.

Joseph Volgemore, farmer of Frederick Co. to appear in March Court 1751. "Case for selling liquors by small m---."

Leonard Albright, farmer of Frederick Co. to appear in March Court 1751. Offense: neglected duty as overseer of the High Way.

Nathaniel Curry, farmer of Frederick Co. to appear in March Court 1751. Offense: breach of peace.

John Rench, farmer of Frederick Co. to appear in March Court 1751. Offense: assaulted Col. Thomas Cresap.

Henry Cain, planter of Frederick Co. to appear in March Court 1751. Offense: swearing.

Rachel Sprigg, Ex. of Osburn Sprigg, deceased, plaintiff vs. William Norris. John Davis and James Dickson to appear in March Court 1750 to testify for Norris.

William Cumming, plaintiff, vs. Henry Gaither. Susanna Starr, wife of William Starr to appear in March Court 1750 to testify for Cumming.

Samuel Duvall, plaintiff vs. Edward Sprigg, Junr. William Luckitt, John Norris the third and Garah Davis to appear in March Court 1750 to testify for Duvall.

William Williams, plaintiff vs. Hugh Gilliland. Rees Price and Sarah Price to appear in March Court 1750 to testify for Williams. Court to be held at the dwelling house of Kennedy Farrell in Frederick Town.

James Gore, plaintiff vs. Hendrick Allison. Ezekiel Gosling, Nathan Veach, and Wadswoth Wilson to appear in March Court 1750 to testify for Gore.

Rees Price, plaintiff vs. Elias Alexander. Revd. William Williams to appear in March Court 1750 to testify for Price.

Lord Proprietary, plaintiff vs. Leonard Albright. Jonathan Hager to appear in March Court 1750 to testify for the plaintiff.

Lord Proprietary, plaintiff vs. Nathl. Curry. Thomas Fletchell to appear in March

Court 1750 to testify for the plaintiff.

Lord Proprietary, plaintiff vs. Joseph Volgamout. John Alum to appear in March Court 1750 to testify for the plaintiff.

Lord Proprietary, plaintiff vs. Henry Cain or Henry Rench. [Henry Cain in body of note, but on back, Cain crossed out and "Rench" written in] Thomas Cresap to appear in March Court 1750 to testify for plaintiff.

Lord Proprietary, plaintiff vs. Michell Risener. John Youngblood to appear in March Court 1750 to testify for the plaintiff.

Richard Beaman, farmer of Frederick Co. to appear in March Court 1751. Offense: felony?. [very hard to read]

Ann Cramptin, spinster of Frederick Co. to appear in March Court 1751. Offense: bastardy.

Mary Hall, spinster of Frederick Co. to appear in March Court 1751. Offense: bastardy.

Mary Jackson, spinster of Frederick Co. to appear in March Court 1751. Offense: bastardy.

Eleanor David, spinster of Frederick Co. to appear in March Court 1751. Offense: bastardy.

Rebecca Wray, spinster of Frederick Co. to appear in March Court 1751. Offense: bastardy.

Phillis Wilson, spinster of Frederick Co. to appear in March Court 1751. Offense: bastardy.

Alexander Wells, farmer of Frederick Co. to appear in March Court 1751. Offense: can't read offense, mentions "Clark" from Virginia.

Christopher Elrode, plaintiff vs. Thomas Douthel. Chidley Mathens to appear in March Court 1750 to testify for Elrode.

Rees Price vs. Samuel Harden. Sarah Selby to appear in March Court 1750 to testify for Price.

Revd. William Williams, plaintiff, vs. James Fowler. Moses Chapline to appear in March Court 1750 to testify for Williams.

John Youngblood, plaintiff vs. Michael Reisner. Mary Ringle, Joseph Hardman, and Boston Tyeshue to appear in March Court 1750 to testify for Youngblood.

Mathew Edwards, plaintiff vs. William Plummer. Thomas Fletcher to appear in March Court 1750 to testify for Edwards.

Rachel Sprigg, Ex. of Osburn Sprigg, vs. John Beall Taylor. Lodowick Davis to appear in March Court 1750 to testify for Taylor.

William May, taylor of Frederick Co. to appear in March Court 1751. Offense: May owed money, apparently to the Province.

Nathan Peadycoart, planter and inn keeper of Frederick Co. to appear in March Court 1751. Peadycoart owed money and tobacco to Matthus Hopkins and

Co.

John Russell, planter of Frederick Co. and Enoch Robinson, planter of Frederick Co. to appear in March Court 1751 to answer to a complaint of Thomas Fletchall. Fletchall claimed that Russell and Robinson owed him money. Note made May 23, 1749. Daniel Dulany, Jr. acted as attorney for Thomas Fletchall.

Andrew Cotterall vs. Isaac Harris of Frederick Co., planter. (March Court 1751)

Nicholas Tavers, schoolmaster of Frederick Co. to appear in March Court 1751 to answer to the complaint of Isaac Risteau.

John Compton, laborer of Frederick Co. to appear in March Court 1751 to answer to the complaint of Richard Smith.

John Keys, planter of Frederick Co. to appear in March Court 1751 to answer to the complaint of Richard Smith.

Joseph Johnston, farmer of Frederick Co., Peter Bonnet, farmer of Frederick Co., Joseph Mounts, farmer of Frederick Co., John Nicholls, farmer of Frederick Co., and Andrew House, farmer of Frederick Co. to appear in March Court 1751 to answer to the complaint of Rachel Sprigg, Ex. of Osburn Sprigg, deceased.

John Lecroy and Lukus Lecroy, planters of Frederick Co. to appear in March Court 1751 to answer to the complaint of Basil Pearl.

Thomas Hawkins, planter of Frederick Co. to appear in March Court 1751. Offense: owed money, apparently to the province.

Peter Laney or Teter Laney, farmer of Frederick Co. to appear in March Court 1751. Offense: owed money, apparently to the province.

Leonard Johnston, lawyer of Frederick Co. to appear in March Court 1751 to answer to the complaint of George Bowles.

Philemnon Church, schoolmaster, to appear in March Court 1751 to answer to a complaint of Nathaniel Knott.

John Foard, farmer of Frederick Co. to appear in March Court 1751 to answer to a complaint of John Ruter.

Neal Ogullion, farmer of Frederick Co. to appear in March Court 1751 to answer to a complaint of William Ervin, Ex. of Joseph Ervin, deceased.

John Jones, farmer of Frederick Co. to appear in March Court 1751 to answer to a complaint that he owed money to the Lord Proprietary and to Evan Shelby.

Heptoe ? Clark, planter of Frederick Co. to appear in March Court 1751 to answer to the complaint of Henry Cower.

Arden Evans, planter of Frederick Co. to appear in March Court 1751 to answer to the complaint of Daniel Carroll, to whom Evans owed money.

Edward Davis, planter of Frederick Co. to appear in March Court 1751 to answer to a complaint of Rachel Sprigg, Ex. of Osburn Sprigg, deceased of Prince Georges County, to whom Davis owed money.

Mathew Howard, planter of Frederick Co. to appear in March Court 1751 to answer to a complaint of James Walker, to whom Howard owed money.

Samuel Wells, planter of Frederick Co. to appear in March Court 1751. Offense: owed money, apparently to the province.

Peter Williams, laborer of Frederick Co. to appear in March Court 1751. Offense: owed money, apparently to the province.

Samuel Beall, Senr. to appear in March Court 1751 to answer to the complaint of Ignatius Digges and John Hepburn.

John Foard, weaver of Frederick Co., otherwise called John Foard, weaver of Cecil Co., to appear in March Court 1751 to answer to the complaint of James Baxter to whom Foard owed money.

Call for jurors from Frederick Co. for George Gordon vs. Thomas Willet. Jurors: Van Swearingen, Dav. Cox, De. Chaney, Lu. Lecroy, Conrad O--tts, Micaj. Plummer, Jno. Jones, P. Butler, J. Harrison, Nick. Bundrick, and Jas. Harrington.

James Cumpton, plaintiff, vs. Henry Davis. Samuel Duvall and William Davis to appear in March Court 1751 to testify for Davis.

William Cumming, plaintiff vs. Henry Gaither. Thomas Newman Roden, Deboror Jones wife of John Jones, Jno. Barber and Frances Hartley to testify for Gaither. Jno. Barber also to appear in March Court 1751 to testify for William Cumming. Samuel Ridgley was also to testify, but it was not stated for which party.

Mary Frederick, plaintiff vs. Matthew Edwards. Edwd. Macken to appear in March Court 1751 to testify for Frederick.

Michael Reisner to appear in March Court 1750 to answer to a complaint of Philip Kinse.

Nicholas Bundrick, merchant of Frederick Co. to appear in March Court 1751 to answer to the complaint of Daniel Jessarang.

William Flintham, farmer of Frederick Co. to appear in March Court 1750 to answer to the complaint of John Beresford.

Nicholas Bundrick, merchant of Frederick Co., otherwise known as Nicholas Bundrick, of Prince Georges County, to appear in March Court 1751 to answer to the complaint of Jacob Collyday, to whom Bundrick owed money. On April 13, 1748, Bundrick made a note with Collyday, but later failed to pay. Henry Darnall acted as attorney for Collyday.

Griffith Davis, planter of Frederick Co. to appear in March Court 1751 to answer to the complaint of Richard Snowden and Richard Thomas, Executors of John Thomas, of Frederick Co. deceased. Davis owed tobacco to the estate.

David Forbes, farmer of Frederick Co. to appear in March Court 1751 to answer to the complaint of Andrew Scott.

William Elrod and Christopher Elrod, farmers of Frederick Co. to appear in

March Court 1751 to answer to the complaint of Richard Dorsey.

John Brensler, blacksmith of Frederick Co. to appear in March Court 1751 to answer to the complaint of Andrew Tannyhill.

Thomas Thompson, planter of Frederick Co. to appear in March Court 1751 to answer to the complaint of Richard Snowden and Richard Thomas, Executors of John Thomas deceased. Thompson owed tobacco to the estate.

John Beall, son of Ninian Beall, planter of Frederick Co. to appear in March Court 1751 to answer to the complaint of Benja. Brookes, to whom Beall owed money.

Joseph Robinson, farmer of Frederick Co. and Sarah Robinson his wife, to appear in March Court 1751 to answer to the complaint of William Aldred.

Alexander Waddall, farmer of Frederick Co. to appear in March Court 1751 to answer to the complaint of John Douthit.

Peter Butler, scrivener of Frederick Co. to appear in March Court 1751 to answer to the complaint of William Fee.

William Wilkey, planter of Frederick Co. to appear in March Court 1751 to answer to the complaint of Richard Dorsey to whom Wilkey owed money.

Nicholas Bundrick, inn holder of Frederick Co. to appear in March Court 1751 to answer to the complaint of Deval Shaver to whom Bundrick owed money.

Philip Griever, farmer of Frederick Co. to appear in March Court 1751 to answer to the complaint of Robert Debutts, to whom Griever owed money.

Jonathan Hagar, blacksmith of Frederick Co. to appear in March Court 1751 to answer to the complaint of Leonard Albright.

Isaac Rees, mason of Frederick Co. also known as Isaac Rees, mason of ? Township, Lancaster Co., PA, to appear in March Court 1751 to answer to the complaint of Joseph Ambrose, to whom Rees owed money. [unable to read name of township]

Robert Perle, planter of Frederick Co. to appear in March Court 1751 to answer to the complaint of David Linn.

Jno. Larkin, Ex. of Pk. McMullen, plaintiff vs. Richard Touchstone. Thomas Johnson and Caleb Touchstone to appear in March Court 1751 to testify for Larkin.

Wm. Slade and others, plaintiffs vs. Thomas Maynard. Chloe Mobberly, Thomas Beatty's wife [unnamed] and Darby Ryan to appear in March Court 1751 to testify for Maynard.

James Burges and others, plaintiffs vs. Joseph Hill. Jacob Vantrease and his wife [unnamed] to appear in March Court 1751 to testify for Burges.

Jacob Fry, plaintiff vs. Phillm. Church and Abraham Miller. Daniel Miller and Frances Miller to appear in March Court 1751 to testify for Fry. [no relationships stated for the Millers]

Joseph Chapline, plaintiff vs. Arthur Charlton. James Mar, Charles Chaney,

Senr. and William Welsh to appear in March Court 1751 to testify for Chapline.

Rees Price, plaintiff vs. Elias Alexander. Joseph Chapline, Alexander Staret and Hugh Barnell to appear in March Court 1751 to testify for Price.

William Cumming, plaintiff vs. Henry Gaither. John Morbley to appear in March Court 1751 to testify for Gaither; another summons stated that John Mobberly [different spelling] was to testify for Cumming . In a summons for William Cumming himself to appear in court for his own case; he was described as an overseer.

Richard Coombes, plaintiff vs. John Jones. Charles Wood and Richard Coombes, Junr. to appear in March Court 1751 to testify for Coombes.

Thomas Scarlit, farmer of Frederick Co. to appear in March Court 1751 to answer to the complaint of Joseph Henley. On October 17, 1747, William Kagel was living in Maryland and "using commerce within the province of Maryland to wit at Frederick County". Kagel made a bill in writing that required Thomas Scarlett [different spelling] to pay to Joseph Henley 600 pounds of tobacco. Scarlett failed to deliver the tobacco. A complaint was filed March 19, 1750. Another document stated that Edward Dorsey acted as attorney for Henley, and that Scarlett was a farmer.

Stephen Julian, farmer of Frederick Co. to appear in March Court 1750 to answer to the complaint of Thomas Cresap to whom Julian owed money.

Hendrick Allison, planter of Frederick Co. to appear in March Court 1750 to answer to the complaint of James Gore.

Isaac Rue/ Isaac Rew, farmer of Frederick Co. to appear in March Court 1750 to answer to the complaint of Col. Thomas Cresap, to whom Rue owed money.

Abington George Colvell, planter of Frederick Co. to appear in March Court 1750 to answer to the complaint of George Gordon, Esq. James Dickson served the summons on February 19, 1750.

Evan Shelby, farmer of Frederick Co. to appear in March Court 1750 to answer to the complaint of Thomas Beall.

Patrick Matthews, farmer of Frederick Co. to appear in March Court 1750 to answer to the complaint of Col. Thomas Cresap, to whom Matthews owed money.

John Cramphin and Kennedy Farrell, inn holders of Frederick Co. to appear in March Court 1750 to answer to the complaint of John Hepburn, to whom they owed money.

Aquilla Cumpton of Frederick Co. to appear in March Court 1750 to answer to the complaint of Nathaniel Correy.

John Champion, carpenter of Frederick Co. to appear in March Court 1750 to answer to the complaint of John Evans.

Thomas Locker, planter of Frederick Co. to appear in March Court 1750 to answer to the complaint of Alexander Lamar. [isssued by Daniel Dulany and John Darnall]

William Davis, farmer of Frederick Co. to appear in March Court 1750 for assaulting Joseph Skidmore.

Wadsworth Wilson, planter of Frederick Co., and Eleanor Wilson his wife, to appear in March Court 1750 to answer to the complaint of James Gore.

William Harrison, planter of Frederick Co. to appear in March Court 1750 to answer to the complaint of Griffith Davis, Junr.

William Elrod, farmer of Frederick Co. to appear in March Court 1750 to answer to the complaint of James Read.

Ann Prather, widow of Frederick Co. to appear in March Court 1750 to answer to the complaint of Robert Dunlop and Thomas Dunlop.

Neal Ogullion, farmer of Frederick Co. to appear in March Court 1750 to answer to the complaint of John Foard.

Stephen Julian, farmer of Frederick Co., and John Clabaugh, farmer of Frederick Co. to appear in March Court 1751 to answer to the complaint of Joseph Wood. Julian and Clabaugh made a note to Wood October 27, 1747 at Frederick Co., but later failed to repay the note. A complaint was filed February 12, 1750. Daniel Dulaney, Junr. acted as attorney for Wood. Julian and Clabaugh to appear in March Court 1750.

John Prather, son of William, planter of Frederick Co. to appear in March Court 1750 to answer to the complaint of Griffith Davis, Junr.

Nathaniel Curry, farmer of Frederick Co. to appear in March Court 1750 to answer to the complaint of Silas Enyard.

Neal Ogulion, farmer of Frederick Co. to appear in March Court 1750 to answer to the complaint of George Gordon.

Thomas Douthit, farmer of Frederick Co. to appear in March Court 1750 to answer to the complaint of Mary Simms, administratrix of the late Cleburn Simms. Cleburn Simms died intestate in Frederick Co.

John Biggs, planter of Frederick Co. to appear in March Court 1750 to answer to the complaint of Gamaliel Butler.

Joseph Belt, son of John, planter of Frederick Co. to appear in March Court 1750 to answer to the complaint of Phillip Hammond.

Bigger Head, planter of Frederick Co., previously of Calvert Co.,MD, to appear in March Court 1750 to answer to the complaint of Kensey Johns and William Harris, administrators of Benjamin Johns. Benjamin Johns, deceased, of Calvert Co. The page has a hole in it, but also mentioned are Kensey Johns, Benjamin Johns and Richard Johns, whom apparently are owed money by Head, according to the will of Benjamin Johns.

Lucas Lecroy, Junr., farmer of Frederick Co. to appear in March Court 1750 to answer to the complaint of Lucas Lecroy. [no generation designation after the second Lecroy, back of the summons states that the case is between "L. Lecroy and L. Lecroy, Junr.]

John Lecroy, farmer of Frederick Co. to appear in March Court 1750 to answer to the complaint of Lucas Lecroy.

Peter Smith, blacksmith of Frederick Co. to appear in March Court 1750 to answer to the complaint of George Grafe.

Paul Noland, planter of Frederick Co. to appear in March Court 1750 to answer to the complaint of William Ross.

George Brown, farmer of Frederick Co. to appear in March Court 1750 to answer to the complaint of Thomas Cresap.

James Hearnden, planter of Frederick Co., to appear in March Court 1750 to answer to the complaint of Henry Maroney.

John Wagwood, planter of Frederick Co., formerly of Anne Aurndel Co., to appear in March Court 1750 to answer to the complaint of Richard Snowden, to whom Wagwood owed money.

Daniel Williams, planter of Frederick Co., formerly of Prince Georges Co., MD, to appear in March Court 1750 to answer to the complaint of Richard Snowden, to whom Williams owed money.

John Thomas, planter of Frederick Co., to appear in March Court 1750 to answer to the complaint of James Douglas.

William Rickets, planter of Frederick Co. to appear in March Court 1750 to answer to the complaint of Richard Snowden, to whon Rickets owed money.

Ardin Evans, planter of Frederick Co., and Thomas Willet, planter of Frederick Co., both formerly of Prince Georges Co., MD, to appear in March Court 1750 to answer to the complaint of Richard Snowden, to whom they owed money.

Abington George Colvirl, planter of Frederick Co., formerly of Prince Georges Co., to appear in March Court 1750 to answer to the complaint of Richard Snowden, to whom Colvirl owed tobacco.

Alexander Mackcoy, planter of Frederick Co. to appear in March Court 1750 to answer to the complaint of Alexander Lamar.

Enoch Robinson, planter of Fredrick Co. to appear in March Court 1750 to answer to the complaint of Philip Key, Esq.

Neal Ogulion, farmer of Frederick Co. to appear in March Court 1751 to answer to the complaint of Thomas Chittam.

David Forbes, farmer of Frederick Co. to appear in March Court 1751 to answer to the complaint of William Cumming, Junr.

Wadsworth Wilson, planter of Frederick Co. to appear in March Court 1751 to answer to the complaint of James Gore.

John Tulse, planter of Frederick Co. to appear in March Court 1751 to answer to the complaint of James Mills.

James Tulse, planter of Frederick Co. to appear in March Court 1751 to answer to the complaint of James Mills.

Hugh Gilliland, farmer of Frederick Co. to appear in March Court 1751 to answer to the complaint of Rachel Sprigg, Ex. of Osborne Sprigg, deceased, to whom Gilliland owed tobacco.

Pierce Noland, planter of Frederick Co. to appear in March Court 1751 to answer to the complaint of Robert Peter.

George Dalyrmpel, farmer of Frederick Co to appear in March Court 1751 to answer to the complaint of John White.

Thomas Thomson, planter of Frederick Co., formerly of Prince Georges Co. to appear in March Court 1751 to answer to the complaint of David Ross, to whom Thomson owed tobacco.

William Ray, Junr., planter of Frederick Co. to appear in March Court 1751 to answer to the complaint of Anthony Smith, whom Ray assaulted.

Thomas Conn, plaintiff vs. Henry Poulson. Robert Patricks to appear in March Court 1751 to testify for Conn.

George Scott, plaintiff vs. Thomas Hunt. Robert Perle, John Delashmet and John Johnson Kittenton to appear in March Court 1751 to testify for Scott.

George Scott, plaintiff vs. Henry Foolney. Robert Perle, John Delashmet and John Johnson Killenton to appear in March Court 1751 to testify for Scott.

Matthew Edwards, plaintiff, vs. William Plummer. Elizabeth Smith and Charles Neal to appear in March Court 1751 to testify for Plummer.

Joseph Chapline, plaintiff vs. Arthur Charlton. William Flintham to appear in March Court 1751 to testify for Chapline.

Jno. Larkin, Admin. of Pk. McMullen, plaintiff vs. Richard Touchstone. Thomas Johnson to appear in March Court 1751 to testify for Larkin.

March Court 1750: George Gordon, Sheriff of Frederick Co. was to command the following to appear in court during that session:

* Robt. Ward.
* Samuel Shipley "to testify for Henry Wades agst. Michael Hodgkiss". [not clear for which party Shipley was to testify]
* [very faded] Thos. Wales "to testify for Jos. Chapline ag. Arthur Charlton." [not clear for which party Wales was to testify]
* John Purdom to testify for Henry Gaither, in William Cumming, Esq. vs. Henry Gaither.
* Henry Maroney to answer to the complaint of Mary Robinson immediately.
* Jno. Darling to testify for Charlton in Jos. Chapline vs. Arthur Charlton.
* Elizabeth Tyeshoe "to testify for John Youngblood against Michael Reisner."
* Christopher Lowndes to testify for Elias Alexander in Rees Price, plaintiff vs. Elias Alexander.

A note written on February 20, 1750 to John Hanson, Sheriff of Charles County from W. Cumming and R. Burdus, Clerk stated that Hauson was to command John Marr of Charles County to appear in March Court 1750 in Frederick Town to testify for the plaintiff. The case involved Joseph Chapline, plaintiff vs. Arthur Charlton. Witness: Benj. Young, Esq.

On October 30, 1749, Nicholas Bundrick borrowed money from Deval Shaver. Shaver filed a complaint that Bundrick had refused to repay the note. Daniel Dulany was the attorney for Shaver.

On August 11, 1750 in Frederick Co., David Forbes, farmer of Frederick Co. made an account with William Cummings, Junr. for sundry articles purchased. Cummings filed a complaint that Forbes had failed to repay the note. The items purchased by Forbes: thread, garlic, barber sisers [scissors], snaffle bridle, razor and case, large pins, medium pins, rum and nails.

Col. Edward Sprigg vs. David Cox of Frederick Co. Cox borrowed money on May 1, 1745; it was to be repaid on May 20, 1746. Sprigg filed a complaint that Cox did not intend to repay the money. Daniel Dulany, Junr., attorney for Sprigg. George Gordon, Sheriff, commanded to bring Cox to court in March 1751.

Ignatius Digges and John Hepburn, plaintiffs, vs Samuel Beall, Senr, planter of Frederick Co. Beall made a note on May 1, 1745 to Digges and Hepburn, due June 19, 1750. Digges and Hepburn filed a complaint that Beall had refused to pay the money and tobacco that he owed.

Silas Pew, plaintiff vs. Joseph Johnson. Johnson, a farmer, late of Frederick Co., known as "Joseph Johnson of the City of Parthlimboy, Eastern Division of the Province of East New Jersey, Coardwain in the County of Middlesex". On August 14, 1741 at Frederick Co., Johnson made a note with Pew, which later he pailed to repay. Daniel Dulany, attorney for Pew.

John Hepburn, plaintiff vs. Conrod Keller. Keller a farmer of Frederick Co. Henry Darnall, attorney for Hepburn, stated that Keller made a note to Hepburn on March 21, 1749 at Frederick Co. Note to be repaid May 1, 1750. Keller failed to repay the note; a complaint was filed. William Cumming and Isaac Brooke witnessed the note. Sheriff George Gordon was to command Keller to appear in March Court 1751.

Rachel Sprigg, Ex. of Osburn Sprigg, deceased, vs. James Ellis, planter of Frederick Co. Ellis made a note to Osburn Sprigg on April 4, 1748 in Frederick Co. for tobacco. Ellis failed to repay the note; a complaint was filed. Henry Darnall acted as attorney for Rachel Sprigg. George Gordon, Sheriff was to command Ellis to appear in March Court 1751.

Rachel Sprigg, Ex. of Osburn Sprigg, deceased of Prince Georges County, MD, vs. Van Swearingen, planter of Frederick Co. Swearingen made a note to Sprigg on October 11, 1749; the note was to be repaid on December 10, 1750. On December 11, 1750, a complaint was filed that Swearingen had failed to pay the note. Col. Beanes witnessed the note. Henry Darnall acted as attorney for Rachel Sprigg. George Gordon, Sheriff, was to command Swearingen to appear in March Court 1751.

Andrew Scott, plaintiff vs. David Forbes, farmer of Frederick Co. David Forbes purchased sundry items of Andrew Scott, including rum, sugar, and salt on August 11, 1750 in Frederick Co. Forbes later failed to repay Andrew Scott. George Scott acted as attorney for Andrew Scott. A complaint was filed December 4, 1750.

Robert Dunlop and Thomas Dunlop, plaintiffs, vs. William Munfoord. The account of William Munfoord stated that on October 22, 1750, he purchased Kersey, India Chintz, cotton, womens' stockings, mohair, small metal buttons, blue broad cloth, silk, a man's fine hat, Irish linen, indigo, and a chamber pot from the plaintiffs. A statement of the account was prepared on February 25, 1750/1 in Rock Creek by Andrew Heugh, who swore before Josi Beall on February 27, 1750/1 that it was accurate. On March 2, 1750, a complaint was filed that Munfoord had failed to repay the Dunlops. George Scott acted as attorney for the Dunlops.

David Linn, plaintiff vs. Alexander Lemar, planter of Frederick Co. On April 24, 1750 in Frederick Co., Lemar made a note to Linn. Thomas Holland witnessed the note. The note was due on October 1, 1750, but Lemar failed to pay. Edward Dorsey acted as attorney for Linn. A complaint was filed on November 29, 1750. George Gordon was to command Lemar to appear in March Court 1751.

Richard Dorsey of Anne Arundel Co., plaintiff, vs. William Wilkey, planter of Frederick Co. On October 28, 1749, Wilkey made a note to Richard Dorsey. Th. Johnson, Junr. and John Briscoe, Junr. witnessed the note. Wilkey later failed to pay the note which was due on October 27, 1750. A complaint was filed on November 29, 1750. Edward Dorsey acted as attorney for Richard Dorsey. The back of the note stated that Wilkey was a tenant of James Brooks and that he lived on Hawlings River.

Richard Snowden vs. John Cramptin of Prince Georges County, planter. Cramptin made a note on December 8, 1746 to deliver tobacco, to be repaid on May 1, 1747. Sam Snowden and Capt. Holland witnessed the note. Cramptin failed to deliver the tobacco, and a complaint was filed on January 24, 1750. Edward Dorsey acted as attorney for Snowden. George Gordon, Sheriff was to command Cramptin to appear in March Court 1750.

Court Appearance Paper prepared November 23, 1751 by Jno. Darnall, Clerk and Daniel Dulany, Chief Justice. George Gordon to command Anthony Smith "late of Frederick Co. taylor, otherwise called Anthony Smith of Frederick County in the province aforesaid planter" to appear in March 1751 Court to answer to a complaint of William Cummings.

Court Appearance Paper November 27, 1749-- Prepared by Jno. Darnall, Clerk Nathaniel Wickham, Junr. Justice. George Gordon, Sheriff to command William Waters, planter of Frederick Co. to appear in March Court 1750 to testify. "Case for not Ret. [returning] in his list one of Saul Selby's taxa. [taxables]."

Matthew Hopkins and Co., plaintiff vs. Nathan Peddycoart, inn keeper of Frederick Co. On February 28, 1749, Peddycoart made a note with Hopkins in Frederick Co. to pay money and tobacco. Peddycoart failed to repay the note. A complaint was filed on August 30, 1750. Henry Darnall acted as attorney for Hopkins.

Andrew Tannehill, planter of Prince Georges County, bound himself to Charles Carroll of Annapolis for 53 pounds current money on October 20, 1744. Witnesses: C. Croxall and Matthr. Coen. In 1750, Tannehill was in Frederick Co. A complaint was filed on February 27, 1750 against Andrew Tannehill, innholder of Frederick Co., also known as Andrew Tannehill, planter of Prince Georges County. Tannehill had failed to repay the note. Daniel Dulaney, Jr. acted as attorney for Carroll.

George Colvin, plaintiff vs. William Capes, also spelled William Kippis. Capes had failed to repay Colvin for items he bought on credit. On September 18, 1750, Capes purchased: one horse, a man's saddle, a man's leather tackett, women's stockings, "a cap handkerchief", one pair of men's shoes, a pair of buckles and stockings, one falling ax, one grubing hoe, one horse bell, one pair of leather britches, and 3 pecks of salt. A complaint was filed on December 1, 1750.

Robt. Dunlop and Thos. Dunlop vs. Pharoch Riley. The Dunlops had extended credit to Riley between April 18, 1749 and August 1, 1749 for: one man's castor hat, powder, fabric, a man's felt hat, rum, a dozen fish hooks, and a snaffle bridle. The account also showed that Robert Peter had accepted 522 pounds of tobacco from Osborn Sprigg, Esq. Jno. Needham took the statement of account from Peter. A complaint was filed on November 20, 1750 when it was discovered that Riley had moved from his place of abode.

Note of John Hathman, made May 9, 1747 in Charles County. Hathman agreed to pay George Maxwell 521 pounds of merchantable tobacco on July 1, 1747. Between May 9, 1747 and January 27, 1748, Hathman purchase the following items on credit, apparently in Charles County: fabric, rum, salt, a felt hat, paper, pepper, a pint mug, needles and pins, 2 thimbles, sugar, a razor, an ivory comb, a castor hat, knives and forks, garlic, and a hair syfter. Statement of account taken on June 9, 1750 before Allen Davies. The account also stated that John Harrison paid on an account in 1748.

On November 17, 1744, Thos. Dulany made a note for two pounds and ten shillings current money due to Elias Delashmutt on May 10, 1745. Dulany apparently failed to repay the note. On February 11, 1750, a complaint was filed after it had been discovered that Dulany had "absconded from the place of his abode".

Mattias Pooley, plaintiff vs. William Lakey. Lakey owed Pooley 218 pounds of tobacco, 4 barrels of Indian Corn and three shillings. Lakey had removed from his last place of abode, such that the usual process of law could not be served upon him.

A statement taken before Joseph Chapline on November 21, 1750 stated that Pharoch Riley owed money to Hugh Riley. Pharoch Riley had "absconded and fled from justice." Pharoch Riley was described as a planter of Frederick Co. No mention of the relationship between Pharoch and Hugh Riley.

A statement taken before Jno. Needham on November 30, 1750 stated that Robert Peter had been informed that Arden Evans had "absconded from his last place of abode" and that he owed 2013 pounds of crop tobacco to Robert Dunlop and Thomas Dunlop. The following account of Arden Evans stated that he had purchased in September, October and November of 1750 these items: a fine hat, women's calf shoes, fabric, men's worsted stockings, one single channelled pump, a bridle, a set of buckles, rum, men's shoes, blue chintz, thread, pins, a fur hat band, and a pair of women's shoes. Also mentioned was James Beall, son of Ninian, and James Smith, blacksmith.

Statement taken before William Griffith: James Lee complained that John Baker [Robert Baker had been crossed out in two places, and John had been written in in both places] owed him money and tobacco. Complaint filed December 14, 1750.

Statement taken before Josi Beall: William Colvin owed tobacco to Robert Dunlop and Thomas Dunlop. The account of William Colvin stated that he had purchased the following items from August 1749 ? to February 1750: men's white thread stockings, men's gloves, women's gloves, chintz, buttons, silk handkerchiefs, Irish linen, men's worsted stockings, steel tobacco box, knee buckles, thread, a frying pan, a snaffle bridle, rum, pepper, woman's coarse shoes, a razor, ribbon, a knife, a man's fine hat, a dozen big buttons, and pins. A complaint was filed on February 16, 1750 after it had been learned that Colvin had removed from his place of abode.

Stephen Julian and John Clabaugh, farmers of Frederick Co. made a note to Joseph Wood on October 27, 1747, but later failed to repay it. A complaint was filed on February 12, 1750.

Transcript of case: Court held August 9, 1748 in Annapolis, Anne Arundel Co. Justices: James Monat, Chief Justice, Alexr. Warfield, son of Richard, John Bullen, Richard Dorsey, John Gassaway, Nicholas Gassaway, William Chapman, Junr., George Steuart, Thomas Jennings, and Humphrey Boone. Jno. Brice, Clerk. William Thornton, Sheriff. Thomas Harrison vs. Thomas

Reynolds. In a case from June 10, 1746, Thomas Reynolds, inn holder of Anne Arundel Co. undertook that if Thomas Harrison should receive judgement against William McClann, inn holder of Anne Arundel Co, that McClann should "render his body to the custody of the sheriff of Anne Arundel County". Harrsion did receive judgement against McClann. Edward Dorsey acted as attorney for Reynolds when Harrison later sued him.

John Bell, farmer of Frederick Co. made a note to Philip Kence on May 1, 1750 but later failed to pay. Henry Darnall acted as attorney for Kence. A complaint was filed January 15, 1751.

Transcript of case: Court held March 28, 1747? at Upper Marlboro, Prince Georges County. Justices: Henry Trueman, John Contee, Francis Waring, Richard Keene, Mordecai Jacob, John Hawkins, Junr. and Thomas Gantt, Junr. Also present: Edward Sprigg, James Russell, George Fraser, Peter Dent, and James Edmonston. Jacob Frye, plaintiff vs. John Cramphin. Cramphin an inn holder of Prince Georges County. In March of 1747, Cramphin made a note to Frye in Prince Georges County. Cramphin failed to repay the note. Thomas Clark acted as attorney for Frye. Judgement for Frye. Filed in Frederick Co. March 22, 1750.

Edward Wyatt, taylor of Frederick Co. made a note to Aaron Price on November 27, 1750 at Frederick Co. Wyatt later failed to repay the note. A complaint was filed March 7, 1750 ?. Daniel Dulany acted as attorney for Price. Witness to the note was John Hammer ?, Junr.

Nicholas Bundrick, merchant of Frederick Co., formerly of Prince Georges Co. made a note to Jacob Coliday on April 13, 1748 at Frederick Co. Bundrick failed to repay the note. A complaint was filed January 15, 1750?.

John Cramphin, inn holder of Frederick Co., formerly a planter of Prince Georges Co. to appear in March 1750 Court to answer to the complaint of Richard Snowden, to whom Cramphin owed money. J. John Cramtin, planter of Prince Georges Co. made a note with Richard Snowden, inn holder for tobacco in Frederick Co. on December 8, 1746. The tobacco was to be delivered on May 1, 1747. Sam Snowden witnessed the note. Cramphin failed to deliver the tobacco. A complaint was filed on January 24, 1750.

Jacob Falkner, farmer of Frederick Co. made a note to George Kershner on March 23, 1748 at Frederick Co. Falkner failed to repay the note. A complaint was filed. William Cumming, Esq. acted as attorney for Kershner.

Abraham Miller made a note to Hugh Parker on August 16, 1749. Witness: P. Butler.

William Norres, farmer of Frederick Co. made a note to Nathaniel Curry on February 3, 1748 in Frederick Co. Norres failed to repay the note. A complaint was filed. Henry Darnall acted as attorney for Curry. According to another document, the note was apparently written to cover the costs of broad cloth and trimmings purchased of Curry.

Kennedy Farrell, innholder of Frederick Co., formerly of West Coller Twp., Chester Co., made a note to Griffith Evans on October 30, 1732 in Frederick Co. Farrell failed to repay the note. A complaint was filed. Mr. Gheselin filled in the blanks for this document. Edward Dorsey acted as sttorney for Evans.

Account of Batholomew Hallon from February 20, 1747 until November 1, 1748. Hallon purchased a man's fine hat, double channel pumps, 6 hand saw files, super fine cotton stockings, fabric, a joist, and a snaffle bridle. Hallon received a credit for 2 1/2 days work in the store. Another notation "To credit Stephenson and Neel". Errors excepted for Daniel Stephenson, signed Wm. Skyrin, Charles County, October 10, 1749. Daniel Stephenson and Thomas Jenifer appeared before Edmd. Sortus on October 11, 1749 in Charles Co.

John Hack made a note to Richard Touchstone on September 19, 1746 or 1748. Witness: Henry Touchstone. Hack failed to repay the note. Hack, a farmer of Frederick Co. was summoned to appear in November Court 1749 in Frederick Co. to answer to the complaint of Touchstone.

Silas Enyart and Stephen Julian made a note to John Middagh and Barbara Hufman on September 7, 1747. The note was to be repaid on September 7, 1748.

Thomas Charter, plaintiff, vs. John Jacobs. Jacobs ordered by the court to pay Charters 562 pounds of tobacco. Signed: Nathan Magruder, Jno. Needham, and Alex Beall. This file also contains the transcipt of the case, which was held in Prince Georges Co., with no mention of Frederick Co. Osburn Sprigg was mentioned as being the sheriff of Prince Georges Co. John Jacobs was described as a farmer of Prince Georges Co. Complaint filed November 27, 1750. Not stated exactly when dispute began.

Jacob Bare, and Abraham Miller, farmers of Frederick Co., made a note to Thomas Palmer on December 4, 1749. Bare and Miller failed to repay the note. Daniel Dulany, Junr. and Henry Darnall acted as attorneys for Palmer. A complaint was filed.

Note of Nathaniel Wickham, signed by his mark, "Pay the contents to Elias Bland, mercht. in London or Order Value rec'd of Hugh Roberts." Witnesses: Edwd. Cole and Luke Morris. Written in Maryland October 4, 1747. Front side of the note very difficult to read, but apparently it was a note payable to Nathaniel Wickham, Senr. from Nath. Wickham, Junr. Mentions: John Buckhanan, merchant in London to whom Wickham, Junr. owed money. A complaint was filed on March 23, 1749 by Elias Bland, against Nath. Wickham, Junr. for the settlement of his account.

John Clagett, gentleman of Frederick Co. made a note to Basil Waring in 1748 in Frederick Co. Clagett failed to repay the tobacco as stated in the note. A complaint was filed. Henry Darnall acted as attorney for Waring.

Nathaniel Beall, Senr., gentleman of Frederick Co. made a note to Stephen Bordley of Annapolis on October 19, 1748. Witness: Ble. Nicholson. Beall failed to repay the 1500 pounds of tobacco according to the terms of the note. A complaint was filed. Henry Darnall acted as attorney for Bordley.

Note of Nicholas Bundrick, merchant of Frederick Co. to Osburn Sprigg, Sheriff of Prince Georges Co. on November 23, 1749. Witness: Reverdy Ghiselin. Later, after the death of Osburn Sprigg, Rachel Sprigg, Ex. of Osburn Sprigg filed a complaint on March 26, 1750 that Bundrick had failed to repay the note. Henry Darnall acted as attorney for Sprigg.

Account of Benjamin Harris form March 27, 1749 until June 27, 1749 with George Hamilton. The debits to Harris' account included a payment of sterling cash, a payment to George Gordon, and the purchase of a gallon of rum. The credit to Harris' account was for 14 bushels of Indian corn. A statement of Harris' account was made on January 22, 1749 in Frederick Co. to George Gordon. Harris was described as a planter of Frederick Co. A complaint was filed about the account of Harris. Daniel Dulany, Junr. acted as attorney for Hamilton.

Neal Ogullion and Jeremiah Jack, farmers of Frederick Co., made an obligation to Charles Carroll on July 28, 1747 in Frederick Co. for tobacco, which was to be repaid on the eastern branch of the Potowmack River. Witness: Wm. Baker. Ogullion and Jack failed to pay the tobacco. A complaint was filed. Henry Darnall acted as attorney for Carroll.

Nathaniel Beall, planter of Frederick Co. made a note to Edward Trafford, Esq. on August 14, 1745 in Frederick Co. for tobacco. Witness: A. Magruder. Beall failed to pay the tobacco. A complaint was filed.

Thomas Baker, farmer of Frederick Co. made a note to Mathias Ambroysey on February 13, 1748 in Frederick Co. Baker failed to repay the note. A complaint was filed.

Thomas Baker, planter of Frederick Co. made a note to Stephen Guthrill on June 21, 1749. Witnesses: John Jacobs and Micjah Plummer. The note was to be repaid on February 21, 1749, but Baker failed to repay it. A complaint was filed.

Neal Ogulion, farmer of Frederick Co. made a note to John Johns on September 20, 1748 in Frederick Co. Witness: William Erwin. Ogullion later failed to repay the note, and a complaint was filed.

Evan Shelby, farmer of Frederick Co. made a note to Frederick Ice on Novmber 6, 1749 for 3 pounds, 1 shilling and 4 pence Pennsylvania money. Witness: Davis Thomson. On November 9, 1749, Ice assigned the note to Peter Hart. On March 29, 1750, a complaint was filed by Hart that Shelby had failed to repay the note.

Account of Casper Winrod for 1748 and 1749. Debits 1748: money paid to the county, payment to Young and Tasker unpaid from last year (1747), and payment to William Mauduiet; Debits 1749: money paid to the county, and payment to J. Bladen; Credits (no year): Conrad Downe. Account from Rachel Sprigg, Ex. from the books of Osburn Sprigg. Casper Winrod, a farmer of Frederick Co. was ordered to appear in court in August Court 1750 to answer to Sprigg's complaint of his unpaid account.

Nathaniel Beall, planter of Frederick Co. made a note to Hilleary Williams on July 2, 1749 at Frederick Co. Williams filed a complaint on July 4, 1750 that the note was unpaid.

Account of William Harbert, planter of Frederick Co. between November 2, 1745 and July 9, 1747. Debits 1745: cloth, silk, worsted hose, thread, payment to Nathan Peddycoat; Debits 1746: 1 boy's castor hat, shoe buckles, cotton cloth, rum, knives, powder goose shot, payment to William Mills Magruder, stockings, broad cloth, 1 fine hat, men's stockings, Irish Linen and a tobacco box; Debits 1747: nails, payment to William Offutt, white wash gloves, buttons, and 1 fine hat; Credits for tobacco. The account went unpaid, and a complaint was filed by George Gordon on August 22, 1749.

Benjamin Hopkins, planter of Frederick Co. made a note to John Rowe on August 1, 1749 for tobacco. Hopkins failed to repay the note. A complaint was filed on April 3, 1750.

William Flintham and Michael Kirkpatrick, planter of Prince Georges Co. made a note to Joseph Skidmore on April 21, 1747. Witnesses: William Wyvill and John Winford. On March 9, 1748, when Skidmore filed a complaint that the note was unpaid, both Flintham and Kirkpatrick were described as planters of Frederick Co.

Abraham Miller, farmer of Frederick Co. made a note to Hugh Parker on August 16, 1749 in Frederick Co. Miller failed to pay, and Parker filed a complaint on January 27, 1750.

Thomas Reynolds, innholder of Frederick Co. made a note to Elizabeth Smith on March 16, 1748 in Frederick Co. Reynolds failed to pay and a complaint was filed.

John Jacobs, farmer of Frederick Co. made a note to Richard Tutchstone September 19, 1746 in Frederick Co. Jacobs failed to pay and a complaint was filed.

The account of Richard Tuchtone for November 21, 1749 stated that he owed money to John Hack for the following: poplar, oak and walnut planks, ten quarts of whiskey, and one day of work for each Hack and his wife. Hack swore before George Gordon on November 21, 1749 that the account was accurate.

Thomas Wilson, laborer of Frederick Co., formerly of Prince Georges Co. made a bond with John Middagh and William Barrick on May 18, 1748 in Frederick Co. Wilson failed to pay, and a complaint was filed.

William Raymon, farmer of Frederick Co. made a note to John Metcaffe on September 4, 1749 in Frederick Co. Raymon failed to pay, and a complaint was filed.

Bartholomew Hatton, joyner of Frederick Co. made a note to Daniel Stephenson on November 4, 1748 at Frederick Co. Hatton failed to pay, and a complaint was filed.

Philip Howard, planter of Frederick Co. made a note to Thomas Harrison on December 10, 1747 in Frederick Co. Howard was described as "then and there using commerce" when he made the note to Harrison for his purchases. A complaint was filed for lack of payment. Mentions William Perkins, merchant in London.

John Brewster, blacksmith of Frederick Co. made a note to Ninian Hamilton on March 13, 1749/50 at Frederick Co. A complaint was filed on April 24, 1750 when Brewster refused to pay.

A letter written on November 11, 1750 by Joseph Beall to John Darnall of the Frederick Co. Court, stated that the suit of John Row had not been properly filed. Witnesses: Robert Beall and Archd. Beall.

Peter Smith, blacksmith of Frederick Co. made a note on January 8, 1748 at Frederick Co. to William Miles. Smith failed to repay the note, and a complaint was filed on September 15, 1749.

Isaac Rees, bricklayer of Frederick Co., made a note to John Mackoy, farmer of Frederick Co. on April 4, 1750 at Frederick Co. Witnesses: Daniel Ryan and Thomas Hayes. Rees failed to pay. A complaint was filed on July 31, 1750.

Robert Debutts, merchant of Frederick Co. made a note to Moses Rutter on October 22, 1748 at Frederick Co. Debutts failed to pay and a complaint was filed.

Account of Nathaniel Curry, farmer of Frederick Co. with John Cooke, for the period of September 5, 1749 until July 18, 1750: purchased one hair sifter, one fine hat, one silk handkerchief, one pair of shears, nails, a furred hat, a laced hat, 2 3/4 yards of beaver coating, 2 felt hats, fabirc, ribbon, a large ivory comb, worsted binding, a linen handkerchief, six pewter basins, six pewter plates, 6 clasp knives, shott and lead, gun powder, calico, gloves, striped flannel, 6 felt hats, and Irish Linen. On August 22, 1750, John Cooke swore before John Darnall that the account was accurate. A complaint was filed on July 19, 1750 that Curry's account was unpaid.

On August 23, 1749, Robert Debutts filed a complaint against John Cramphin, innholder of Frederick Co., Admin. of the deceased Henry Cramphin who died intestate in Frederick Co. Henry Cramphin had made a bond with Debutts in December 1747 in Frederick Co. and it was yet unpaid. The account of Henry Cramphin with Robert Debutts stated that Cramphin had purchased narrow boards, brown sugar, 2 sticks of hair, and 1 stick of mohair between November 24, 1747 and December 3, 1747. Account proved November 21, 1748 in Prince Georges Co. before Henry Munday.

John Richardson and Nicholas Bundrick, farmers of Frederick Co. made a note to John Middagh and Wm. Barrick on May 18, 1748 at Frederick Co. Richardson and Bundrick failed to pay, and a complaint was filed January 27, 1749.

Silas Enyart and Stephen Julian, farmers of Frederick Co. made a note to John Middagh, John Hufman, and Barbara Hufman his wife, September 7, 1747 at Frederick Co. Enyart and Julian failed to pay, and a complaint was filed.

John Shephard, farmer of Frederick Co. to appear in court to answer to the complaint of Thomas Caton. Issued August 23, 1749 by Daniel Dulany, Chief Justice and Jno. Darnall, Clerk. Shephard to appear in November Court 1749.

The following items were court summons issued by Nathaniel Wickham, Junr., Justice of Frederick Co. Court, and Jno. Darnall, Clerk. Issued November 1750; those summoned to appear in March Court 1751. [11 items]

* Evan Shelby, farmer of Frederick Co. to appear in court to answer to the complaint of Hugh Parker.

* Leonard Johnson, farmer of Frederick Co., formerly a planter of St. Marys Co., to appear in court to answer to the complaint of James Mills to whom Johnson owed tobacco.

* Seth Hyat, Junr., planter of Frederick Co. to appear in court to answer to the complaint of Rachel Sprigg, Ex. of Osburn Sprigg, deceased.

* John Hopkins, Senr., planter of Frederick Co. to appear in court to answer to the complaint of Rachel Sprigg, Ex. of Osburn Sprigg, deceased.

* William Flintham, farmer of Frederick Co. to appear in court to answer to the complaint of Rachel Sprigg, Ex. of Osburn Sprigg, deceased.

* John Hathman, carpenter of Frederick Co. to appear in court to answer to the complaint of George Maxwell.

* Joseph Crongelton, farmer of Frederick Co. to appear in court to answer to the complaint of John Jones, whom Crongelton assaulted.

* William Ricketts, planter of Frederick Co. to appear in court to answer to the complaint of Rachel Sprigg, Ex. of Osburn Sprigg, deceased, to whom Ricketts owed tobacco.

* William Ladd, planter of Frederick Co. to appear in court to answer to the complaint of Rachel Sprigg, Ex. of Osburn Sprigg, deceased.

* Isaac Hardee, planter of Frederick Co. to appear in court to answer to the complaint of Jno. Owen.

* Hugh Parker vs. Angus M. Pherfer ?. The ink in which the key points were

22

written in has faded completely. Apparently Parker and Pherfer made a note in the 1740's which was unpaid on November 20, 1750 when the complaint was filed.

Arden Evans, planter of Frederick Co. made a note to Daniel Carroll May 10, 1749 at Frederick Co. Evans failed to pay and a complaint was filed.

John Harp, laborer of Frederick Co. made a contract with William Cumming, Junr. on July 30, 1750. Harp contracted to work for two months for Cummings. Harp was to work for 26 days each month, providing that it did not rain, and that he was not sick. Cumming was to pay Harp a wage, and to provide sufficient food, drink, washing and lodging during the term of the contract. Witnesses: Blandy ? Brown, and James Sewell.

Phillemon Church, schoolmaster of Frederick Co., and Abraham Miller, farmer of Frederick Co. made a note with Jacob Fry on February 21, 1748 or 1749. Church and Miller failed to pay. Witness Daniel Miller and Frances Miller, both noted as having made his mark. A complaint was filed on August 7, 1750.

Thomas Baker, farmer of Frederick Co. made a note with Thomas Hargus on November 30, 1748 in Frederick Co. Baker failed to pay, and a complaint was filed.

On February 9, 1748, Joseph Belt, son of Benjamin made a note with Daniel Carroll of Marlbro. The note is signed Joseph Belt, Jr., and mention is made in the body of the note to Joseph Belt, Jr. Witnesses: Wm. Magan and Daniel Carroll, Junr. Another document refers to "Joseph Belt Jr. late of Frederick County planter otherwise called Joseph Belt son of Benjamin". Belt failed to pay and a complaint was filed on October 20, 1750. The back of the document refers to "Joseph Belt Jr. son of Benja." On March 26, 1750, a letter signed "Jos. Belt son of Benja." to Mr. Carroll stated that Belt did not have the money to repay the note, but would have the money as soon as he got his tobacco to market, which would be as soon as possible.

Abington George Calvin made a note to Thomas Gittings on January 30, 1745. Witnesses: John Mardin and John Piborn ?. On October 23, 1750, Nathaniel Wickham, Junr., Justice, and Jno. Darnall, Clerk, issued a summons to Abington George Calvin, planter of Frederick Co to appear at November 1750 court to answer to the complaint of Rachel Sprigg, Admin. of Thomas Gittings, deceased of Frederick Co., to whom Calvin owed money.

William Leakey, farmer of Frederick Co. made a note to William Daliom on April 24, 1747 at Frederick Co. Dallom later assigned the note to Jacob Trisell. Leakey failed to pay and a complaint was filed.

John Eaton, farmer of Frederick Co. made a note to William Cumming, Junr. on August 31, 1750. Eaton failed to pay. A complaint was filed on November 7, 1750. The account of John Eaton stated that he had purchased powder, swan shott, 500 large pins, and a dozen pipes of William Cumming, Junr.

The account of Chidley Matthews with Osburn Sprigg for 1748 and 1749 stated that payments had been made to the county and to Wm. Magruder. On August 16, 1750, Rachel Sprigg, Ex. of Osburn Sprigg, deceased stated that the account was accurate. Statement taken in Prince Georges Co. before Morda. Jacob. Filed November 21, 1750.

Peter Smith, blacksmith of Frederick Town, was summoned to answer to the compaint of Robert Debutts. Smith made a note to Debutts on March 22, 1748 in Frederick Co. and later failed to pay. A complaint was filed.

Henry Sayers, merchant of Frederick Co., heir at law of James Sayers, deceased of Frederick Co. to appear in court to answer to the complaint of Christopher Lowndes. The account of James Sayers proven before Richard Snowden on October 30, 1746, stated that James Sayers had purchased the following items between June 1743 and October 1746 of Lowndes: men's gloves, a waistband buckle, bacon, a hunting horn, soap, payment to Mr. Robinson, Spanish snuff, 1/2 bushel of salt, payment to Benja. Belt, order on Geo. Robinson payable to Willm. Sherlock, rum, payment to Wm. Tannehill, flask of oil, lump sugar,. glass buttons, payment to Elias Delashmet, linen handkerchief, payment to Capt. Loocker, a loafe of sugar, a pen knife, fishing lines, 2 bottles flower mustard, payment to Edward Owen, molasses, sundries in Jno. Lancaster's books, bridle, boots, and men's stockings. Credits: paid by Thomas Lemar, Senr., paid by Geo. Robinson, paid by Easter Offutt, paid by Robert Horner's order on the books of Jno. Lancaster and Joseph Lancaster.

Article of Agreement between James Sewell and William Cumming, Junr. Sewell to work for Cumming for three months, for twenty-six days per month, providing that it did not rain and that Sewell was not sick. Cumming was to pay wages and to provide sufficent food, drink, washing, and lodging. Agreement made July 26, 1750.

John Brewster made a note to Lawrence Owen on October 13, 1750. Witness: Henry Wright Crabbs. A complaint was filed on October 18, 1750. William Griffith, a justice, wrote a letter stating that Owen claimed that Brewster was indebted to him, but that Brewster had moved from his place of abode.

A complaint was filed on November 25, 1750 by Moses Chapline against Benjamin Catton. On October 20, 1750, Thomas Prather, Justice, wrote a letter which stated that Catton was indebted to Chapline, but that Catton had "absconded and flown from Justice". An account of Benjamin Catton, which was sworn before Joseph Chapline on November 20, 1750, stated that in May of 1750, Catton bought one horse, and in July of 1750 "one mare sold to your brother Robert at your request" [Robert apparently a brother of Benjamin Catton] The account also stated that Benjamin Catton had worked on the plantation of Chapline.

Thos. Beatty wrote a letter on September 3, 1750 which stated that John Bateman was indebted to Joseph Hardman, but that Bateman had absconded.

Thos. Beatty wrote a letter on September 4, 1750 which stated that William Lakey was indebted one thousand pounds of tobacco to James Dickson, but Lakey had absconded from his place of abode. In 1749, William Lakey had made a rental agreement with Dickson for his plantation called Matthews Lot.

Thos. Beatty wrote a letter on October 20, 1750 which stated that John Brewster was indebted to William Wallace, but that he had absconded from his last place of abode.

On October 8, 1749, Thomas Baker, farmer of Frederick Co. made a note with John Howard, son of Benjamin. Baker failed to pay and a complaint was filed.

Thomas Nicholls, carpenter of Frederick Co. made a note with Matthew Hopkins on May 12, 1749 at Frederick Co. Nicholls failed to pay and a complaint was filed.

William Breshear, farmer of Frederick Co. made a note with Rachel Sprigg, Ex. of Osburn Spirgg of Prince Georges Co. on May 12, 1750. Witness: Thomas Hilleary. Breshear failed to pay and a complaint was filed on July 3, 1750.

Thos. Brown and James Harrison, planters of Frederick Co. made a note to George Gordon, Esq., Sheriff on August 15, 1750 for tobacco. Thos. Fletchall was a witness. Gordon filed a complaint against Brown and Harrison on August 31, 1750.

Peter Venemon, a carpenter, made a note with Daniel Dulany, Esq. of Annapolis on July 2, 1747 while he was a resident of Prince Georges County. Witnesses Ben. South and Henry Munday. No date of filing was noted, but Dulany later filed a complaint against Venemon who then resided in Frederick Co.

John Jones, planter of Frederick Co. made a note with Charles Ridgely on May 9, 1747 at Frederick Co. The witnesses were John Deane and John Hedding. A complaint was filed that Jones had failed to pay. The back of the note which had been submitted for evidence states that the case is between Henry Gaither and John Jones, but there is no mention that the note had been assigned to Gaither.

John Stafilmire, carpenter of Frederick Co. made a note with Martin Whitsell on March 8, 1749 in Frederick Co. A complaint was filed on May 7, 1750 that Stafilmire had failed to pay.

Thomas Burshers, planter of Frederick Co. purchased "a beef" from Duncan Ogullion of Frederick Co. the past fall. Ogullion later purchased items from Kennedy Farrell, a merchant. Ogullion ordered Burshers to pay Farrell, in return for the cost of the beef. A complaint was filed by Farrell against Burshers on September 5, 1750. Micajah Plummer was ordered to testify on

August 13, 1751.

Richard Smith, innholder of Frederick Co. made a note with Godferett Mung on October 29, 1749 in Frederick Co. Witnesses Richd. Reynolds and Jas.? Smith. A complaint was filed on September 5, 1750 that Smith had failed to pay.

Isaac Garrison, farmer of Frederick Co. to appear in November 1750 court to answer to charges that he assaulted Daniel Ryan of Frederick Co. Issued by Nathaniel Wickham, Junr., and Jno. Darnall on September 1, 1750.

Richard Churby made a note with Grove Tomlisson on April 13, 1749. Witness: Richard Graddick.

John Candler and Arden Evans, planter of Frederick Co. made a note with Daniel Carroll of Prince Georges Co. on May 10, 1749 in Frederick Co. Witnesses: Benj. Becraft and William Condon. A complaint was filed against Candler only for failing to pay.

Henry Merony, planter of Frederick Co. made a note with Stephen Rainabergh on November 11, 1748 in Frederick Co. for tobacco. Witness: Saml. Duvall. A complaint that Merony had failed to pay was filed.

Thomas Heath, planter of Frederick Co. made a note with Robert Wilson on October 12, 1748 for items purchased. The items purchased were: cloth, ribbed stocking, shoe buckles, a buckhorn knife, and metal buttons. On April 8, 1749, Wilson swore before William Griffith that Heath's account was accurate. On August 7, 1750, Wilson filed a complaint in court that Heath had failed to pay.

No year stated, however, this document was filed with another document which appears to be the same case. That document was dated November 20, 1750. [see below] "Novr. 14th before John Fletchall and Mark Edwards have attached in the hands on Thomas Oseburn the sums within mentioned; before Thomas Davis and Mark Edwards have attached in the hands of William Wheet the sums within mentioned. Novr. 16th before Hugh Reily and Thomas Oseburn had attd. in the hands of Even Jones the sum of five shillings; before Will. Offut and James Murphy have attached in the hands of Sarah Offut eleven shillings and I further verify that I made known to the above said James Derry, Thomas Kelly, Thos. Lemar, Henry Kenn, Thos. Williams, Nehemiah Wade, John Baal, Grove Harden, Thomas Oseburn, William Wheet, Even Jones and Sarah Offut that they should be at the time and place within mentioned to show cause if any they have why the within mentioned Lawrence Owen should not have condemnation; as by the within receipt I am commanded. So answers Geo. Gordon, Sheriff."

[Goes with above] November 20, 1750: Statement of William Griffith, Justice of Frederick Co.:

John Bruister had moved from his place of abode, but was indebted to Lawrance

Owen. Bruister's goods and chattels were attached by the court. "You make known unto the person or persons in whose hands you make this attachment that he she or they be and appear before our said justices at the day and place afsd. [aforesaid] to shew cause if any he she or they have why the sums in their or any of their hands attached should not be condemned and the said Lawrance Owen thereof have Execution if to him her or them it seem met..."

Persons affected: Capt. Henry Wright Crabb, Wm. Williams, Thos. Williams, Evan Jones, Wm. Burton, Luke Barnet, Thos. Kelly crossed out, William Chamberlain crossed out, Jno. Chamberlain crossed out, Widow Collier, James Matthews, Thos. Allison, Thos. crossed out William Pritchett written in, Jno. Pritchett, Thos. Offutt crossed out, Michael Jones crossed out, Grove Hardin crossed out, Jeremiah Haysson, Sarah Offutt, Jno. Hughes, Nehemiah Wade crossed out, Wm. Hays, Robt. Lamar, Eliz. Norris, Jno. Boyd, Wm. Cammell, Wm. Needham, Peter Guynn, Leonard Hall, Wm. Wheat, Jas. Renfirm, Benja. Harris, Saml. Lamar crossed out, Jno. Lemar crossed out, Thos. Lamar crossed out, Benja. Perry, Caleb Litton, Brock Mackibee, Thos. Howard, Mary Kelly, Robt. Mitchel, Jno. Wooford, Thos. Johnson, and Jno. Belt. sent to Geo. Gordon, Sheriff by Lawrance Owen on October 18, 1750.

[Also on the above document] November 20, 1750 "I hereby certify to the justices within mentioned that by Virtue of the within receipt to me directed on the 18th of October last before Edward Owen and William Williams, have attached in the hands of James Perry eight pounds five shillings, before Samuel Waste? or Samuel Wade? and John Bucy had attached in the hands of Thomas Kelly for two shillings. October 20th before Henry Kenn and Andrew Tannyhill have attached in the hands of Thos. Lemar for eight shillings; before Gowen Hamilton and Thos. Lemar have attached in the hands of Henry Kenn for two shillings and six pence; before Nathaniel Wickham and Robert Strawbridge have attached in the hands of Thos. Williams for sixteen shillings and six pence; before Thos. Edmonson and Saml. Drouit have attached in the hands of Nehemiah Wade for four shillings and six pence. Novr. 6th before James Dowell have attached in the hands of John Baab for eight shillings; before Charles Cleckett and William Beall have attached in the hands of Grove Harden the sums within mentioned."

John Shephard appeared in court on November 21, 1750 to make bail for Thomas Thornburgh, millwright of Frederick Co., formerly of Lancaster Co. [apparently Lancaster Co., PA]. Thornburgh owed money to Jacob Wybright.

Abraham Miller, planter of Frederick Co., formerly of Prince Georges Co., to appear in November Court 1750 to answer to the complaint of Onorio Razolini, to whom Miller owed money.

Aaron Price, innholder of Frederick Co. to appear in November Court 1750 to answer to the complaint of Robert White, to whom Price owed money.

George House, farmer of Frederick Co., formerly of Prince Georges Co. to appear in November Court 1750 to answer to the complaint of Henry Touchstone, to whom House owed tobacco.

William Bowell appeared in court on March 20, 1750 to make bail for David Watson, weaver of Frederick Co., formerly of Prince Georges Co. Watson owed money to John Cooke.

Wm. Smit, farmer of Frederick Co. to appear in November Court 1750 to answer to the complaint of David Magraw, to whom Smit owed money.

Paul Cox, of Frederick Co., formerly of Carniwacko [Conewago], Lancaster, Pennsylvania, yeoman, to appear in November Court 1750 to answer to the complaint of Sebastian Tyshoe, to whom Cox owed money.

Nathaniel Wickham, Junr. of Frederick Co. to appear in November Court 1750 to answer to the complaint of John Hepburn, to whom Wickham owed tobacco.

Neale Odonnell and Aarter McKenna, farmers of Frederick Co. to appear in November Court 1750 to answer to the complaint of Benjamin Chambers, to whom they owed tobacco.

Thomas Kelly, farmer of Frederick Co. to appear in November Court 1750 to answer to the complaint of William Webb, to whom Kelly owed tobacco.

Uncle Uncles, farmer of Frederick Co. to appear in November Court 1750 to answer to the complaint of Caleb Dorsey, to whom Uncles owed tobacco.

Joseph Skidmore, farmer of Frederick Co. to appear in November Court 1750 to answer to the complaint of John Cooke, to whom Skidmore owed tobacco.

Peter Smith, blacksmith of Frederick Co., formerly of Prince Georges Co. to appear in November Court 1750 to answer to the complaint of Daniel Dulany, to whom Smith owed money.

Richard Smith, innholder of Fredrick Co. to appear in November 1750 Court to answer to the complaint of John Brunner, to whom Smith owed money.

Basthin Tyshowe, farmer of Frederick Co., formerly of Prince Georges Co. to appear in November Court 1750 to answer to the complaint of John Cooke, to whom Tyshowe owed tobacco.

Charles Cleggett, planter of Frederick Co., formely of Prince Georges Co. to appear in November 1750 Court to answer to the complaint of Matthew Hopkins and Co. to whom Cleggett owed tobacco.

John Hopkins, planter of Frederick Co., formerly of Prince Georges Co. to appear in November 1750 Court to answer to the complaint of Matthew Hopkins and Co., to whom John Hopkins owed tobacco.

John Hopkins, planter of Frederick Co., formerly of Prince Georges Co. to appear in November 1750 Court to answer to the complaint of John Beall, Junr. to whom Hopkins owed tobacco.

August 24, 1750: The goods and chattels of William Davis, planter of Frederick

Co., formerly of Prince Georges Co. were to be attached because he owed tobacco to Thomas Lancaster.

William Lakey had "removed in a secret manner from the place of his abode", but was indebted to James Dickson for tobacco. The goods and chattels of Lakey were attached August 24,1750.

John Cramptin, innholder of Frederick Co. was the administrator of Henry Cramptin, deceased. John Cramptin was ordered to appear in November Court 1750 to answer to the complaint of George Scott, to whom money was owed.

August 21, 1750: The goods and chattels on Uncle Uncles were attached to pay his debt to Caleb Dorsey.

August 24, 1750: William Lakey "had removed in a secret manner from his place of abode", but was indebted to Matthias Pooley for tobacco. The goods and chattels of Lakey were attached.

John Beatman "had removed in a secret manner from the place of his abode", but was indebted to Joseph Hardman. The goods and chattels of Beatman were attached.

Nehemiah Ogdon, blacksmith of Frederick Co. to appear in November Court 1750 to answer to the complaint of Ignatius Digges and John Hepburn to whom he owed tobacco.

Patrick Mathews, farmer of Frederick Co. to appear in November Court 1750 to answer to the complaint of Peter Williams. Mathews owed money to Williams, as adjudged by the court in Prince Georges Co. in March of 1750.

John Maccarmack, farmer of Frederick Co. to appear in November Court 1750 to answer to the complaint of Peter Williams. Maccarmack owed tobacco to Williams as adjudged by the court in Prince Georges Co. in March 1750.

Robert Evans, farmer of Frederick Co. to appear in November Court 1750 to answer to the complaint of Thomas Wilson. Evans owed tobacco to Wilson, as adjudged by the court in Prince Georges Co.

John House, farmer of Frederick Co., formerly of Prince Georges Co. to appear in November Court 1750 to answer to the complaint of Richard Kune, to whom House owed tobacco.

Abraham Miller, farmer of Frederick Co. to appear in November Court 1750 to answer to the complaint of Benjamin Becraft, to whom Miller owed money.

Michael Kirkpatrick, farmer of Frederick Co. to appear in November Court 1750 to answer to the complaint of Henry Charlton and Thomas Charlton, to whom Kirkpatrick owed tobacco.

Barnet Waymer, farmer of Frederick Co. to appear in November Court 1750 to answer to the complaint of Robert Debutts, to whom Waymer owed tobacco.

John Brewster "had removed in a secret manner from the place of his abode", but was indebted to William Wallace. The goods and chattels of Brewster were attached on August 24, 1750.

August 24, 1750: William Bowell, Admin. of John Roberts to appear in November Court 1750 to answer to charges of contempt.

James Gore, plaintiff vs. Wadsworth Wilson. Jane Gore, Mary Allison and Mary Gatton to appear in November Court 1750 to testify for the plaintiff.

Issued September 24, 1750 to the sheriff of Anne Arundel Co.: Wm. Cumming (overseer of Wm. Cumming, Esq.), Richard Young, and Susanna Starr, wife of Wm. Starr to appear in November Court 1750 in Frederick Town to testify for the plaintiff. Case: Wm. Cumming, plaintiff vs. Henry Gaither. Witness: Benjamin Young, Chief Justice.

Issued November 14, 1750 to the sheriff of Prince Georges Co.: The Revd. George Murdock, Thomas Cramphin, Isaac Brooke and Baruch Williams to appear in November Court 1750 in Frederick Co. to testify for the defendant. Case: Rachel Sprigg, plaintiff vs. John Bell Taylor.

John Veach, Ex. of Ann Weaver, to appear in November Court 1750 to answer to a matter of the settlement of the estate of Weaver.

John West, Ex. of Benjamin West, to appear in November Court 1750 to answer to a matter of the settlement of the estate of Benjamin West.

William West, Admin. of John Magee to appear in November Court 1750 to answer to a matter of the settlement of the estate of Magee.

Samuel Duvall, planter of Frederick Co. to appear in November Court 1750 to countersecure William Davis. Davis was responsible for the balance of the estate of John Harding.

Michael Reisner, farmer of Frederick Co. to appear in March 1751 Court to answer to a misdemeanor that he committed.

George Scott, plaintiff vs. Henry Futney. Robert Pearl to testify in November Court 1750 for Futney. John Delashmeet and John Johnson Kittocton to testify for Scott.

George Scott, plaintiff vs. Thomas Hunt. John Delashmutt, Robert Perle, James Dukson and John Johnson Kittocton to appear in November Court 1750 to testify for the plaintiff.

Thomas Conn, plaintiff vs. John Tinney and Henry Poulson. Robert Patricks and William Beall, Senr. to appear in November Court 1750 to testify for the plaintiff.

Francis Hartley and others, plaintiffs vs. John Clark. George Gue, Elizabeth Peterson and Samuel Mount to appear in November Court 1750 to testify for the plaintiffs.

Jonathan Hagar, Michael Ruff, and David Jones to appear in November Court 1750 to testify for Geo. Kersher vs. Jacob Falker. Not stated for which party they were to testify.

Jno. Rawlins, Josias Beall, and Nathan Magruder to testify for Basil Waring vs.

Jno. Claget. Not stated for which party they were to testify. No date.

Chs. Bussey to testify in November Court 1750 for Jno. Jacobs vs. Ths. Charters. Not stated for which party Bussey was to testify.

Chas. Chaney to testify for the grand jury immediately, November Court 1750.

John McFaden to testify for the grand jury immediately, November Court 1750.

Clement Davis to testify for the grand jury immediately, November Court 1750.

Wm. Cumming, Junr. and Dr. And. Scott to testify for the grand jury immediately, November Court 1750.

Matthew Edwards, plaintiff vs. William Plummer. Elizabeth Smith and Charles Neal to appear in November Court 1750 to testify for Plummer.

Eunice Brown, plaintiff vs. Benjamin Barton. Jeremiah Elrode to appear in November Court 1750 to testify for Brown.

The Proprietary, plaintiff vs. Richard Smith. William Webb, Thomas Scarlett, Henry Charlton and Arthur Charlton to appear in November Court 1750 to testify for the plaintiff.

Joseph Chapline, plaintiff vs. Arthur Charlton. William Flintham, William Welsh, James Mar and Charles Chaney, Senr. to appear in November Court 1750 to testify for Chapline.

Jacob Fry, plaintiff vs. Phill. Church and Abr. Miller. Frances Miller, a woman, and Daniel Miller to appear in November 1750 Court to testify for Fry.

James Burgess and others, plaintiffs vs. Joseph Hill. Jacob Vantrease or Jas. Vantrease (front says Jacob, back says Jas.), also the unnamed wife of Jacob Vantrease, to testify in November Court 1750 for Burgess.

Wm. Slade and others, plaintiffs, vs. Thos. Maneyard. Chloe Mobberly and Darby Ryan to testify in November Court 1750 for Maneyard. Jemima Stevens, wife of Willm. Stevens and James Crouch and the unnamed wife of Thomas Beatty to testify for Slade in November Court 1750.

Jno. Larkin, Admin. of Patrick McMullen, plaintiff, vs. Richard Touchstone. Thomas Johnson and Caleb Touchstone to testify in November Court 1750 for Larkin.

James Compton, plaintiff, vs. Henry Davis. William Lucket to testify in November Court 1750 for Compton.

Thos. Cresap, Admin. of Wm. Griffith, plaintiff, vs. Patrick Mathewes. Richard Chapman to appear in November Court 1750 to testify for Mathewes.

Thomas Cresap, Admin. of Wm. Griffith, plaintiff, vs. Wm. and Eliz. Mitchel, Admins. of Jno. Mitchel. Richard Chapman to appear in November Court 1750 to testify for Cresap.

The Proprietary, plaintiff, vs. Thomas Richardson. Ninian Beall, son of Ninian to appear in November Court 1750 to testify for the Proprietary. No offense stated for Richardson.

The Proprietary, plaintiff, vs. Thomas Beatty. William Robert Hinton and

Gabriel Hughs to appear in November Court 1750 to testify for the case. Not stated for which party Hinton and Hughs were to testify. No offense stated for Beatty.

The Proprietary, plaintiff, vs. Richard Beaman. William Robt. Hinton, Arthur Parr and Gabriel Hughs to appear in November Court 1750 to testify. Not stated for which party the witnesses were to testify. No offense stated for Beaman.

Richd. Coombes, plaintiff, vs. John Jones. Richd. Coombes, Junr. and Charles Wood to appear in November Court 1750 to testify for Coombes.

Wm. Cumming, Esq., plaintiff, vs. Henry Gaither. John Mobberly, Deborah Jones, wife of John Jones, Francis Hartley, Thomas Newman Roden and John Barber to appear in November Court 1750 to testify for Gaither. William Cumming to testify for himself. Richard Young, John Barber (also testified for Cumming) and Samuel Ridgley to testify in November Court 1750 for Cumming.

Rees Price, plaintiff, vs. Elias Alexander. Alexander Staret to appear in November Court 1750 to testify for Alexander. Hugh Barnet and Joseph Chapline to appear in November Court 1750 to testify for Price.

Thomas Charter, plaintiff vs. John Jacobs. Stephen Newton Chiswell and Lawrance Owens to appear in November Court 1750 to testify for Charter. John Rolls, Charles Bussey and James Veatch, Senr. to appear in November Court 1750 to testify for Jacobs.

James Compton, plaintiff, vs. Henry Davis. Samuel Duvall and William Davis to appear in November Court 1750 to testify for Compton.

Thomas Cresap, Admin. of William Griffith, plaintiff, vs. George Croghan. William Mitchell to appear in November Court 1750 to testify for Cresap.

John Clark, plaintiff, vs. Francis Hartley. William Star to appear in November Court 1750 to testify for Clark.

Mary Frederick, plaintiff, vs. Mathew Edwards. Edward Macknew to appear in November Court 1750 to testify for Frederick.


## TOBACCO INSPECTION PROCEEDINGS OF FREDERICK CO., MD
## 1748-1769

*Maryland Archives C894-1 1/40/14/1*

March 10, 1748  Met in Frederick Town. Justices: Daniel Dulaney, Esq., Nathaniel Wickham, Junr., Thomas Owen, Henry Munday, and George Gordon. John Darnall, Clerk. George Gordon and John Rawlins appointed to inspect the weights and scales at Rock Creek Warehouse in Frederick Co.

March 21, 1748  Met in Frederick Co. Justices: Daniel Dulaney, Esq., Nathan Wickham, Junr., Henry Munday, William Griffith, Thomas Prather, Thomas Cresap, John Rawlins, and Joseph Chapline. John Darnall, Clerk. Alexander Magruder and Alexander Beall to inspect warehouse at Rock Creek. Samuel Beall was one of the inspectors for the warehouse at Bladensburg in Price Georges County. John Thomas, Sheriff took an oath prescribed by an "Act of Assembly to prevent the Clandestine Exportation of Tobacco." George Gordon and John Rawlins, Justices, appointed to adjust the weights at Rock Creek Warehouse.

June 20, 1749  Met in Frederick Co. Justices: Nathaniel Wickham, Junr., George Gordon, William Griffith, John Rawlins, Thomas Prather and Thomas Beatty. John Darnall, Clerk. Basil Beall, an "under Sheriff" of Frederick Co., took an oath.

Another entry also dated June 20, 1749  Met in Frederick Town. Justices: Daniel Dulany, Esq., Nathaniel Wickham, Junr., Henry Munday, John Rawlins, Joseph Chapline, Thomas Prather, William Griffith, Nathan Magruder, Thomas Beatty and John Clagett. John Darnall, Clerk. Bonds for inspectors of Rock Creek Warehouse: Bond of Alexr. Beall, Nathl. Beall, and John Claggett of Frederick Co., made January 25, 1749, for Inspector Alexr. Beall. Bond of Alexr. Magruder, Nathl. Beall and John Clagett, of Frederick Co. made January 25, 1749; for Inspector Magruder. Alexander Beall, Inspector of Rock Creek Warehouse, and Samuel Beall of Bladensburgh Warehouse took oathes.

November 21, 1749 Met in Frederick Co. Justices: Nathaniel Wickham, Junr., Thomas Prather, George Gordon, William Griffith, and John Rawlins. Jno. Darnall, Clerk. Alexander Beall and Alexander Magruder, Inspectors of Rock Creek Warehouse, reported:
* George Gordon and Henry Threlkield were paid for sundries.
* Joshua Bucey and Nathl. Magruder, son of Ninian, were paid for 10 dozen hoops.
* John Bickels was paid for the use of his horses and trucks to bring ropes and blocks.

November 27, 1749 Justices ordered that Alexander Beall and Alexander Magruder be paid for the deficiencies at the warehouse. Also ordered that John Darnall, Clerk, be paid for services. Sent order to the Honorable Charles Hammond, Esq., Robert Gordon, Esq. and George Stuart, Esq., commissioners of the loan office.

August 21, 1750 Met in Frederick Co. Justices: Nathaniel Wickham, Junr., Thomas Beatty, Joseph Chapline, James Doull, John Needham, Thomas Prather, Nathaniel Alexander, John Rawlins and William Griffith. John Darnall, Clerk. John Needham, Josias Beall, John Clagett, and James Doull, or any three of them, appointed to inspect the Rock Creek Warehouse.

November 20, 1750 Met in Frederick Co. Justices: Nathaniel Wickham, Junr., Thomas Beatty, Joseph Chapline, John Rawlins, James Doull, Nathaniel Alexander, Josias Beall, Henry Munday, Thomas Prather, William Griffith, Nathan Magruder, John Needham, John Clagett, and Alexander Beall. Report made by Alexander Beall and Alexander Magruder of old tobacco from before 1747.

March 19, 1751 Met at Frederick Town. Justices: Daniel Dulaney, Esq., Thomas Beatty, Nathaniel Wickham, Junr., William Griffith, Nathan Magruder, Alexander Beall, John Rawlins, Nathan Alexander, Joseph Chapline, Thomas Prather, and John Needham. John Darnall, Clerk. Samuel Beall, Inspector of Bladensburgh Warehouse in Prince George's County, and Alexander Beall, Inspector of Rock Creek Warehouse took oathes. Bonds for inspectors of Rock Creek Warehouse: Bond of Alexr. Beall, Zacha. Magruder, and Josiah Beall of Frederick Co. made November 27, 1750 for Inspector Alexr. Beall. Bond of Alexr. Magruder, Josiah Beall and John Clagett, of Frederick Co. made November 27, 1750 for Inspector Magruder.

June 18, 1751 Met at Frederick Town. Justices: Nathaniel Wickham, Junr., Thomas Beatty, Thomas Prather, John Rawlins, Josias Beall, John Needham, Joseph Chapline, Alexander Beall, Nathan Magruder and William Griffith. Jno. Darnall, Clerk. John Clagett, an inspector the the Rock Creek Warehouse took an oath. Bond for inspector of Rock Creek Warehouse: Bond of John Clagett, George Gordon and Nathl. Magruder son of Alexr., made May 17, 1751 for Inspector Clagett.

November 19, 1751 Met at Frederick Town. Justices: Nathaniel Wickham, Nathaniel Alexander, Thomas Prather, William Griffith, John Rawlins, and Josias Beall. John Darnall, Clerk. The inspectors of the Rock Creek Warehouse reported for the 1751 books. Bonds for inspectors at Rock Creek Warehouse: Bond of Alexander Beall, Thomas Prather, and Josiah Beall made November 23, 1751 [sic], for Inspector Alexander Beall. Bond of John Clagett, Thomas Prather and Josiah Beall made November 23, 1751 [sic] for Inspector Clagett.

November 21, 1752 Met at Frederick Town. Justices: Nathaniel Wickham,

Josiah Beall, Thomas Prather, John Needham, John Rawlins, Henry Wright Crabb, William Griffith, and Nathan Magruder. Jno. Darnall, Clerk. Bonds for inspectors of Rock Creek Warehouse read and approved: Bond of Alex Beall, Willm. Wallace, Senr., and Joshua Bucey of Frederick Co. made December 7, 1752 [sic] for Inspector Beall. Bond of John Clagett, Willm. Wallace, Senr. and Joshua Bucey of Frederick Co., made December 7, 1752 for Inspector Clagett.

November 20, 1753 Met at Frederick Town. Justices: Nathaniel Wickham, Joseph Wood, William Webb, John Rawlins, John Clagett, Alexr. Beall, Joseph Smith, Wm. Griffith, Thos. Prather, and W. Crabbs. Jno. Darnall, Clerk.

March 19, 1754 Met at Frederick Town. Justices: Nathaniel Wickham, Henry Wright Crabb, Thomas Prather, Joseph Wood, Wm. Griffith, William Webb, John Rawlings, Thomas Beatty, and Alexander Beall. Bonds read and approved for insectors of Rock Creek Warehouse: Bond of John Clagett, Henry Wright Crabb and Robert Lamar, Senr. of Frederick Co. made January 16, 1754, for Inspector Clagett. Bond of Alexander Beall, Henry Wright Crabb, and Robert Lamar, Senr. of Frederick Co., made January 7, 1754, for Inspector Beall. Bond of George Gordon and Henry Wright Crabb to Nathaniel Wickham, made March 22, 1754 [sic] in the presence of Jno. Stone Hawkins; Gordon and Crabb obligated to keep the warehouse and wharf in George Town in good repair. Alexander Beall and John Clagett, Inspectors of Rock Creek Warehouse, Samuel Beall, Sheriff of Frederick County, Peter Butler, Ginsey Gittings and Joseph Beall, Sub-Sheriffs of Frederick Co. all took an oath appointed by an Act of Assembly to Suppress the Exportation of Trash Tobacco. John Rawlins and William Griffith appointed to view the scales and weights at Rock Creek Warehouse.

November 19, 1754 Met at Frederick Town. Justices: Col. Nathaniel Wickham, William Webb, Thomas Prather, Thos. Beatty, William Griffith, Joseph Smith, John Rawlins, David Lynn, Joseph Wood, Jno. Smith Prather, and Charles Jones. John Darnall, Clerk. Bonds read and approved for inspectors of Rock Creek Warehouse: Bond of John Clagett, Henry Wright Crabb, and William Pritchett of Frederick Co., made November 4, 1754 [sic], for Inspector Clagett. Bond of Nath. Magruder, William Pritchett and Zachariah Magruder of Frederick Co. made November 4, 1754 [sic], for Inspector Nathan Magruder. Report of the inspectors of the Rock Creek Warehouse in November 1754:
* Robert Peter was paid for new rope.
* George Kiger was paid for bringing rope from Bladensburgh.
* Thomas Snowden was paid for two figure irons.
* Archibald Henderson paid.

* Robert Mundel paid.
* John Crosthwarte paid for hammers.

March 18, 1755 Met at Frederick Town. Justices: Nathaniel Wickham, John Rawlins, Thomas Beatty, Joseph Wood, Thomas Prather, William Webb, William Griffith, David Lynn and Charles Jones. Jno. Darnall, Clerk. John Clagett and Nathan Magruder took an oath to suppress the exportation of trash tobacco.

November 18, 1755 Met at Frederick Town. Justices: Nathaniel Wickham, Joseph Wood, Thomas Beatty, Joseph Smith, William Griffith, David Lynn, John Rawlins, and Charles Jones. John Clagett and Nath. Magruder, Inspectors of the Rock Creek Warehouse reported that Archd. Henderson was paid for sundry items. Bonds for inspectors of Rock Creek Warehouse read and approved: Bond of Jno. Clagett, Joshua Bucey, and Thomas Clagett, planters of Frederick Co., made November 1, 1755, for Inspector John Clagett. Bond of Nath. Magruder, Zach Magruder and George Beall, planters of Frederick Co., made November 1, 1755, for Inspector Nath. Magruder.

March 16, 1756 Met at Frederick Town. Justices: Thomas Beatty, John Rawlins, William Griffith, David Lynn and Joseph Wood. Jno. Darnall, Clerk. Luke Barnard, James Coffee, James Fyffe, and William Norris, Constables of Frederick Co. took an oath to suppress the exportation of trash tobacco.

November 16, 1756 Met at Frederick Town. Justices: Thomas Beatty, William Griffith, Charles Jones, David Lynn, Joseph Wood, Thomas Cresap, Thomas Prather, James Dickson, Andrew Heugh, and John Dagsworthy. Jno. Darnall, Clerk. Bonds for inspectors of Rock Creek Warehouse read and approved: Bond of John Clagett, Zacha. Magruder and Andrew Heugh of Frederick Co., made November 1, 1756, for Inspector John Clagett. Bond of Nathaniel Magruder, son of Alexander, Zacha. Magruder, and George Beall, Junr. of Frederick Co., made November 1, 1756, for Inspector Nathaniel Magruder. Report of the inspectors of the Rock Creek Warehouse November 1756 stated that George Theger was paid by order of Lynn and Jones.

November 15, 1757 Met at Frederick Town. Justices: Thomas Prather, Joseph Smith, Joseph Wood, Charles Jones, Andrew Heugh, David Lynn, Peter Bainbridge, William Luckett and Thomas Norris. Bonds presented for inspectors of Rock Creek Warehouse: Bond of John Clagett, Wm. Williams son of Thomas, and Lawrance Owen, all of Frederick Co., made November 17, 1757 [sic] for inspector Clagget. Bond of Nathaniel Magruder, William Williams son of

Thomas, and William Wallace, Junr. of Frederick Co., made November 17, 1757 [sic] for inspector Magruder. Report of Clagget and Magruder for Rock Creek Warehouse:
* Robt. Mundell account paid.
* Andrew Heugh paid for irons and scales.
* James Moore paid for wood work.
* Thomas Clark paid for "fetching the notes from Annapolis".
* Robert Peter account paid.
* John Darnall paid for seal of bonds.

March 21, 1758 Met in Frederick Town. Justices: Thomas Beatty, Thomas Prather, Joseph Wood, Charles Jones, Andrew Heugh, Joseph Smith, David Lynn, Moses Chaplin, Jacob Duckett, William Luckett, and Thomas Norris. Jno. Darnall, Clerk. Lynn and Heugh appointed to examine weights and scales at Rock Creek Warehouse. John Clagget and Nathaniel Magruder addressed objections to the account they had presented in November Court.

November 21, 1758 Met at Frederick Town. Justices: Thos. Beatty, Thos. Prather, Dav. Lynn, Thos. Norris, Pet. Bainbridge, Chs. Jones, Jos. Smith, Andrew Heugh, and Mos. Chapline. Bonds presented: Bond of Jno. Clagett, Col. Sam Beall, and Wm. Williams all of Frederick Co., made November 22, 1758 [sic] for inspector Clagett. Bond of Nathan Magruder, Wm. Williams and Law. Owen, all of Frederick Co., made November 22, 1758 [sic] for inspector Magruder. John Clagett and Nathan Magruder son of Alexander reported for Rock Creek Warehouse:
* Josn. Belt account paid.
* George Vandevers paid for repairing the Brandy Irons.
* Andrew Heugh paid for adding to a chain.
* Wm. Johnson paid for an iron hand spike.
* Robt. Peter paid for sundries.
* Error accepted by Robert Peter, Attorney for Jno. Glassford and Co.

November 20, 1759 Met at Frederick Town. Justices: Thos. Beatty, Jos. Wood, Thos. Norris, Wm. Luckett, Chas. Jones, And. Heugh and Petr. Bainbridge. Bonds approved for inspectors of Rock Creek Warehouse: Bond of John Clagett, Josi Beall and Nath. Magruder son of Alexander, of Frederick Co., made November 6, 1759 for inspector Clagett. Bond of Samuel Wade Magruder, George Beall, Junr., and Nath. Magruder son of Alexander, planters of Frederick Co., made November 6, 1759 for inspector Samuel Magruder. Report of Rock Creek Warehouse accounts stated that the accounts of Josiah Beall and Robert Peter had been paid. John Darnall, Clerk, was to be paid for sundry services.

November 18, 1760 Met at Frederick Town. Justices: Thos. Beatty, Thos. Prather, Jos. Wood, Chas. Jones, Petr. Bainbridge, Thos. Norris and Mos. Chapline. Inspectors' bonds approved: Bond of Samuel Wade Magruder, Andrew Heugh and Even Jones, planters of Frederick Co., made November 4, 1760 for inspector Magruder. Bond of Nicklas Baker and John Baker, planters of Frederick Co., made November 4, 1760, for inspector Nicklas Baker. report of Rock Creek Warehouse stated that Josiah Beall and Robert Peter were paid. John Darnall, Clerk was to be paid for services.

November 17, 1761 Met at Frederick Town. Justices: Thomas Beatty, Thomas Prather, Peter Bainbridge, David Lynn, Joseph Wood, Moses Chapline, William Luckett, Thomas Norris and Charles Jones. Jno. Darnall, Clerk. Inspectors' bonds for Rock Creek Warehouse presented: Bond of Nicklas Baker and David Lynn, planters of Frederick Co., made November 18, 1761[sic] for Inspector Baker. Bond of Samuel Wade Magruder, Clement Beall, and Walter S. Greenfield, planters of Frederick Co., made November 18, 1761 [sic]for Inspector Magruder. Report of Magruder and Baker stated that Josiah Beall, Robert Peter and Chris. Lowndes were paid.

November 16, 1762 Met at Frederick Town. Justices: Thomas Beatty, Joseph Wood, William Luckett, Thomas Norris, David Lynn, and Charles Jones. John Darnall, Clerk. Inspectors' bonds for Rock Creek Warehouse presented: Bond of Samuel Wade Magruder, Erasmus Gill and John Clagett, planters of Frederick Co., made November 17, 1762 [sic] for Inspector Magruder. Bond of Nicholas Baker, Erasmus Gill and John Clagett, planters of Frederick Co., made November 17, 1762 [sic], for Inspector Baker.

November 15, 1763 Met at Frederick Town. Justices: Thomas Beatty, Charles Jones, William Luckett, James Dickson, Peter Bainbridge, Samuel Beall, Josiah Beall, David Lynn, Evan Shelby, James Smith, Joseph Wood, Thomas Price and Samuel Postlethwait. John Darnall, Clerk. Bonds presented for Rock Creek Warehouse: Bond of Nichs. Baker, David Lynn, and Capt. William Williams, planters of Frederick Co., made December 14, 1763 [sic] for Inspector Baker. Bond of Samuel Wade Magruder, Col. Saml. Beall, Junr., and Erasmus Gill, planters of Frederick Co., made December 14, 1763 [sic] for Inspector Magruder. Report of Inspectors Magruder and Baker stated that Josiah Beall and Robert Peter had been paid.

November 15, 1764 Met at Frederick Town. Justices: Peter Bainbridge, David Lynn, Charles Jones, William Luckett, William Blair, Thomas Price, James Smith, Samuel Beall, Josiah Beall, Andrew Heugh, Kinzy Gittings, Joseph Smith

and Joseph Warford. John Darnall, Clerk. Bonds for inspectors of Rock Creek
Warehouse presented: Bond of George Beall, Junr., Josiah Beall, and Erasmus
Gill, of Frederick Co., made November 17, 1764 [sic] before Chas. Jones and
Samuel Beall, Junr. for Inspector George Beall, Junr. Bond of Saml. W.
Magruder, Josiah Beall, and Erass. Gill of Frederick Co., made November 17,
1764 [sic] for Inspector Magruder. Report of Inspectors Magruder and Beall:
* Robert Peter, Stephen West, Josiah Beall and Chris. Lownds, accounts paid.
* Thos. Cleland paid for mending scales.

November 17, 1765 Met at Frederick Town. Justices: Thomas Beatty, Peter
Bainbridge, William Luckett, Charles Jones, David Lynn, Thomas Price, James
Dickson, William Blair, Samuel Beall, Josiah Beall, Andrew Heugh, and Joseph
Smith. John Darnall, Clerk. Bonds for inspectors of Rock Creek Warehouse
presented: Bond of Saml. W. Magruder, John Oime and Brooke Beall, of
Frederick Co., made October 31, 1765 for Inspector Magruder. Bond of George
Beall, Junr., John Oime, and Brooke Beall, of Frederick Co., made October 31,
1765 for Inspector George Beall, Junr. Inspectors Magruder and Beall reported:
* Richard Thompson, Josiah Beall, Chris. Lownd and Robt. Peter accounts paid.
* John Elias Martin Sadlor account paid. [not clear if "Sadlor" was last name or
    occupation]

November 18, 1766 Met at Frederick Town. Justices: Joseph Wood, Charles
Jones, David Lynn, Josiah Beall, Samuel Beall, William Luckett, Thomas Price,
Joseph Smith, William Blair, Evan Shelby and Peter Bainbridge. John Darnall,
Clerk. Inspectors' bonds presented: Bond of George Beall, Junr., Hezekiah
Magruder, and Clemt. Beall of Frederick Co., made November 14, 1765 [1765 is
recorded for both bonds], for Inspector George Beall, Junr. Bond of Samuel
Wade Magruder, John Oime and Hezekiah Magruder, of Frederick Co., made
November 14, 1765 for Inspector Samuel Wade Magruder. November 6, 1766,
report of Inspectors Magruder and Beall: Accounts paid for Robert Peter, Josiah
Beall, Richard Thompson, Christn. Lownds and Nichlas Dawson.

November 12 or 18, 1767 Met at Frederick Town. Justices: Joseph Wood,
Charles Jones, Peter Bainbridge, William Luckitt, Andrew Heugh, David Lynn,
Josiah Beall, Samuel Beall, Thomas Price, James Smith, Joseph Smith, and Evan
Shelby. John Darnall, Clerk. Bonds for Inspectors of Rock Creek Warehouse
presented: Bond of Samuel Wade Magruder, Joseph Wilson and Nathaniel
Magruder, of Frederick Co., made November 18, 1767 for Inspector Samuel
Wade Magruder. Bond of George Beall, Junr., Joseph Wilson and Nathaniel
Magruder, of Frederick Co., made November 18, 1767, for Inspector George
Beall, Junr. Report of Inspectors Magruder and Beall: Accounts for Josiah Beall,

William Deakins, Stephen West, John Glasford, and John Swinson paid.

November 18, 1768 Met at Frederick Town. Justices: William Luckett, David Lynn, Eaneus Campbell, Thomas Price, Thomas Prather, Charles Jones, Andrew Heugh, T. Sprigg Wooten, Evan Shelby and Joseph Tomliston. John Darnall, Clerk. Bonds for inspectors of Rock Creek Warehouse presented: Bond of Samuel Wade Magruder, Zachariah Magruder, and Wm. Deakins, Junr., of Frederick Co., made November 5, 1768 for Inspector Samuel Wade Magruder. Bond of George Beall, Junr., Zachariah Magruder, and William Deakins, Junr., of Frederick Co., made November 5, 1768 for Inspector Beall. Inspectors Magruder and Beall reported:
* Accounts of William Deakins, Edward Perkinson, Adam Stuart, and Robert Peter paid.
* Benj. Ray paid for making new scales.
* Jacob Mounts " and Boon" paid for smith's work.

Thomas Sprigg, Clerk of Frederick Co. ordered to be paid for sundry services.

November 21, 1769 Met at Frederick Town. Justices: Thomas Prather, Thomas Price, Eneas Campble, Thomas Sprigg Wootton, Joseph Tomlinson, Joseph Wood, David Lynn, William Blair, Andrew Heugh, and Samuel Beall. John Darnall, Clerk. Bonds of Inspectors of Rock Creek Warehouse presented: Bond of Samuel W. Magruder, Adam Stuart, and Anthony Holmead of Frederick Co., made November 6, 1769, for Inspector Magruder. Bond of George Beall, Junr., Adam Stuart and Anthony Holmead, of Frederick Co., made November 6, 1769 for Inspector Beall. Report of Inspectors stated that accounts had been paid for William Deakins, Junr., Edwd. Perkison, Robert Peter, Ardon Mariarte, Thomas Pindle "and Low", John Mount, and Christopher Lowndes. Ordered that Thomas Sprigg, Clerk of Frederick Co., be paid for sundry services.

## 1761 TAX LIST, OLD TOWN AND SUGARLAND HUNDREDS

[The tax lists for the other hundreds have been lost. The original document for Old Town Hundred listed only personal names with no explanation of what was taxed.]

*Maryland Archives Series C244-16 Location 1/32/1/53*

A list of the taxables in Fred. County in Old Town Hundred taken by Providence Mounts, Constable.

| | | | |
|---|---|---|---|
| Francis Spencer | 2 | James Winters | 1 |
| Abraham Teagarden | 2 | Timothy Sweet | 1 |
| Joseph Mounts | 2 | Solomon Terpen | 2 |
| Frederick Dunfield | 2 | Andrew Hendricks | 1 |
| John Castell | 1 | John Connel | 3 |
| Adam McCarte | 1 | Casper Everly | 1 |
| John Slater | 1 | James Spurgeon, Sr. | 4 |
| Saml. Plump | 1 | James Craptree | 2 |
| John Nichols, Jr. | 2 | Andrew Sinn | 1 |
| Edward Anderson | 1 | Nathan Friggs | 1 |
| John Nichols, Sr. | 2 | Richard Morris | 1 |
| Providence Mounts | 2 | William Spurgeon | 1 |
| John Trotter | 1 | Jno. Spurgeon | 1 |
| Isaac Colyer | 1 | James Spurgeon, Jr. | 1 |
| Nehemiah Martin | 1 | Jno. Morris | 1 |
| Aron Moore | 2 | John McDonald | 1 |
| Thomas Cresap | 4 | Thos. Spencer | 1 |
| George Wade | 1 | Edmd. Martin | 3 |
| Philip Mason | 1 | "A true copy. Saml. Beale, Sherrif" |  |
| Samuel Welder | 2 | | |
| Daniel Pruiel | 4 | | |

A list of the taxables taken in Sugarland Hundred by Arthur Hickman, Constable, for the year 1761.

Henry Allison, Alex Allison, John Allison, James Peters - taxed as 4

Capt. George Beals Quarter, Francis Clark, Slaves Phebe and Maria - taxed as 3

Leonard Beale, Slave Fortune - taxed as 2

Charles Blackmore, Slave Abigail - taxed as 2

Sam. Bowman — 1

Rich. Bryan — 1

Phillemon Bryan — 1

John Baxter, Willm. Evan, Joshua Hickman, Jr. - taxed as 3

John Beale 1
Jacob Baker 1
Adam Burris 1
Henry Beeding, Thos. Beeding, Edward Beeding - taxed as 3
Enos Campbell Quart[ers]: Slaves Tom, Mornica & Sarah - taxed as 3
Willm. Cotteral 1
Andrew Cotteral, Jr., Saml. Cotteral - taxed as 2
Andrew Cotterale, Sr. 1
Wm. Clary 1
Henry Cole 1
Tunis Cole 1
Simon Case 1
Silvester Clearwater 1
Chas. Coats, Andrew Williams - taxed as 2
Philip Dowel 1
Jno. Draper 1
Jno. Dowden, Sr., Jno. Dowden, Jr. - taxed as 2
Nathl. Dowden 1
Michl. Cashford Dowden 1
Wm. Douglas Quarter, Gowen Hembleton, David Ryan, Slaves Jack, Peg Windsor & Dinch - taxed as 6
Saml. Ellis, Solomon Ellis - taxed as 2
Zach. Ellis 1
John Ellis 1
Sarah Eltinge, Joshua Davis, Moves Coleman, Slaves Peter, Jack, Kate, Leah, Hal - taxed as 7
John Fletchal, John Frederick, Slaves Frank & Phillio - taxed as 4
James Fife 1
Saml. Frederick 1
James Gore, Sr., Michl. Gore, Slave Jenny - taxed as 3
James Gore, Jr. 1
Clemsias Gore 1
Thos. Gore 1
James Getton, Gideon Paramour - taxed as 2
Benj. Getton 1
Joseph Groves 1
Thos. Grimes 1
Ezekiel Goslin, Joshua Goslin - taxed as 2
Wm. Galford, Wm. Neal, Slave Kate - [tax missing]
Ann Genkins, Beadow Philips - [tax missing]
William Hickman, Slaves Sampson & Sib - [tax missing]
Joshua Hickman, Sr., Joseph Paramour, Slaves George & Moriah - taxed as 4
Stephen Hickman, Saml. Douglas, Slave Harry - taxed as 3
Henry Hickman, Slaves Tom, Rose & Kate - taxed as 4
David Hickman 1
Solomon Hickman 1
Arthur Hickman, Willm. Hickman, Slave Rose - taxed as 3
James Harbin 1
Sam Hardy 1
Chas. Houkmson, Geo. Farlindinhiem - taxed as 2
Peter Hoggins 1
John Harris 1
John Henwood 1
Geo. Jewile, Moses Jewile, Jesse Allison - [tax missing]
David Jewile 1
Willm. Jewile 1
Francis Kannedy, Jerh. Stokes - taxed as 2

Daniel Kelly, James Burrows - taxed
as 2
Capt. Wm. Lucket, Wm. Lucket,
Jr., John Sample, Slaves Hannah,
Will, Nel, Joseph - taxed as 6
Locker Joseph                1
Robt. Mouten                1
Rich. Merrick, John Miles - taxed as
2
Thos. Martin                1
Nich. Minor's Quarter, John
Crumpton, Slaves Nat., Tom,
Sarah, Inda, Frank, Jack &
Harry - taxed as 8
Benj. Mackal, Sr., Henry Talbert,
Slaves Mason, Harry, Sarah, Ken
& Luce - taxed as "7"
Benj. Mackal, Jr.                1
Charles Nisbet                1
John [?torn] Nobs                1
Spicer Owen                1
Thos. Duborn & Wm. Osborn    2
Benj. Duborn                1
John Owen, John Collier - taxed as 2
Chas. Collier                1
James Riggs, Sr., John Riggs - taxed
as 2
Edmd. Riggs                1
James Riggs, Jr.                1
Benj. Riggs, James Walloxen - taxed
as 2
James Rimmer, Slave Hannah -
taxed as 2
James Robinson                1
Wm. Roads                1
Wm. Saunders                1
Dan Smith                1
Dan Stuart                1
James Tear, Slave Bess - taxed as 2
Wm. Sears                1
John Shelton, James Shelton - taxed

as 2
Wm. Shelton                1
Richd. Self                1
John Swam                1
Francis Street                1
Willm. Vears                1
John Vears, John West - taxed as 2
John Veach, Rich. Veach, Slaves
Jones & Hannah - taxed as 4
Silas Veach                1
Thos. Veach, Slave Eve - taxed as 2
James Veach, Jr., Josiah Dann -
taxed as 2
Benj. Veach                1
Wm. Veach                1
William Willson                1
Wadsworth Willson, Slave Bess -
taxed as 2
Josiah Willson                1
Elisha Williams, Slave Tom - taxed
as 2
Agnes Wilcoxin, Slave Judith - taxed
as 1
Wm. Wafford                1
Daniel Walter, David Walter, Joseph
Jones - taxed as 3
John Walter                1
Saml Walter                1
Geo. Walter                1
Geo. Wilson                1
John Young                1
"A true copy. Sam Beale, Sheriff of
Fred. County"

## RENT DUE ON LAND IN FREDRICK COUNTY, 1768- 1769

"A list of persons who stand charged with lands on Frederick county Rent Rolls which are under such circumstances as renders it out of the power of George Scott Farmer afsaid County to Collect the Rents, and therefore claims allowance under his articles for the same from March (?) 1768 to March (?) 1769"

Alexander Adams, himself and land in PA
John Adamson
Ann Agnew
Samuel Agnew
Christian Allbaugh
Eve Allbaugh
William Alldreidge all uncultivated and himself no constant place of abode and will not pay
William Allerburton
William Almary
William Anderson
Daniel Arshcraft's heir unknown
Thomas Awbrey, lives in Virginia
Alexander Bailey
Abram Baker
Peter Baker, says is charged to Saml. Baker
Daniel Baldwin living in PA
James Baldwin
John Bukurduke Ball, Balt. Co.
Jacob Ballsell
Richard Barnes
Thomas Bassett, lives in PA
Thomas Bassett, Phila (addl)
David Beagler
Mark Beagler
Captain Alexander Beall's heirs
Archibald Beall
Benjamin Beall's heirs
Edward Beall

George Beall Junr.
James Beall of Ninian
John Beall of Robert
--hn Beall's heirs
William Beall's heirs
William Beall of Ninian
Thomas Beane, lives in PG Co.
Jacob Bearur, lives in PA
James Beatty
Susanah Beatty, is dead and they who own the land say she owned no more than 81 ½ acres and will pay no more
Benjamin Becraft
Mary Belt
Joseph Bennett
Thomas Bentley, gone to Carolina
Jacob Bishop
---m Black, in England
John Bob
Andrew Booker
Peter Booker
John Boone, 1 lot in Geo. Town
William Boyd
Solomon Brewer
James Brooke's heirs
James Brooke (addl)
Lucey Brooke
Mary Brookes
Henry Brothers, lives in PA
Benjamin Brown, gone to Carolinas
David Brown, himself and land in PA

John Brown of Joshua
William Brown, he and land in PA
Edward Browns
Peter Bruner
Everhart Bumgardner
Richard Bumgardner
Yost Bunkle
Elizabeth Burcham, VA
Matheas Burkett's heirs
George Burnes
William Burnes, lives in VA
Peter Butler's heirs
Tobias Butler
Henry Byer
Philip Caffee, dead
John Campbell
John Carr
William Chadd, a stroler
William Chapline
Henry Charlton, lives in PA
Saml. Chase
Greenbury Cheany, dead
Zachariah Cheany
Josiah Claphan, lives in VA
George Clark
Thomas Clarkson
Johny Clary
William Clary
William Deveron (?) Clary
Tiel Clements
John Cochran, him and land in PA
William Cochran, himself and land in PA
John Colwell's heirs, VA
Thomas Conn, gone to Carolina
Devall Coonce
George Coonce, PA or Balt. Co.
Frederick Cooper
Nicholas Corben
John Cowman
Henry Wright Crabb's heirs

John Crawford, him and land in PA
Michael Creager, Senr.
Jacob Creasy, is dead
--- Crise
William Cumming's heirs
George Dagan
Henry Darbey
Ann Davis
David Davis
Meredith Davis's heirs
Phenehas Davis, lives in PA
Sarah & Mary Davis, Sarah is in AA Co.
Wm. Davis's heirs
Thomas Davison, PA
Leonard Decaes, dead
James Decker
James Dickson's heirs
Edward Diggis & Ralph Taney
Henry Diggis, lives in PA
John Diggis's heirs
Basil Dorsey's heirs
Captain John Dorsey's heirs
John Dorsey's heirs
The Honble D. Dulany Esq.
Samuel Dullenbaugh
John Dunn's heirs unknown
Christian Dyer
George Easter
William Eastub
Ninian Edmonston
Ulerick Ekler
John Emmetts
John England
Joseph Ensor
Adam Erchard
Walter Evans, in PG Co.
John Everet, lives in PA
Henry Fight, lives in Balt. Co.
Peter Fine, lives out of the Province
John Flint, is dead, his son the heir

lives in VA
Simon Foy
Nicholas France
Jason Frizzle, gone to Carolina
Richard Gabriel, himself and land in
    PA
Benjamin Gaither, in AA Co. or Balt.
    Co.
Fielder Gantt
Fielder Gantt (addl)
John Gardner
Isaac Garrison
Jacob Giles, belongs to Jos. Waters, a
    stroler
Thomas Gilliland's heirs
George Gordon's heirs
Josiah Gordon, PG Co.
George Graff
Philip Grambler
Jacob Grams            .
Benjamin Griffith, AA Co.
Orlander Griffith, AA Co.
John Gronon
Joseph Groves
Jonathan Hagan
Henry Hall, is dead
Joseph Hardman's heirs
Shedrech Harmon
George Hartman
George Frazier Hawkins
Margaret Hern, both her and land
    suppd. in PA
Martin Hilderbrand
Patrick Hinds (addl)
John Howard, Carolina
John Hyer
John Larkins
Valentine Larsh
James Lemar, gone to Carolina
Saml. Lewellin, PA
Charles Lewis

Philip Litzinger, VA
Jonas Luby
Wm. Lucas
Alexander Magruder
John Magruder
Nathaniel Magruder
Ninian Magruder
Samuel Magruder
Paul Mark's heirs
Edmond Martin
James Martin
George Matthews
Rowland May
William McClary, all in PA
William McCrachan, VA
William McCray
Moses McCubbin, Balt. Co.
Wm. McGaughy, a stroler
Thomas McHaine
John McIntire
Saml. McKeene, himself and land in
    PA
Thomas McKeene, both him and land
    in PA
Thomas McLane
William McLane
Patrick McManning
Alexander McNear
Honest Medley
Conrod Miller
Isaac Miller
Jacob Miller, Jr.
John Miller
Lodwick Miller
Michael Miller heirs
Oliver Miller, Balt. Co.
Oliver Miller Balt. Co. (addl)
Thomas Miller
Morris Millhouses heirs, part lies in
    Pen.
George Valentine Milsgars

Isaac Milton's heirs
Mary Anne Mislin
John Mitchel, a minor in Chas. Co.
David Mitchell
Thomas Morris
Samuel Mount, VA
Thomas Mullineux, Balt. Co.
Philip Murphy's heirs
George Neale
Raphael Neale, St. Marys Co.
Benjamin Nearson
George Neat
Mathias Need
Christian New
Jacob Nicholls
Samuel Nicholls
Thomas Nicholls
Thomas Nicholls' heirs
John Nichols, in AA Co.
Benjamin Nickring
Thomas Noble's heirs
William Norris' heirs
Andrew Nubinger
Jacob Null
Nathaniel Offutt, Junr.
Major Joseph Ogle's heirs
Thomas Orbison, lives in Pen
Joshua Owen, Balt. Co.
Samuel Owings, Junr.
William Paca
George Pack's heirs
Thomas Palmer, in PA
Richard Pernall
James Perry, PG Co.
Elias Pettitt - runaway
Nicholas Philips, VA
Thomas Philpot, London
Thomas Pickerton
Jacob Piper
Peter Praig
Thomas Claget Prather's heirs, gone

to Red Stone
Samuel Price
William Price of Rheese Run
Casper Primore
John Radford's heirs
John Ralston, himself and land in PA
William Raven
John Ray, AA Co.
Valentine Reap
John Reddick, Balt. Co., land in PA
Andrew Reed
Frederick Reel
John Richards
John Ridgeley, Balt. Co.
Mary Ridgeway
Elisha Riggs
Aaron Riley, belongs to merchant in
    Phila.
Jeremiah Riley
John Riley
Peter Ritcher
William Rivert, said to live in PA
Stephen Robert
Lawrance Rombarah
Doctor David Ross
John Row, dead
William Rugdon, both himslef and
    land in PA
John Ruister, Balt. Co.
William Rusk, himself and land in PA
Thomas Rutland, AA Co.
Nicholas Samuel
John Sausar, is run away
Andrew Scott's heirs
William Scott, lives in VA
James Sears, dead
John Sharra
David Shelbey, lives in PA
Captain Evan Shelbey
Jacob Shilling
William Shoup, VA

John Shudey
Isaac Simmons
John Simple, lives in VA
Andrew Simpson
John Sittern's heirs
Richard Skith
George Slator
George Sloy
George Smith
Jacob Smith, a stroler
John Smith's heirs
Frederick Sower
William Spartis
Conrad Spaw
Leonard Spong
Captain Edward Sprigg
Colo. Edward Sprigg's heirs (the
  widow pays for 593 acres)
Gilbert Sprigg's heirs
Joseph Sprigg, PG Co.
Osburn Sprigg's heirs
James Spurgeon
James Spurgeon, both him and land in
  PA (addl)
John Spurgeon
Benjamin Spyker
Tobias Stansbury's heirs
William Starr, gone to Carolina
James Stephenson, both him and land
  in PA
William Stewart, PA
Thomas Stoddert's heirs
Henry Stolae
Henry Stone
William Stroope, VA
Jacob Sunfrang
Edward Swaney
Benedict Swope, Balt. Co.
Benedict Swope, (addl)
Alexander and Andrew Symmers
Thomas Tallbert

Ralph Taney with Edward Diggis
George Tayler
Anthony Thompson
Cornelius and Ann Thompson
John Thompson, dead
Captain Wm. Tipple
Edward Totheral, lives in England
Caleb Touchstone
Sampson Trammell, VA
Widow Tranceway
Jacob Trout
John Trundle
Frederick Tryor
Edmond Turner, PG Co.
Frederick Unsell
John Vammons, Pen, both him and
  land
James Verdie
Jeremiah Virgin
Hance Waggoner, gone to Carolina
George Wales
William Wallace's heirs
Edward Ward
Basil Warfield, Eastern Shore
James Warford, gone to Carolina
Joseph Warford, both him and land in
  PA
William Warford, Carolina
Joseph Waters, a stroler
Nathan Waters, AA Co.
William Waters, is gone
John Watts, both him and land in PA
William Waugh's heirs
John Weaver
John Webster, AA Co.
Alexander Wells, Balt. Co.
Thomas Wells, Balt. Co.
Stephen West
William West's heirs
Nathaniel Wickham, Senr.
William Wilkins

Thomas Willet
Eleanor Williams, in PA
Esther Williams, in PA
John Williams
Gerard Willson
John Willson, PG Co.
Thomas Willson

William Willson, Greenwood
John Wilmot, Junr., AA Co.
Francis Wise's heirs
Jane Wivell
John Woolf
John Worthington, Junr., Balt. Co.

## RENT DUE ON LAND IN FREDERICK COUNTY, 1771-1772

"A List of Persons who stand charged with lands on Fredk Co which are under such circumstances as rendered it out of the Power of George... Farmer of the said County to collect the Rents and therefore Claims Allowance under his articles for the same - from Michael mass 1771 to Michael mass 1772"

Thos. Abrey, lives in VA
Mark Alexander and Andw. Stigar,
    they live in Balt. Co.
Christian Allbaugh
Eve Allbaugh
John Alldridge (addl)
William Alldridge, a single man and
    no place of abode
William Allerberton's heirs
William Allmary
Daniel Ashcraft's heirs
James Baldwin, lives in PG Co.
Jacob Banker
Jacob Barnes
Richard Barnes
Thos. Bassett, lives in PA
Alexander Bayley
Michael Beagler
Capt. Alexr. Beall's heirs
Edward Beall, no constant place of
    abode
John Beall's heirs
John Beall of Robt. heirs
Patrick Beall, lives in PG Co.

Robt. Beall (of Jas.) (addl)
William Beall's heirs
William Beall's heirs, this land
    belongs to minors
William Murdock Beall
John Beane
Richard Beard, man and land in PA
Chas. Beatty
Chas. Beatty and Geo. Fraser
    Hawkins, lots in Geo. Town
Susannah Beatty, she is dead
William Beatty
Benjamin Belt Junr., lives in PG Co
Col. Joseph Belt's heirs, lives in PG
    Co.
Mary Belt (wife of Col. Jeremiah),
    she lives in PG Co.
Thos. Belt, lives in PG Co.
William Thos. Benson
Thos. Bentley
--- Best
John Bishop, lives in PA
Samuel Biusey
William Black, lives in London

Brice Blair
Allen Bowie, he lives in PG Co.
John Bowman
David Bowser
Abram Boyd's Children, minors
Robert Brightwell's heirs
--- Brooke's heirs
Henry Brothers, lives in PA
Benjamin Brown
Edward Brown
James Brumlee, lives in PA
William Buchanan
John Buckerduke
Elizabeth Burcham
Jehew Burkhart
Peter Butler's heirs
Richard Butler
Philip Butman
Henry Byer
Patrick Caile
Messrs. Benedict Calvert & Compy.
John Campble, lives in AA Co.
Neil Campble, a poor man, no effects
John Carehart (addl)
John Carmack
Chas. Carroll, Esq.
Jacob Carsner
William Chadd, a stroller
George Chairman, lives in PA
Joseph Chapline
Capt. Moses Chapline's heirs
Henry Charlton, lives in PA
Samuel Chase (addl)
Michael Clapsaddle, a stroller
George Clark
Wm. Devorn Clary, runaway
Tule Clements
Philip Coffee
Geo. Coleman
Geo. Coonce, lives in PA
Jacob Coonce

Peter Coonce
Nicholas Corbin
Henry Wright Crabb's heirs
Mrs. Crabb's heirs
Jacob Crasey, dead, land lies in PA
Michael Creger Junr., gone to VA
Stephen Crise
James Cross
Frederick Crouse, lives in PA
Aron Crusey
John Cuirtain
Joseph Cumberlidge, poor man, no
    effects
Henry Darby
John Darnall, lives in Chas. Co.
Thomas Davidson, lives in PA
David Davis, lives in PA
Isaac Dawson, moved to Red Stone
    Settlement
Francis Deakins (addl)
William Deakins (addl)
Leonard Decoes, man dead
William Dent
Peter Detlinger
James Dickson's heirs
Dudley Diggs, lives in St. Mary's Co.
Edward Diggs, and Ralph Tawney
Ignatius Diggs
John Diggs' heirs
James Docker
Calib Dorsey
William Downey, a poor man, no
    effects
Richard Duckett and Thos. Williams
Daniel Dulany
Walter Dulany
John Dunn's heirs
William Dunwoody, has gone to Red
    Stone Settlement
John or Samuel Durbin
--- Dyer

Adam Easter
Ninian Edmonston
Rachel Edmonston
Ulerich Eikler
John England
Joseph Ensor, lives in Balt. Co.
Walter Evans, lives in PG Co.
Jacob Eversole
Peter Fine
John Flint Senr., is dead, son lives in VA
Charles Allison Foard, lives in Charles Co.
Edward Fotterall's heirs, heirs in Ireland
Jacob French, gone to VA
Benjamin Gaither, lives in AA Co.
John Gardner
Isaac Garrison
Thos. Gassaway, lives in AA Co.
Fielder Gaunt
William Gibson, no effects on the land
Jacob Giles, lives in Balt. Co.
Mordecai Gist, man gone to the West Indies
Geo. Gordon's heirs
Michael Gore, gone to Carolina
Geo. Graff
Francis Grandadam
Thos. Green, gone to Carolina
Orlander Griffith, lives in AA Co.
Joseph Groves
Jacob Gunter, lives in PA
Jonathan Hagar, says char'd to Peter Ridenour
William Hall
Charles Hammond (addl)
Nathan Hammond's heirs, heirs live in AA Co.
Edward Willers Harbine, lives in PG

Co.
William Hardey
Charles Harding
Josiah Harper's heirs, lives in VA
Robert Harper, lives in VA
Robert Harrison, lives in VA
William Harrison
Conrod Hartsog
Nicholas Haslum
Geo. Haun
John Haun
Lodwick Haun
Fredk. Wm. Hawker, lives in VA
Geo. Fraser Hawkins, land in PA
Joseph Hayes
Biggar Head's heirs
Martin Hildebrand
Thos. Hilleary, lives in PG Co.
John Hisler
Peter Hisson, lives in PA
Hanor Holmes
John Howard, gone to Carolina
Samuel and John Howard, these people live in AA Co.
Ulerick Huffstadler, lives in PA
John Hughes
Abram Hull
David Hurley
Thos. Hutchcraft, run away
Samuel Hyde's heirs, he lives in England
William Ingleman
Daniel Jenkins' heirs, belongs to an orphan, no effects
John Evan Jenkins
John Jessey
Mathew Jones
William Jones
Mountz Justice
John Geo. Keedman
Jacob Kegg, lives in PA

Charles Kelley
Samuel Kelley, a stroller
Thos. Kellor, lives in PA
Thos. Kennard
John Kennedy's heirs, minors
Martin Kersner's heir
John Keys
William Kimball
Christopher Kitterman, lives in PA
James Lamar, lives in Carolina
Valentine Larsh, lives in Balt. Co.
Geo. William Laurance, lives in VA
Patrick Law (addl)
John Layman
Henry Lazenby (addl)
Frederick Leatherman
Philip Ludwell Lee, lives in VA
Geo. Lemmon
Samuel Lewellen, land lays in PA
Evan Lewis, lives in PA
John Logsdon (addl)
Laurence Logsdon, gone to Carolina
Ralph Logsdon, is gone to Carolina
John Long
Christopher Lowndes
Jonas Lutz
William Lux, lives in Balt. Co.
Joseph Lynn
Samuel Lyon, lives at Red Stone
Jonathan Madding
Hezekiah Magruder
Charles Martin
Edmond Martin
John Martin Junr.
John Mason, man run away
Leigh Master
Geo. Mathews
Jacob May
Rowland May
William May, a very poor man, no
    effects

Andrew Mayes
William McClary, lands in PA
William McCray
Capt. Angus McDonald
William McGaughy, lives in PA
Thos. McKain
Hugh McLane
Thos. McLane
Alexander McNear
Honesty Medley
Peter Melattoe
Isaac Miller's heirs
Michael Miller's heirs
Oliver Miller's heirs
Solomon Miller's heirs
Thos. Miller
Morris Millhouse's heirs, lays in PA
Mary Ann Misline
David Mitchell
John Mitchell, belongs to a minor
Thos. Morris
Samuel Mount, lives in VA
Thos. Mullineux, lives in Balt. Co.
Philip Murphey's heirs
Christian Myers
Ralph Neall, lives in St.
Sarah Needham, she is dead
William Needham, he is ---
Christian New
Margaret Newsbaume
John Nicholls Junr., gone to VA
Thos. Noble's heirs, possessors live
    in PG Co.
Laurence O'Neill (addl)
William O'Neill
Thos. Ogle, Senr., lives in Cecil Co.
John Oliver, a stroller
John Jas. Owen, gone to VA
Joshua Owen, lives in Balt. Co.
Geo. Pack's heirs
Hugh Parker's heirs, possessor lives

52

in PA
Richard Parnall, lives in AA Co.
James Patterson, lives in PA
John Pearce, man run away
Thos. Pecker's heirs, minors
Joseph Perry
Robert Peter (addl)
Elias Petitt, runaway
Thos. Philpott, lives in London
William Pidgeon, lives in PA
John Christian Pinkley
David Pot's heirs, they live in VA
William Powell, man run
Peter Praigg
John Smith Prather's heirs
Thos. Clagett Prather's heirs, he is at
    Red Stone (sole heir)
Elders of Presbyterian House
Casper Primore
John Radford
Goslip Ratt
John Ray, lives in AA Co.
Andrew Reid
John Reister, lives in Balt. Co.
Nicholas Rhoads, is a mad man, no
    effects
John Richards
Benjamin Riddle
Henry Ridenour
John Ridgely, lives in Balt. Co.
Mary Ridgway, alias Ridgely
John Riley
Valentine Rinehart
Daniel Robbins, land in PA
John Robbins, lives in VA
William Roberts
Anthony Roof
John Harmon Rosenplatt
Doctr. David Ross, lands in PA
William Rugdon, lives in PA
Thos. Rutland, lives in AA Co.

Alexander Rutter
John Sammons
John Sausar, run away
Andrew Scott's heirs
John Semple, lives in VA
William Sergeant
John Settern's heirs
Horatio Sharp, Fort Frederick, stands
    on this land
David Shelby, lives in PA
Isaac Shelby (addl)
John Shepherd's heirs, live in VA
Laurence Shock
David Shriver (addl)
Michael Shultz
Andrew Simpson, lives in PA
Geo. Sly, is dead
John Smith's heirs
Joseph Smith
Philip Smith
Richard Smith
Peter Snider
Doctor Henry Snively
Richard Snowden's heirs
Frederick Sower
Conrod Space ?
William Sparks
Jeremiah Spires, gone to Carolina
Col. Edward Sprigg's heirs, heirs live
    in PG Co.
Gilbert Sprigg's heris, heirs live in
    PG Co.
Joseph Sprigg
Ozburn Sprigg's heirs, land belongs
    to minors
James Spurgeon, lives and has pt of
    his land in PA
William Spurgeon, lives in PA
Henry Stall
Geo. Stanier
Tobias Stansburg's heirs, live in Balt.

Co.
Thos. Stansbury
William Starr, in Carolina
Simon Stickle
Andrew Stigar, lives in Balt. Co. [see Mark Alexander]
Thos. Stoddert's heirs, they live in PG Co.
Henry Stole
John Stoner's heirs, the heir PA
William Stroope, lives in VA
John Hance Stullman
Edward Swaney
Alexander and Andrew Symmer's assignees
Thos. Talbert, lives in PG Co.
Geo. Taylor
Richard Tedd's heirs, a poor man, no effects
Christopher Thomas, man in Carolina
Samuel Thomas
Anthony Thompson
Cornelius & Ann Thompson
John Thompson's heirs
Capt. William Tipple, lives in London
Joseph Tomblinson, lays in PA
Caleb Touchstone
Alexander Tracey, man in Carolina
Goodheart Trisler
John Trundle
Samuel Tulaghpan ?
Robt. Twigg, lives in PA
Peter Ulamer
Christian Valentine
Richard Vandike, lives in PA
Daniel Vears' heirs
Jeremiah Virgin
Hancy Waggoner
James Waling Senr.
Zachariah Walker
William Wallace's heirs
Jacob Walter
Edward Ward
Joseph Ward, lives in Calvert Co.
Alexander Warfield's heirs, they live in AA Co.
Bazil Warfield, lives on the Eastern Shore
James Warford, is in Carolina
Joseph Warford, land and man in PA
John Waters (addl)
Nathan Waters, lives in AA Co.
Samuel Waters, a stroller
John Watts, lives in PA
John Webbster & Compy., they live in Balt. Co.
Benjamin Welch, lives in AA Co.
William Welch, is dead, no effects on land
Alexander Wells, lives in Balt. Co.
Bernard Wertenburgh, lives in PG Co.
William West's heirs
John White, gone to Carolina
Abram Whitmon and others
Peter Wiesinger
John Wiles
William Wilkins
Edward Willett
Ninian Willett (addl)
Thos. Willett
Elisha Williams
John Williams, Junr.
James Williamson
Thomas Willson
William Willson
John Wilson, he lives in PG Co.
Thos. Wilson
Geo. Winder
Jacob Wise, gone to Carolina
Jane Wivell
Peter Yeater

James Young                                    Henry Younger
Notley Young
John Youngblood

## ESTRAYS

*Maryland Archives C788-1 1/40/14/1*

Richard Acton July 1 76
Andrew Adams May 17 76
George Adams Oct 26 85
Robert Addison July 25 80 living at
    Bush Creek Forge
Thomas Affutt Apr 25 74 near the
    Grate Fall on Pot'k. River
Valentine Ailer June 13 74 lives near
    Joseph Woods, Jr.'s Mill on
    Israels Creek
John Albaugh Feb 21 83
William Albaugh May 23 83
Zackariah Allbaugh July 15 73
Elizabeth Allen Dec 8 72
Moses Allen Nov 8 74
John Allison Aug 14 69
Henry Ambrose May 27 78
Richard Ancrum, Junr. May 31 80
Alexander Anderson May 23 66
    brought by his son William (father
    sick)
Elizabeth Anderson May 5 74 lives
    about Perry Creek Hundred
William Anderson Aug 15 78
Philip Angleburgher June 11 70
Dawalt Ankney Jan 15 73
John Ankrom Aug 6 65 (recorded his
    mark)
Balser Arbough May 19 70
Daniel Arnolt May 3 74
Benjamin Artmore Aug 4 69
Henry Ash Mar 17 72
Thomas Ash Sept 19 67

Charles Atkins Apr 20 68
Thomas Austin Sept 25 75
Benjamin Baggerly Oct 31 68 lives
    near Mr. Snowden's Manor
Peter Bainbridge Mar 21 70, June 8
    81
Peter Bainbridge, Senr. Aug 22 83
Peter Baker Oct 26 74, Nov 8 74
John Balinger Jan 26 75
John Ballinger May 7 77
Jacob Balsell Dec 6 81 of Middle
    Monokasy Hundred
Henry Baltzel May 5 73
John Barber Apr 2 74
John Barber, Junr. Sept 8 68
George Bare Dec 31 84
Thomas Barlow Nov 19 83
John Barrick Aug 19 71
John Barrick, Senr. Dec 7 85
Peter Barrickman July 31 67
Walter Basil Oct 22 66
John Bateman May 6 76
Samuel Bayard Jan 22 67
John Baylie Nov 16 68
Edward Beading Nov 19 66
Basil Beall Sept 26 71, Dec 6 74
Brooke Beall May 11 75
Elisha Beall May 28 67, Apr 2 74,
    May 3 84
Col. George Beall July 14 66
George Beall June 16 67
John Beall Aug 25 74, June 25 66,
    Sept 24 70

John Beall June 4 72 of Bennett's
    Creek
Nathan Beall Apr 18 82
Nathan Beall Aug 9 84 of Bennett's
    Creek
Ninion Beall July 3 73
William Beall Nov 26 66, June 17 67
Samuel Bearle-- see Samuel Pearl
Edward Beatton July 21 73 lying in
    the upped end of the sugar land
Charles Beatty Aug 19 76
John Beatty Aug 5 76
Thomas Beatty, Junr. Nov 29 84
George Beckwith June 7 77
George Beckworth July 7 67
George Becraft June 17 65 of Pipe
    Creek
George Becraft Apr 27 75
Peter Becraft Apr 29 73, July 14 83
Peter Becraft, Senr.June 9 79
Thomas Beeding Aug 17 65
Charles Beggarly Dec 24 84
John Bellough Dec 20 71
Capt. Jeremiah Belt May 24 83
Christian Benchley May 27 82
Abraham Benjamin Aug 6 69
Abner Bentley June 10 83
William Bentley May 12 72, Nov 14
    77
Mrs. Susanna Berrier June 29 79
Susanna Berryer Oct 30 81 near Little
    Pipe Creek
Michael Billmoyer Oct 21 82
Daniel Biser June 11 77, June 22 80
John Blair Feb 29 68, Dec 18 71
George Bond May 7 65
Thomas Bonton Oct 6 70 lives in
    Frederick Co. near John Branch
Andrew Bostian Oct 1 84
Alexander Boteler June 27 67
Thomas Bowles June 24 73, Jan 24

82
John Bowlon (?) May 27 72 son of
    Zech.
Baltis Bowman Oct 18 73
Baltsor Bowman June 13 74
Henry Boydsell May 27 74
Hubortis Boys July 21 65 of Israels
    Creek
Frederick Bramberger Oct 12 77
Jacob Brangle Nov 26 66
Ludwick Brickner Apr 7 81
Robert Briscoe Apr 30 66
Richard Brooke June 14 73
Roger Brooke May 5 85
William Brooks Dec 4 65
Antoney Brost July 18 67
Henry Brothers Mar 22 79
Edward Brown Feb 26 68, May 27 77
Henry Brown May 26 85
James Brown May 29 76
John Brown Apr 19 83
Richard Brown June 18 66
Robert Brown June 20 82 of Toms
    Creek Hundred
Thomas Brown July 20 76
Joseph Browning Jan 3 76
Valentine Bruner Aug 27 78, Feb 6
    81
William Buchanan Aug 15 69
John Buckias Sept 24 76
John Buckie Dec 18 82
Creek Budge Nov 25 73
Thomas Burgee June 20 75
Peter Burghart Feb 11 75
William Burton Jan 20 68
Edward Butler Apr 1 82
Elixander Butler June 26 69
Samuel Butt Oct 25 68
John Buxton Sept 13 74
Andrew Buzzard Nov 26 85
David Buzzard May 18 84

David Buzzart Sept 26 82

--- Byall June 12 69

Henry Caldwell June 5 76

Anne Callorigs (?) Sept 27 70 lives near Ogles on Owens Creek

Leanard Cammel Aug 10 65

Capt. Eanos Campbell June 7 68

John Campbell Dec 21 65 of Lenganore

Kneas Campbell Nov 21 71

Kneas Campbell June 19 71 lives at upper end of the Sugar Lands

Evan Carmack Jan 7 85 on Little Pipe Creek

Evin Carmack June 15 68 lives near Little Pipe Creek

Capt. Samuel Carrick May 25 65

John Carroll Sept 17 77

James Carsey July 2 65

Shadrach Case Aug 29 71, Mar 24 75

John Casel Jan 13 75

Thomas Castle June 16 78

William Cecill Dec 8 85 of near Sugar Loaf Mountain

John Cellars, Jr. Mar 15 73

Ninean Chamberlain Dec 16 66

Nathen Chaney June 24 66

Samuel Chen Mar 20 66

William Chilton Nov 3 66

John Chisholm, and overseer, Joseph Jean Jan 6 66

Benjamin Chittey Nov 26 68

Conrad Chreichbaum June 25 81 of Middle Monokasy Hundred

Conrad Chreichbaum Dec 12 82

George Chriesman May 4 81

John Chriesman June 9 80 a tanner

George Church July 25 66

Thomas Clagett June 15 65

John Clarey Nov 16 84 lives near William Hobbs

William Clarey Sept 21 78

Henry Clark May 26 69

Neal(e) Clark July 18 68, June 19 69

William Clark Dec 10 67

Henry Clem May 5 84

Oswald Clements Dec 18 71

Elley Clime Jan 23 77

Peter Cline Nov 30 81

Michael Cober (Coler?) Feb 4 66

James Coffy July 15 67

James Cole Apr 20 73

Richard Collins Nov 15 73

William Condon Dec 9 72

James Conn, son of Hugh June 18 66

Stephen Constable Jan 1 72

Ambrose Cook July 1 69

Capt. George Cook May 18 84

John Cookerly Nov 21 85

Martin Coonce Apr 19 75

Mary Ann Cooper June 17 65

Henry Cork Feb 17 74

Robert Corsleble Oct 14 68

John Cottrel Mar 31 66

Jeremiah Covel Nov 29 68

Nehemiah Covell July 1 75

Christian Cox June 10 74

Ezekle Cox Dec 19 74

John Cox July 4 74 living on Friends Creek in the South Mountain near Province Line

Richard Crabb Jan 23 75, Sept 4 73

David Crabell Dec 20 80

David Crawford, Junr. May 25 84

Joseph Craycraft Nov 19 66

Adam Creager May 31 77

Christian Creegar Aug 10 65, of Monocacy Manor, recorded by his wife Mary

Christian Creeger July 11 68

Peter Creger Feb 20 68

Peter Crider June 2 73

George Criesman July 3 77
Richard Cromwell Dec 10 85
Jacob Crook Jan 29 70
Charles Crouch June 12 72
Michael Crouse July 29 69 lives on
    Monocacy Manor
Devault Crowley May 19 74
William Crum Sept 13 70
Jacob Crumbecker Oct 5 77
Paul Cruse Apr 29 77
John Cryder Aug 12 82
Christian Cumber May 6 82
William Cumming June 2 67
George Curch (Carch?) July 25 68
George Custer June 9 81
Edmund Cutler Dec 17 77
John Cypher Nov 17 77
Thomas Darnall July 8 78
Jacob Darner Aug 19 71
William Daveler Aug 10 76
Abraham Davenport Nov 3 74
William Davey May 12 81
Charles Davis July 4 66
Francis Davis, Junr. June 26 71
Gerard Davis Mar 9 80
Gerrard Davis Oct 14 67; also on
    another occasion for which the
    date was not recorded
Griffith Davis June 16 73
Leonard Davis Oct 6 69, June 4 71
Richard Davis Aug 3 71
Vachal Davis May 22 65, Aug 21 66,
    Mar 20 70, Aug 22 71
Walter Davis June 8 82
William Davis May 8 65; also on
    another occasion for which the
    date was not recorded
William Davis, Junr. May 12 67, Dec
    14 68
George Dawson June 17 67
Henry Dawson Nov 7 85

Nicholas Dawson May 11 85 on the
    Monocacy in Lower Monocacy
    Hundred
Moses Deaslin Jan 26 71
Abraham Deerdruff Apr 3 83 of
    Middle Kittoctin Hundred
John Delander May 16 69
Elias Delashmitt Nov 9 79
Lindsey Delashmitt Mar 9 82
Capt. Elias Delashmutt Jan 9 76
Elias Delashmutt Oct 13 84, May 5
    85
John Delauder Feb 27 73
David Delauter May 3 81
Laurence Delonder Apr 16 71
William Denis Nov 17 66
Thomas Denney Apr 29 76
John Depue Aug 19 66
George Derr Nov 10 80
Casper Devilbess Apr 22 71
Serrat Dickenson July 9 71
Thomas Dickison May 9 69
John Dodson Apr 12 83
Michael Dodson May 22 78
Richardson Donaldson July 3 66
Basil Dorsey June 12 73
Charles Dorsey Apr 7 80, Oct 8 84
Michael Dottro Apr 5 70
James Douley, Junr. Apr 18 71
Rachel Dowden Nov 27 74
Richard Dowden Sept 28 65
Peter Dowell Oct 15 70
Joseph Draik Oct 9 71
William Drone, Senr. Sept 7 84 lives
    on Trammel's Island
Thomas Duly Nov 28 70
George Dutterow Aug 21 82
Conrod Dutton July 20 69
Alexander Duvall June 5 69, July 6
    69
Lewis Duvall May 3 65, Sept 8 75

Lewis Duvall, son of Benjamin July 30 65

William Duvall May 27 66, June 7 85

Capt. William Duvall May 27 80

Capt. William Duvall, Senr. July 5 80

Philip Dycus May 13 83 lives near upper part of Monocasy Manor

Harmon Eagle Sept 30 72

John Eason June 14 69

George Easter Sept 24 65

John Easton Jan 6 68

Christian Eaverhart Apr 28 73

John Eck June 9 83

Christopher Edden Jan 3 82

Robert Edes Dec 12 70

Frederick Eison June 13 68, Dec 12 68

Aloysius Elder Aug 21 82

William Elerburten June 24 65

Mark Ellett May 14 67

Samuel Ellis Aug 15 67

Zachariah Ellis June 26 72

Zachariah Ellis June 11 71, lives about 5 miles below the mouth of the Monococy

Melchor Endley Aug 18 81

William England Jan 14 68

Barbara Engle Oct 29 83

John Engle Aug 6 76 of Middle Monokasy Hundred

Richard Ensey Apr 6 80

Philip Ensmuger May 24 70

Philip Entsminger Apr 13 76

Adam Estor Aug 8 67

Edward Evans Jan 5 75

Joseph Evans Apr 23 66, near the Great Falls, Potomack

Joseph Everit Mar 19 73, lives near Little Pipe Creek

Baltis Fait Jan 24 74

Samuel Farmer Nov 3 73

Allen Farquhar Aug 18 84

Moses Farquhar May 15 75

William Farquhar Sept 1 72

Barnet Faud Aug 30 75

John Ferguson June 12 73, lives between two Pipe Creeks

John Fetherly June 2 77

Mathias Fickle July 28 74, lives near Tawney Town

Mathias Fickle Aug 2 74

Matthias Firestone June 1 85 of Monocacy Manor

Adam Fischer Aug 22 85 of Frederick Town

Adam Fisher Sept 24 65

Martin Fisher Dec 6 69

Henry Fister July 7 70, May 17 76

George Fivecoat Nov 13 82 also written George Finffrock in same entry

James Flemming Aug 30 73

John Fletchall May 16 69, May 21 71

Martin Fletcher-- see Cornelius Hickey

William Flinthem Mar 27 67

Jacob Flook July 30 76 near Middletown

Robert Flora June 2 68

Albright Florey May 29 79

Ann Foard Jan 22 73, lives on Rock Creek, 9 miles from Geo. Town

Philip Fogel Dec 4 65

Andrew Fogle July 27 72

Jacob Foner Nov 23 79

John Ford Feb 4 66

Peter Ford Sept 20 65

Henary Fore Feb 8 70

John Forman June 17 65

Jacob Foute Sept 9 67

John Fowler Dec 1 85

Frederick Fraise Apr 5 65, June 19 66

Michael Frank May 12 66
Joseph Franklin July 18 75
Henry Frazier June 19 75
Jonathan Frazier Dec 5 81
Capt. Thomas Frazier Apr 27 82
Jacob French Mar 8 70
Thomas French Dec 5 70, Feb 14 71
Andrew Frey July 24 67
Michael Fundalin Aug 11 72, near
   Taney Town
Henry Funk Jan 20 78
Michael Funk Mar 20 66
James Fyfe July 24 66
James Fyfe Apr 20 69, lives on
   Seneca near the Sugarlands
Basil Gaither June 17 67, Mar 21 72,
   Oct 7 72
Edward Gaither May 21 70, son of
   Benjamin
Henry Gaither June 21 68
Mony Galford June 17 65
John Gallaway May 28 70
James Galt May 27 69
Benjamin Galton May 14 64, June 17
   67
Jacob Gance Dec 7 76
Barton Garrett Feb 3 79
Richard Gatton Apr 8 67
Peter Gaver July 4 76
Albright George Dec 28 69
Peter Ghiss Aug 18 78
Ashmon Ginkings Jan 8 65
Ashmon Ginkins May 15 66
Samuel Glaze Oct 17 70
Humphrey Godman June 28 74, May
   27 75
William Goforth July 4 69
William Good July 30 66
Philip Goodman Sept 12 77
Benjamin Goodrick June 22 71
Thomas Graham June 4 76

Alexander Grant Dec 6 65, Aug 7 70
Thomas Graves Sept 17 71
Thomas Graves Oct 2 66, lives on the
   road near Georgetown
William Graves June 26 71
John Gray Aug 8 70
John Gray June 14 70, lives on tract
   called Pourk (?) Hall, on Little
   Pipe Creek
Robert Green Aug 3 82 lives near
   Plummer's Mill
Samuel Green Apr 28 85
Thomas Green May 15 66
William Green Sept 19 65
Walter Smith Greenfield May 22 65
William Grey Mar 10 68
Charles Greenbury Griffith May 5 74
Orlando Griffith May 8 78
Jacob Gripe, Junr. Aug 11 68
Robert Guinn Sept 10 81
Abraham Haff June 27 67, May 9 71,
   June 29 72, Apr 5 73, Apr 21 75,
   Oct 9 75, June 4 81, July 19 84
Garret Haff Sept 19 76, Mar 26 82
John Haff Sept 30 76
Richard Haff Apr 29 73, Sept 20 73
Edward Hagan Sept 9 80
Jonathan Hager Sept 18 65, Apr 24
   67
Benjamin Hall July 27 65, of Burnt
   Housewood Hundred
Benjamin Hall, Junr. July 4 68
Edward Hall Nov 21 84 lives "on or
   near Monocacy and about 3 miles
   from Fred. Town"
Elijah Hall May 1 79
Michael Hall Apr 22 71
Ralph Halt June 13 69
John Hamel Dec 22 73
Francis Hamilton Aug 16 72
John Hammond July 27 80

William Hanker Apr 20 65
Samuel Hanson May 29 72
Christian Harbaugh Apr 17 84
Francis Harbaugh Dec 8 77
William Harbert Nov 8 70
Jacob Harbough Mar 23 76
Samuel Hardesty July 19 71
John Hardin, Junr. June 8 68
Charles Harding May 6 71
Gary Harding Oct 24 78
Francis Hardister July 12 69
George Peter Hargate Nov 1 85
Conrod Hargawder Nov 16 72
William Harison July 6 65, near the
    Widow Hobbs
Isaac Harlan Sept 8 66
Jacob Harman May 31 75
Josiah Harper Sept 2 66
Josiah Harper Apr 15 65, near
    Harper's Ferry
Aaron Harris May 22 74
William Harris Oct 21 66
Thomas Harrison June 11 82
Michael Hartman Nov 30 67
Henry Hartsock Dec 7 71, lives near
    Conrod Dottros
Peter Hauver July 26 85
George Haver Nov 4 85
Henry Hawk Aug 29 68
William Hawker May 20 72
John Hawkings Apr 19 68
Alexander Thomas Hawkins Apr 26
    76
John Hawkins Aug 16 75
Andrew Hawne Aug 17 79
Jonathan Hayes Aug 31 81
William Hays Aug 16 68, Aug 24 70
Jeremiah Hayse July 7 68
William Edward Head Aug 24 71
William Head, Junr. Apr 8 69
Michael Heavly Nov 14 75

Jacob Hedges Nov 11 80
Joseph Hedges June 11 77, Oct 18 84,
    Aug 20 78
Joseph Helm Aug 21 66
Hendrick Hendrickson Sept 30 68,
    Dec 2 77
John Hennongirth July 30 65
Fortnoy Henry Aug 23 73
Abraham Hergert Dec 9 83
Marks Hermon Mar 8 66
John Herring June 13 81
Mathious Herschman Dec 3 67
Bernard Hershberger May 21 79
Joshua Hervin July 21 69
Jacob Hess Feb 23 70
Michael Heyler Feb 17 74
Cornelius Hickey July 4 83 horse put
    into possession of Martin Fletcher
Edmund Hickey May 27 80 of Middle
    Monokasy Hundred
David Hickman Feb 2 69
David Hickman May 9 69, lives in the
    Sugarland
Margaret Hickman May 8 71, lives
    about 10 miles below the mouth of
    Monococy
John Higgins July 5 74
Abm. Hill Mar 30 75
Isaac Hill June 16 71
James Hill Jan 25 74
Richard Hill July 21 79
Ralff Crabb Hilleary Dec 8 66
Andrew Hime June 4 71
Ballsor Hinkle June 8 74
Boltzer Hinkle Feb 18 78
John Hinkle Oct 2 84
Richard Hinton May 12 84 lives on
    Bennett's Creek
Thomas Hinton June 19 67, May 19
    70, June 14 74
Adam Hisung Aug 16 75

Ephraim Hobbs May 31 82 horse trespassed on land of his father, John Hobbs

Joseph Hobbs Feb 29 67

Joseph Hobbs and Nathan Magruder Apr 12 75

Leonard Hobbs Jul 5 79

Nicholas Hobbs Oct 2 72

Josua Hobs May 21 73

Capewell Holland, Junr. Mar 24 69

Anthony Holmead Aug 23 65

Fredrick Holtshoble Nov 16 68

Benedict Holtz Aug 22 78

Jacob Holtz June 12 82 of Middle Monokasy Hundred

Henry Holtzman June 30 83

Thomas Horner Feb 21 81

Adam Hoover June 12 76

Henry Hoover July 24 75, near Shockeys Gap

Jacob Hoover Nov 11 75

Richard Horner July 26 77

Peter Houbert Sept 7 78 of Piney Creek Hundred

Andrew House Mar 15 68

George House June 18 66

Isaac Houser Jan 26 70

Isaac Houstie Nov 12 71

George Howe Nov 1 81 of Frederick Town

Paul Hoy(e) Aug 1873, May 9 74

Henry Huffman Aug 30 70

Rudolph Huffman Feb 15 66

Thomas Hughes Feb 27 81 of Upper Monokasy Hundred

James Hughs Aug 2 73

John Hughs June 16 69, June 16 73

Jacob Hull Apr 25 85 of Burnt House Woods Hundred

Jacob Human July 24 73

Michael Humbert June 10 76, Jan 4

79

Jacob Hummer June 7 66, June 19 82, Oct 5 84

John Hummer May 4 76

Elisha Hyatt July 25 76

Andrew Hyme Sept 22 84

David Hymes May 19 81 of Middle Monokasy Hundred

Rudy Hynes Sept 22 77

Jacob Inch Sept 3 78

Peter Ingle July 11 75, a farmer

William Ingram Aug 23 69

Edward Inman Nov 6 83

Alexander Ireland Apr 20 82

Jeremiah Jack Aug 15 74, June 20 75

John Jackson June 19 75

Elizabeth Jacobs July 12 71, July 8 74, May 13 75

John Jacobs June 30 66, June 8 81, May 8 84

Joseph Jacobs June 4 85

Grifey James Dec 24 74

Benedict Jameson Nov 7 82

Leonard Jameson Nov 1 85

Joseph Jean, overseer of John Chisholm Jan 6 66

Thomas Jeans Sept 7 76

William Jeans Mar 22 67

Thomas Jennings, Esq. Aug 21 66

John Jerdon Apr 7 70

John Jessper Nov 29 69

Thomas Johnson, Junr. Mar 14 72

Josiah Jones May 16 69

Peter Jones Mar 22 67

Thomas Jones Nov 5 68

Mosis Juel Mar 24 70

William Juel Nov 1 68

Isaac Julin Sept 7 71

Conrad Kareas Nov 7 67, lives near head of Linganore & Sams Creek

Adam Karr Nov 2 71, lives near

Christian Koonces
Conrod Katuldy Mar 22 75
John Kearsler Apr 22 79
Peter Keephart May 9 67
John Keeser May 27 74
William Keley Jan 9 75
Samuel Kelly May 2 67, July 7 68
John Kemp Oct 10 76
John Kemp Oct 13 84 lives on
    Carroll's Manor
Peter Kemp Nov 28 67
John Kennedy Oct 15 76
Joseph Kennedy June 24 79
George Kepheart Oct 28 80 had a
    plantation on Carroll Manor
Peter Kepheart Nov 26 76 of Lower
    Monokasy Hundred
Martin Keplinger Apr 3 69
Valentine Ker Oct 6 79
Henry Kernheart Apr 17 81
John Ross Key Nov 10 84
John Keysinger May 31 67
John George Kidaman July 4 70
George Kiler Feb 13 84
George Adam Killiberger July 30 77
John Kincer Apr 17 71
Richard King Aug 10 72
Shredreck Kinley July 23 85
George Kirk Dec 18 76, June 16 72,
    June 8 73
Thomas Kirk, Junr. May 10 69
Jacob Klein Dec 29 71
Nickolus Kline Aug 5 69
Thomas Knotts Aug 17 69
Jacob Koonce Dec 16 78
Isaac Krall Sept 8 83 of Upper
    Monokesy Hundred
William Kritezer Oct 12 85
Jacob Lagaser June 26 84
Robert Lamar May 26 77
Henry Lamb May 6 85

William Lamb May 24 77 near
    Westminster Town
John Laney Aug 26 85
Mathew Laney Jan 20 69
John Larain May 21 73, lives near the
    mouth of Manocacy
George William Laurance Aug 6 66
Mary Lawrance Jan 17 70
Thomas Laysur Nov 5 68
Henry Lazenby July 14 67
Philip Leace Apr 24 76
Jacob Lear Oct 12 71
Godfrey Leatherman Nov 22 68, Oct
    13 85
Henry Leatherman Aug 6 70
Nicholas Leatherman Jan 27 69
Peter Lebegh Oct 23 72
Aaron Lee June 9 67
Robert Lee Nov 4 69
Jacob Leece Sept 11 70, Oct 25 73
Robert Lemar Dec 6 71
Abraham Lemaster June 2 77
Aaron Lenham Aug 20 71
Zachariah Lenthicum Oct 26 74
Henry Letherman Sept 2 73, Oct 30
    73
Michael Letton Apr 17 70
Henry Levens Aug 25 72
Andrew Levingstone Aug 19 79
David Levy Dec 27 84
Jonathan Lewis Dec 12 70, Aug 13
    76
Henry Liday May 29 76
Adam Lighty June 20 67
John Lindsey Jan 6 81 3 miles from
    Harper's Ferry
Bernard Linganfelter May 9 82
James Lingo Sept 15 68
Andrew Link July 24 67
Philip Linn Sept 1 85
Joseph Linthicom Sept 6 65, Oct 14

67
Samuel Linton June 8 74
Michael Litton Apr 3 65
John Livingston May 7 66
Andrew Livinston July 13 73
Michael Lofter May 16 74
James Logen Aug 6 66
Matthias Long July 25 68, lives near
    Smiths Mill, upon Pipe Creek
John Lookinpeel May 31 82 horse
    trespass. on land of father, Peter
Peter John Luckett Apr 23 76
William Luckett June 27 67, Mar 9
    68
William Luckett, Junr. May 27 65,
    Mar 28 69
John Ludey June 23 85
Moses Luman Aug 18 75
George Lutes May 29 77
Mary Lydy Aug 24 71
Philip Lynn July 16 85
James Macatee Aug 9 73
Thomas Maccubbin May 28 70
John Macginnis Nov 14 67
Benjamin Mackall Feb 12 66
James Mackey Apr 19 75, July 28 75
Philip Macklefish May 16 82
Benjamin Mackrell Feb 16 76
John Madam Sept 2 68
Mordecai Madden Nov 11 71
Thomas Magers Oct 15 79
Alexander Magruder May 17 66, May
    9 76
Mary Magruder July 28 65
Nathan Magruder with Joseph Hobbs
    Apr 12 75
Ninian Beall Magruder July 21 66
William Magruder Oct 20 79, May 25
    82
William Beall Magruder June 10 71
James Makall May 22 75

William Manford Dec 18 67
George Mann Dec 15 74
Joseph Mannakey June 3 80
James Manningore June 24 65
James Mantz Mar 29 75
John Marker Aug 4 75
William Marsch May 6 78
James Marshall Nov 21 77
Philip Marshall Sept 27 79
William Marshall, Junr. Dec 6 77
William Marshall Nov 7 84 lives on
    Carroll's Manor
Matthias Mart July 24 69, lives near
    Paul Woolfs near Little Creek [did
    not say Little Pipe Creek]
John Mason Sept 28 65, Aug 30 68
Valentine Matter May 12 77
Jacob May Sept 12 66, June 21 68
Nathan Maynard June 10 85
Samuel McAtee Apr 9 76
James McBride Mar 15 69
James McCay June 27 67
James McClain Aug 31 65
John McClain Oct 25 77
William McClellan June 22 65
Daniel McCoy Aug 2 70
James McCoy Nov 29 72
Joseph McDonald May 29 73
William McGaughey Aug 15 66
John McGinnes Nov 28 69
James McGuire July 2 77
John McKarkle May 13 76
Joseph McKillup Sept 5 80
Peter McMullen Sept 28 67
Robert McNutt June 22 68
John Meal Dec 15 69
Thomas Meek May 7 76
John Mefford Dec 17 84 of Piney
    Creek Hundred
Charles Menix Aug 29 78
Joseph Mershon Nov 5 74

Thomas Metcalf Apr 17 79
John Meyer Apr 2 66
James Michael June 27 76
John Mifford May 26 71, lives near
  Paul Woolf's Tavern
Anthony Miller July 19 81
Conrad Miller May 27 82
Daniel Miller Aug 12 72
David Miller Aug 12 71, Sept 14 71,
  Sept 25 75
Isaac Miller Aug 8 70
Isaac Miller Sept 26 65, Fishing
  Creek
Jacob Miller Dec 7 67, May 19 76
Jacob Miller Dec 31 71, of Kittocton
Michael Miller Sept 8 65
Peter Miller May 25 79
Robert Miller Nov 14 85 lives on
  Linganore
Solomon Miller Apr 12 81
Thomas Miller Nov 7 67
James Mills Aug 21 84
Casper Missell Aug 11 83
John Mitter May 27 69
Phillipseany Moarner Mar 11 74
Lewis Mobberly Nov 15 84
John Moore July 25 68
John Mooth Aug 28 80
Felix Morgan July 19 70
Richard Morgan Dec 15 70
Joseph Morris Aug 2 84
William Morris July 1 75
Joseph Morriss Aug 12 80
Jarvis Moss Jan 9 75
Thomas Mounts Dec 5 69, June 4 71
Jacob Moyer Nov 23 76
John Moyer Jan 13 81
Luke(r) Mudd Aug 5 67, July 9 69,
July 16 71, May 26 73, May 21 81
Charles Murphy Oct 21 71, Mar 18
  72

Henry Musgrove Aug 18 77
John Musgrove Jan 1 71
Samuel Musgrove Mar 11 74
Peter Musser Jan 23 73
Henry Myers July 7 70, lives near
  Ludowick Yost
Jacob Myers June 22 82
Joseph Myers June 28 82
Conrod Myre Oct 26 73, lives about
  10 miles below mouth of
  Monocacy
Nathan Nabors July 15 66
Thomas Narrison Nov 28 74
Rudy Naughtinger Nov 21 71
George Nead Apr 22 71, lives near
  mouth of Pipe Creek
Jacob Neaff, Junr. Oct 16 69
George Need June 1 67
Doctr. Charles Neel July 18 68
Nathan Neighbours Nov 20 76 of
  Lower Monokasy Hundred
Arthur Nellson Apr 23 82
Arthur Nelson May 16 82
Benjamin Nicholls Nov 7 73, May 24
  80, Jul 11 80
James Nicholls Nov 28 72, near the
  Lower Falls
Thomas Nicholls Jan 7 73
Thomas Nicholls, Junr. June 13 71
Beckett Nichols Sept 4 74
William Nicholson Oct 17 72
John Nickols Feb 27 70
Jonathan Nixon Aug 7 70
Samuel Noland June 16 69
Samuel Noland Apr 5 71, lives about
  8 miles below mouth of
  Monococy
Thomas Noland May 12 72, May 17
  74, July 11 80
Benjamin Norris, Junr. May 25 69
Joseph Norris May 5 70, Oct 29 71

William Seir Norris Mar 4 66
Benjamin Norriss, Senr. Aug 3 67
Richard Northcraft Jan 2 72
Richard Norwood May 2 65
Michael Null, Senr. Sept 8 66
Adam Ocks Dec 11 80
Michael O'Donnall Dec 8 72
John Odaniel Oct 14 75
David John Oden Oct 23 70
James Offutt June 10 71
Nathaniel Offutt May 12 72
Mrs. Sarah Offutt Aug 24 69
Thomas Offutt Dec 14 68, Mar 20 71,
    May 18 71
Alexander Ogle June 25 85
Benjamin Ogle Aug 6 67
Joseph Ogle May 14 69, lives at
    mouth of Toms Creek
Thomas Ogle Feb 14 69
Christopher Ohaven July 22 65
Henry Old May 29 77
Levin Olliver Apr 27 82
William Oneal Oct 25 66
Jeremiah Orme June 3 71, lives near
    Walter Beall's Mill
Moses Orme June 2 73
Christian Orndorff June 21 68
Henry Orndorff Oct 15 67
Mathias Otto Aug 25 67
Adam Oulenbaugh June 27 78, July 4
    78
John Owen Mar 23 71
Robert Owen May 21 70
Sarah Owen Jan 10 68
Rachel Owens Apr 21 83
Rachel Owings Mar 6 71
Richard Owings May 21 83 son of
    Samuel Owings Nov 19 66
Rachel Owins Aug 6 66
Flayll Pain Dec 29 67
Frail Pain Apr 6 65, Aug 10 68

John Pain Aug 28 67
Gideon Palmer Aug 8 67
William Pancrass Aug 21 76
James Paradice Nov 1 69
Jeremiah Patrick June 28 66
John Patterson Oct 30 66
Thomas Patterson Oct 6 84
George Peack May 4 68
Samuel Pearl Aug 2 82 also written
    Samuel Bearle in the same entry
Jacob Peckelshimer May 27 72
Leonard Peckinpaugh Sept 16 76
Sarah Pedecord Sept 5 67
Harrison Pelley Apr 23 66
William Perkabile Sept 22 66
Samuel Perle Feb 1 71
Samuel Perry May 3 71
Robert Peter Oct 17 72
Thomas Pettey Aug 1 67
John Philips Apr 1 75
Nicholous Phillips June 17 65
Barton Philpott May 15 76
Leonard Pickenpaugh Apr 10 71
Peter Pickingpaw Sept 3 70
James Piels Dec 14 68
Clement Pierce May 17 73
John Pigman June 26 71
Nathaniel Pigman Aug 3 71
James Piles May 9 68
Thomas Pindall Aug 15 69
Peter Pinkley May 22 65, Aug 25 67
Joseph Piper Aug 24 68
Adam Pitinger July 8 77
John Pittinger May 28 85 lives at the
    mouth of Pipe Creek
Joseph Plumer June 26 65
George Plummer May 3 66, May 1
    71, Mar 18 73
John Plummer Nov 14 72
Joseph Plummer Aug 11 81 of
    Linganore

Philamon Plummer Apr 21 68, Nov 14 72

Thomas Plummer July 15 73, son of Samuel

Thomas Plummer Nov 10 77 of Sugar Loaf

George Poe May 28 85

Conrad Poole May 7 78

Henry Poole July 5 75

Philip Porter Oct 27 66, near Sarah Hobbs (Fred Co)

John Pottenger June 17 65

Richard Powel June 4 68

Thomas Powell Sept 4 67, Oct 10 75

John Power June 14 71

Laurence Prangle Aug 31 71

Thomas Price Nov 14 72, at the head of Bennet's Creek

Henry Priest May 14 67

Joseph Prigmore Nov 17 66

David Prisch July 31 76

James Prosser Mar 8 68

Henry Prout Oct 13 70

John Quadrent Aug 9 66

John Quartan Feb 5 85

Joshua Ragon Sept 30 79

John Raitt July 13 72

Jacob Ramsberg May 21 73

Elias Ramsbergh Sept 17 83

Adam Ramsower May 29 83

Henry Ramsower Jan 16 84

Aquilla Randle June 6 76

Michael Rape (Ratie?) Mar 21 70

John Rawlings May 16 68

Andrew Redrug May 9 74

John Reed June 5 84

Samuel Reed Aug 21 65

Andrew Rentch Sept 5 68

John Reyley May 22 72

Joseph Reynolds July 23 70

Thomas Reynolds May 23 65

Christian Rhorar Mar 2 66

John Rhorar Mar 3 66

Samuel Rhorar Jan 8 73

John Rhorrar Apr 26 69

Christian Rhorrer Feb 23 68

George Rice Aug 7 68

Philip Rice June 20 85 of Upper Monocacy Hundred

Daniel Richards July 8 71

Isabella Richards June 9 78

Jesse Richards Oct 9 78

Arabella Richardson Sept 5 73

Thomas Richardson Mar 19 65, June 1 71, Nov 30 81, Dec 29 81

William Richardson July 27 80

Isaac Richey June 6 68, Nov 21 80

Thomas Richford June 29 70

Conrad Ricker Oct 1 85

Anthony Rickets June 16 67

Henry Ridenour Aug 16 70

Jacob Ridenour Feb 20 75

Adam Ridenower Jan 3 70

Thomas Rider Dec 8 67

Richard Ridgely Dec 14 75

Joseph Ridgeway June 22 71

Conrad Rigar Dec 17 76

John Riggs Sept 8 70

Philip Rimel Dec 3 65

Ludwick Rimmell Oct 28 80

Jacob Ringer Apr 12 85 of Israel's Creek Hundred

Mathias Ringer Oct 12 67, May 13 71, Sept 6 75

Samuel Roarer July 30 73

William Robason July 27 73

William Roberts Aug 12 72

James Robinson June 26 69

Christian Rode May 25 65

Jacob Rode or Jacob Road Aug 26 68

Philip Rodebeler Aug 5 73

Phillip Rodenbiller May 6 65

Philip Rodenpeler June 18 72
Lodowick Roderick July 4 74
Andrew Roderock Apr 5 65
George Rodger Oct 29 79
Alexander Rogers Nov 21 76, Mar 20 78
Arron Rollins May 21 85
Michael Roof Nov 17 73
Jacob Rossell Aug 19 66
Daniel Rudey Aug 11 68
Gilbert Rudolph May 6 82 of Linganore Hundred near Mr. Johnson's Forge
James Rugles Dec 7 67
Michael Runer July 17 73
Michael Runner June 2 83
Joshua Ryley May 25 79
John Saffell July 1 75
Abraham Sagkim Apr 9 66
Frederick Sallyday May 29 76
William Sander May 26 69, lives on Potomack below the mouth of Monocacy
George Saxton July 23 73
James Scot Jan 18 75
John Scott Aug 22 71
Thomas Scott Aug 20 71
Peter Seddy July 24 67
James Sergent May 31 73
Casper Shaaf July 12 78
John Shaffer Apr 26 84
Sarah Shall (Shaw?) Apr 19 74
Michael Shanebergher Jan 18 83
Frederick Shaneholtz Jan 5 78
George Sheafer Dec 3 79 had a plantation in the spring of 1779
Jacob Shearman Nov 8 82
Christian Sheaver May 24 72, lives near West Minster Town
Sarah Shepherd July 21 65
Thomas Shepherd May 7 76

Simon Shever Aug 5 68
John Shilling May 10 75
Henry Shneboly June 10 73
Christopher Shockey May 31 65
Bartholomew Shoemaker Nov 14 78, Dec 13 81
George Shour May 22 71
Peter Shover July 31 75
Christian Shryock May 22 71
Lamuel Shryor Nov 28 80
Daniel Shults Aug 23 66, July 21 67
Samuel Shurts Sept 17 72
Jacob Sigler Apr 21 73
Samuel Silver July 16 78
John Silvers June 12 73
George Simmerman Nov 12 83, Feb 5 85
Samuel Simons May 10 69
John Simpson Oct 11 74
Richard Simpson, Junr. Dec 9 80
Philip Sinn May 29 72
Sabra Siscel Apr 15 72
Richard Skaggs, Junr. Apr 16 72, Jan 11 75
Walter Skiner Jan 8 66
Richard Skuggs June 22 73
Samuel Smedley Sept 6 84
Adam Smelser June 23 85
Daniel Smith Oct 9 70
George Smith Nov 12 85
Henry Smith May 8 79 near the Wind Falls of Monokasy
Jacob Smith Jan 2 72
James Smith Dec 6 69
James Smith May 6 83 manager at Legh Furnace
Leonard Smith July 22 80, July 25 81
Michael Smith Jul 19 82
Middleton Smith May 2 67
Philip Smith Apr 30 83
Phillip Smith Jan 5 67, May 22 71

Robert Smith Sept 6 66
William Smith Dec 10 83
Simon Snooke June 4 85
Thomas Spalding July 8 74
Richard Speak Aug 12 72
William Speake Nov 1 69
Jeriniall Spiers Feb 9 69
Jeremiah Spires Nov 16 72
Benjamin Spycher Aug 17 74
Jacob Staley May 4 75
Jacob Stallings Jan 14 75
Joseph Stallion Feb 14 66
James Starrett Aug 17 78
George Staup Aug 18 85
Dinel Stephenson Aug 16 72
James Sterrett Dec 2 78
Thomas Steuart May 17 66
John Stevenson July 3 77
Richard Stevenson May 25 78
Jacob Stimmell Nov 26 85
Jacob Stitely Jan 9 83
Adam Stone July 25 85
Henry Stoner Nov 23 71
David Stottlemire Oct 2 80
George Stottlemyer Feb 14 85
Joyham Straffer June 30 79
George Stricker June 3 71, June 15
    72, June 7 73
Michael Stricker June 4 71, Nov 18
    75
Killeon Strider Apr 20 75
Michael Striker June 6 74
Christopher Stull June 16 71, June 23
    78
Valentine Sumer July 31 69
Valentine Sumers July 21 77
Valentine Summer Apr 22 80
Felty Summers May 18 65
Edward Swainy May 27 65, May 11
    73
Andrew Swan June 6 75

Charles Swearingem Aug 16 69
Van Swearingem, Jr. June 29 73
Joseph Swearingen June 18 85 lives
    "adjoining Middle Town"
Samuel Swearingen July 24 69
Van Swearingen July 2 74
Mary Swinford Jule 18 66
Melchor Tabler May 27 71, May 6 74
William Talbott July 7 66, Aug 10 67,
    May 18 71
John Tanehill Nov 13 71
Ninian Tannehill June 12 71
Ninian Tawnihill Aug 16 68
Thomas Taylor Aug 30 81
John Teem Aug 21 72
Jacob Terner Aug 30 85
Benjamin Thomas May 18 65
Edward Thomas July 14 83
Elizabeth Thomas Aug 31 71
Francis Thomas June 20 82 of Middle
    Monokasy Hundred
John Thomas Mar 19 84 also written
    John Tomms in same entry
Jonathan Thomas Oct 2 69
Doct. Philip Thomas, Esq. Jan 18 85
Rebecca Thomas July 27 74
Samuel Thomas Nov 21 83
Richard Thrall July 9 70
Thomas Tobery Nov 27 82 lives at
    Monocasy Manor
Jesse Tomlinson Sept 5 70, lives near
    Elias Delashmutt, Junr.
John Tomms-- see John Thomas
Henry Toms Apr 5 65
John Toms July 26 85
Robert Toon Sept 19 67
William Tracey, Junr. Jan 2 69
John Trammel June 10 71
Philip Trine July 16 82 of Ketoctin
    Hundred
Adam Troup Mar 7 74

Adom Troup Dec 19 74

Jacob Trout Mar 11 76, May 22 84

Michael Troutman May 17 66, Aug
28 67, May 25 70, Dec 4 77, July
1 78, Aug 26 84

Christian Troxell Dec 27 66, May 27
67, July 26 68

John Trucks May 29 82

Ann Trundel, widow Apr 15 71, lives
near Walter Beall's Mill

Josiah Trundell Apr 29 73

John Trundle Aug 17 68

Thomas Trunnel Sept 9 77

Goodheart Trussels July 28 67

John Tucker June 14 77

Jonathan Tucker June 15 71, May 12
74

William Tucker Aug 10 70, July 31
71

Charles Turner Apr 7 68

William Turner May 6 65, Sept 8 81
of Linganore

Casper Turst (?) Apr 23 72

Michael Tutaror, Junr. Sept 8 66

Philip Udia Sept 30 79

Nicholas Umstid June 9 69, lives near
Sams Creek

Unkle Unkles July 8 66 of Pipe Creek

Henry Unsell Dec 17 66

Henry Unstatt July 22 80

Joseph Vandriess Jan 20 83 also
written Joseph Virtries in same
entry

Daniel Vanhorn Nov 19 81

Dennis Vanhorn Oct 19 81

John Veatch May 2 66

Nathan Veatch July 10 71

George Viley Jan 4 77 near the Great
Falls of the Potowmack

Daniel Vince July 6 70, lives near
mouth of Linganore

Daniel Vines May 10 73

Joseph Virtries-- see Joseph
Vandriess

Charles Walker June 27 65, June 11
66, Oct 22 67

Michael Walker Jan 13 65

Zephaniah Walker Apr 26 69

Francis Wallace May 26 68, Jan 18
71

James Wallace, Senr. June 19 66

John Walling May 10 78

Joseph Walls June 9 85 lives near
William Hobbs' Tavern

Daniel Walter May 23 65

George Walter June 21 69, lives in
the Sugarlands

Jacob Walter May 18 65

John Walter July 27 67

Josephus Walters Aug 11 73

Joseph Warford Apr 19 65

Jacob Warnfields Apr 28 75

Samuel Warters Mar 20 70

Richard Waters June 3 69

Thomas Waters Apr 5 65

John Watson July 14 66, near Rock
Creek

Richard Watts Aug 3 65

Richard Watts June 20 74, lives near
Mr. (Mrs.?) Dowden

Isaac Wayne July 29 82 of Israels
Creek Hundred

Peter Wayrey June 4 74

Peter Wayrey ? Oct 4 69

William Wealer June 18 76

Peter Weary Jan 8 81

Conrad Weaver July 8 80

George Weaver Feb 7 80, June 29 82

John Weavor Dec 7 74

John Web Apr 26 75

Peter Weddel Aug 1 70

Jacob Weddle June 11 78

George Weentz Apr 10 80

Thomas Welch July 12 70

Jacob Weller, Junr. Aug 11 66

Thomas Wells Feb 6 67, May 7 73

John West, son of William June 17 67

Joseph West, Sr. May 4 74

Joseph West, Junr. Oct 2 66 recorded his mark

Christopher Westenhaver May 15 82

Thomas What Aug 28 82

George Noble Wheeler July 31 81

David White July 28 72

John White Aug 27 67

Joseph White June 16 67

Joseph White Aug 6 70, lives near the Lower Falls

Leonard White June 24 70

George Whitmore Nov 20 79

John Whitmore May 14 70, July 31 72

Andrew Wigart May 22 84

Charles Williams Apr 20 74

Francis Williams Jan 20 74

Henry Williams June 10 75

John Willson Jan 6 66

Josiah Willson June 28 74

Michael Willson Jan 15 82 of Tom's Creek Hundred

Wadworth Willson Dec 28 69, lives about 5 miles below mouth of Monococy

Thomas Willson Jan 28 67

William Willson June 27 72, May 21 76

William Willson May 8 81 of Lower Monokasy Hundred

Henry Wilson May 15 71

Isaac Wilson July 4 71, June 19 82

Thomas Wilson May 7 71

Wadswoth Wilson Nov 16 73

Walter Wilson Mar 19 73

William Wilson Aug 20 82 of Lower Monocasy Hundred

Thomas Winder Jan 14 74

Christian Winebrenner May 13 80

Henry Winnigler May 24 84

Francis Winrod Nov 20 73

Peter Winrode June 20 72

George Winter Oct 5 69

Ignatious Wisner Jan 13 68

Mary Wisner June 22 69

Benjamin Witmore Sept 12 69

George Witterick June 17 76

James White Apr 26 82

James White Apr 26 83 of Middle Kittocton Hundred

Paul Wolf May 11 69

Conrad Wolford June 6 74

Charles Wood Apr 27 65

John Wood Sept 14 65, June 11 74

Joseph Wood Apr 30 84

Richard Wood June 10 83

Robert Wood May 22 75

Thomas Wood Nov 3 70, lives near where Collo. Samuel Beall lives

William Wood May 3 84

Francis Woodward May 23 74, lives near Rock Creek Church

Paul Woolf Sept 2 68

Conrad Woolfkill Nov 13 75

George Worner Aug 21 76

Thomas Sprigg Wotton June 18 66

Amos Wright Nov 21 70

Christian Yesterday May 3 79

Harman Yoot July 9 74

George Young May 11 79

James Young June 7 68

Lodowick Young Nov 8 75

Samuel Young Jan 3 76

Daniel Zacharias Nov 20 65

Jacob Zieglar May 15 84

## CORONER'S INQUESTS 1778-1789

*Maryland Archives C772-1 1/41/7/34*

Notes: The coroners' inquests consist of a piece of paper for each case. On one side of the paper there is the report written by the coroner to explain his and the jury's conclusions about the cause of the deceased individual's death. At the bottom of the report, the coroner and each juror signed his name or mark, or someone signed on behalf of a juror who could not sign his name. Many of the signatures were difficult or impossible to read. Sometimes the coroner listed the names of the men who served on the jury in the body of the report. When this was the case, the name written by the coroner was compared to the name signed by the juror, and differences were noted in the following abstracts.

On the back of the case report paper, the following items were usually written: name of deceased, cause of death, date of inquisition and the name of the coroner who investigated the death. This summary was apparently a label recorded by a clerk, which was used to identify the case report after it was folded and filed. There were many discrepancies in the spellings of the deceased person's name between the summary and the body of the report. When there was more than one spelling for the name of the deceased, variant spellings are denoted in the abstracts with slash marks between them.

Deceased: Coonrod Cotuldyin/ Coonrod Cotuldy/ Conrad Gadultich
Date of death: June 4, 1778, inquisition on June 7, 1778
Coroner: William Beatty
Cause of death: Suicide by hanging with a hemp rope valued at six pence.
Jury: Matthias Ringer, Jacob Ramsburg, David Shawen, Jacob Trout, Henry Ramsburg, David Harvey, Frederick Mesel, Jacob Mesel, Phillip Shoppart, Jacob Culler, James Steel, Adam Snoke, and Baltzer Getzendaner, all residents of Frederick Co.
Comments: Death occurred at home of Coonrod Cotuldyin in Frederick Co.; inquisition held there as well. Deceased was said to have been depressed and not in his right mind since the death of his wife. Statement of Dr. Adam Fisher before Jacob Young, Justice of the Peace: Deceased's wife [unnamed] died after an "application of severe medicine"; this event caused Coonrod Cotuldyin distress and depression. Deceased was unable to support his family in the manner to which he was accustomed [no family members named]. Statement of

Jacob Kidner before Young: Kidner lived with Cotuldyin for 18 months prior to his death; Kidner at the time of Cotuldyin's death was living on the same plantation. Kidner stated that deceased had been depressed since the death of his wife, and that 5 days prior to his suicide, had been kicked by a horse and was in severe pain as a result. A few hours before the suicide, Cotuldyin came to the house of Kidner, who believed that the deceased was not of sound mind and understanding. Kidner described Cotuldyin as a "hearty man" prior to his wife's death. Statement of John Ramsburg before Young: Ramsburg stated that he frequently saw Cotuldyin, and that the deceased was "not the man he used to be." Statement of George Hackethorn before Young: Hackethorn stated that the deceased was often at his house, and that he "talked in a very simple manner." [Folder 40298-1]

Deceased: Bridget Cronkelton/ Bridget Cochron
Date of death: March 15, 1778, inquisition March 16, 1778
Coroner: William Beatty
Cause of death: Burns.
Jury: Abraham Haff, James Beatty, John Weavour, Thomas Whitting, Peter Stinnel, James Hooper, Thomas Majors, John Tenner, John Cain, Henry Hines, Daniel Hines, John Wagoner, Henry Tenner, John Cassell or John Carson [coroner wrote "Cassell", witness signed "Carson"], Ezekiel Beatty, all residents of Frederick Co.
Comments: Inquisition taken at residence of James Beatty. The deceased became drunk while at the residence of John Hinds on March 2, 1778, then "received a burn on her knees, side and rump." The cause of the burn was unknown. [Folder 40298-1]

Deceased: John Middaugh/ John Middagh
Date of death: July 30, 1778, inquisition August 1, 1778
Coroner: William Beatty and Leonard Smith
Cause of death: "Wandering in a fit of insanity was found dead without marks of violence."
Jury: Francis Pierpoint, Sr., Francis Peirpoint, Jr., Daniel Miller, Obed. Peirpoint, Richard Haff, John Cronise, Abraham Faw, [crossed out Henry Barton and Jesse Pritchard], Jacob Snoudegle, Christopher Guin, Anthony Stuck, Henry Zealor, Nicholas Tice, and Conrad Grosh, all residents of Frederick Co.
Comments: Inquisition taken near Frederick Town. Middaugh was insane and at time of death and was wandering in a field owned by Odebiah Peirpoint when his death occured. Residence of Peirpoint was near Frederick Town. [Folder 40298-1]

Deceased: Mary Goff
Date of death: Not stated, inquisition March 5, 1778
Coroner: William Beatty
Cause of death: Wound to head.
Jury: Conrad Grosh, John Shellman, Jacob Crigger, Thomas Beatty, Nicholas Tice, Joseph Jones, Johannes Gomber, Johannes Hebner ?, John Jacob Schley, Christian Weaver, John Adlum, Saml. Boone, Peter Grosh, Abraham Faw, Ja. Smith, Jacob Schley [a different man], Chas. Beatty, Christopher Hines.
Comments: Inquisition taken at Frederick Town. How and when wounds received was not determined. [Folder 40298-1]

Deceased: George Hutchzel/ George Hutzell
Date of death: May 2, 1778 at dusk, inquisition May 3, 1778
Coroner: William Beatty
Cause of death: The jury determined that the deceased had been "struck with the dead palsy" as he was purple and his blood had settled to his skin.
Jury: Alexander Ogle, Jacob Trout, Jacob Ramsburg, John Meek, Matthias Ringer, Adam Keller, Christian Ramsburg, Peter Hedges, Michael Hafner, Valentine Brunner, Joachim Shaifer ["Shaifer" written by coroner, looks like Joachim Strever signed by juror], John Stoner, Andrew Bohman ["Bohman" written by coroner, Andrew Baughman signed by juror], and Peter Shaffer, all residents of Frederick Co.
Comments: George Hutchzel and wife Magdalene were on the way to the home of a neighbor [unnamed] to conduct business, when the deceased told his wife that he was "out of wind", that she should go along by herself, and that he would follow. Mrs. Hutchzel continued on her way, but Mr. Hutchzel did not arrive at the neighbor's house. When Mrs. Hutchzel returned home, she found her husband dead. [Folder 40298-1]

Deceased: Magdalene Ahalter
Date of death: Not stated, inquisition April 4, 1778
Coroner: William Beatty
Cause of death: Drowned while crossing "Catockton Creek."
Jury: Van Swearingen, Jacob Kerlinger, Frederick Hempel, Michael Shaneberger, Philip Knuler ["Knuler" written by coroner, juror signed Phillip Noller], Jacob Dotter, Casper Beckinbaugh, Michael Rudisill, William Roberson, Henry Colmon, George Poe, George Markel, Jacob Keaver, Jacob Peter, Andrew Peter, Harmon Yost, all residents of Frederick Co. [Folder 40298-1]

Deceased: Sevilla Mock
Date of death: Sunday, March 8, 1778, inquisition March 10, 1778
Coroner: William Beatty
Cause of death: Drowned after falling into a spring. Was in "a fit" when fell.
Jury: Abraham Haff, "foreman", William Dern, Christopher Waggoner, John
Link, William Rice, Michael Late, Edward Salmon, Adam Hoover, George
Curtz, Richard Haff, William Barrick, John Barrick, Jr., Andrew Bockman,
Adam Waggoner Sr., John Ringer, and Adam Snook, all of Frederick Co.
Comments: Deceased was subject to "fits". At the time of her death, deceased
was attempting to retrieve water from the spring. [Folder 40298-1]

Deceased: Thomas Cooper
Date of death: About 3 o'clock May 9, 1779, inquisition same day
Coroner: John McAllister
Cause of death: Murder
Jury: Jacob Good, Adam Good, Abraham White, James Holliday, Abraham Fife,
Eli Bentley, Joseph McKaleb, Pat. ? [can't read first name] Watson, John
Buchanan, [can't read first name] Herr, William Pepple, and William Cornell.
Comments: Body found on the "Great Road" near Taney Town early that
morning by Melcer Knave. No method of murder or suspect mentioned. [Folder
40298-2]

Deceased: John Boochler, Jr./ John Boogher, Jr./ John Buchgar, Jr.
Date of death: Not stated, inquisition June 23, 1779
Coroner: William Beatty
Cause of death: Drowned
Jury: Steven Ramsburg, John Stoner, Abraham Haff, Adam Fisher, Jesse
Pritchett, Henry Ramsburg, Henry Brothers, George Snertzell, Henry Howard,
Joseph King, Ephraim Ridge, and Jacob Buchgar [last juror's name is written the
same way as that of the deceased in the inquisition report], all residents of
Frederick Co.
Comments: Deceased was an infant about 16 months old. He had been missing
for a short time when his body was found. Inquisition held at house of John
Buchgar, Sr. [Folder 40298-2]

Deceased: Negro Man Fortune
Date of death: Not stated, inquisition January 25, 1780
Coroner: William Winchester, Jr., Justice of the Peace, who conducted the
inquisition in the absence of the coroner
Cause of death: Accident which was not stated specifically.
Jury: Thomas Beatty, David Gist, Elias Major, Jacob Lemman, William Chadd,

Joseph Matthias, Ludwick Shrier, Francis Grandam, James Esthup, Robert Mason, Samuel Chadd, William David, Casper Bayer, and Nathan Esthup, all residents of Frederick Co.

Comments: Fortune was a slave of Mordecai Gist, Esq. Inquisition taken at Westminster Town Hundred, Frederick Co. Witnesses to the accident: Mary Creely, John Bumgardner, and John Snaufer. [Folder 40298-3]

Deceased: Catharine Stoner
Date of death: Not stated, inquisition May 4, 1780
Coroner: William Beatty
Cause of death: Drowned in a spring.
Jury: Joseph Wood, Jr., Philip Smith, Jr., Thos. Reynolds, Jacob Stidley, Jacob Christ, Levi Carmack, Benj. Norris, Christian Snider, Frederick Snider, Michael Snider, John Shumaker, Martin Mickault, Johan Snider, and one other name that is illegible, all residents of Frederick Co.
Comments: Catharine Stoner was a child less than 2 years of age. Inquisition taken at the house of John Stoner. The jurors determined that it was "accidentally, casually and by misfortune" that Catharine Stoner came to her death. [Folder 40298-3]

Deceased: Johannes Paulmare
Date of death: Not stated, inquisition August 21, 1780
Coroner: William Beatty
Cause of death: Suicide by hanging with a hemp rope while "in a fit of insanity". Value of rope was six pence sterling.
Jury: Conrad Peters, Samuel Gandy [clearly reads "Gandy" as written by coroner, might be "Samuel Gantz" as signed by juror], William Deakensheets, Sr., Youst Greenwood, Jacob Stripe, Henry Baker, Frederick Snider, George Winters, Michael Hains, Jacob Fisher, Michael Kitner, Thomas Mollinham, David Plain, and Benjamin Davis, all residents of Frederick Co.
Comments: Inquisition taken at the house of Henry Landis of Frederick Co. Death of Paulmare occured at a mill owned by Henry Landis. Johannes Paulmare was described as "not having the fear of God before his eies [eyes], but being seduced by the instigation of the devil." The jury determined that Paulmare "voluntarily and feloniously did hang and strangle" himself. [Folder 40298-3]

Deceased: George Mumma
Date of death: Not stated, inquisition May 11, 1781
Coroner: William Beatty
Cause of death: Accidentally killed by a falling tree.
Jury: Christophel Stull, Henry Garnhard, Jacob Baltzell, John Ridenour, Conrad

Creagebaum, Jacob Holtz, Bortill Shumaker, Adam Reese, David Shawen, Balser Ketchataner, Benedict Holtz, Jacob Holtz, Sr., John Dottro, and Michael Christ, all residents of Frederick Co.
Comments: Inquisition held at George Headerck's house in Frederick Co. George Mumma was employed to cut timber by Headerick. The accident occurred when a recently cut tree fell onto another tree, causing the second tree to come up by its roots. Mumma tried to run, but the uprooted tree fell in the direction that he ran. [Folder 40298-4]

Deceased: Margaret Westenhaver
Date of death: April 17, 1781, inquisition April 18, 1781
Coroner: William Beatty
Cause of death: Shot in the head by accident.
Jury: Luke Mudd, Samuel Cock, Samuel Shirtz, Raphael Thompson, Edward Hagon, Michael Snider, Philip Coon, Peter Bruner, Peter Oats, George Oats, Guy Elder, and Thomas Elder, all residents of Frederick Co.
Comments: Inquisition held at the house of Monica Hagon. Margaret Westenhaver went to the home of Monica Hagon on April 17, 1781; several other people were present. Two young men had been having target practice with their guns; they then reloaded the guns, brought them into the house and laid them down. Misses Elenore Machetu and Susannah Hagon each picked up a gun; neither was aware that the guns were loaded. The gun held by Elenore Machetu went off accidentally. The ball that was fired went through the left eye of the deceased and out through the back of her head; she died instantly. [Folder 40298-4]

Deceased: Adam Spon/ Adam Spoon
Date of death: Not stated, inquisition May 27, 1781
Coroner: William Beatty
Cause of death: Drowned.
Jury: Robert Dean, Matthias Shrup, Alexander More, Conrad Horse, Frederick Holtzman, Henry Holtzman, Balser Duttro, Matthias Ringer, Adam Frushour, Thomas Flemming, Jacob Christ, John Collins, Biggar Head, and Thomas Horner, all residents of Frederick Co.
Comments: Inquisition taken at the house of John Spon in Creagers Town. Adam Spon was two years and seven months of age. The deceased fell into a flooded cellar that had no cover and drowned. [Folder 40298-4]

Deceased: Robert Harris
Date of death: Not stated, inquisition August 19, 1781
Coroner: William Beatty

Cause of death: Killed when fell from his horse.

Jury: William Bentley, John Coocherly, George Brown, Daniel Shealor, William Logan, George Boner, Evan Carmack, George Trucks, John Trucks, Patrick Donnelly, John Wickham, Peter Aulbough, and Benjamin Barnhart, all residents of Frederick Co.

Comments: At the time of his death, Robert Harris was riding his horse in a race. [Folder 40298-4]

Deceased: Elizabeth Blickenstaff

Date of death: Not stated, inquisition December 5, 1781

Coroner: William Beatty

Cause of death: Suicide by hanging. Deceased was said to have hanged herself "in a fit of insanity". Value of rope was six pence.

Jury: Samuel Cock, George Huff (? writing ran off the page), Isaac Double, Andrew Hamen, Albert Flory, Andrew Pothowen, David Garringer, Samuel Thomas, Peter Grosnickle, Henry Miller [in between Henry and Miller, the name "Thomas" is crossed out], George Custard, and David Swigen, all residents of Frederick Co.

Comments: The deceased was described as having been insane for some time. She "not having the fear of God before her eyes but being seduced by the instigation of the Devil in her own house then and there being alone" hanged herself with a rope made of hemp. [Folder 40298-4]

Deceased: Matthias Young

Date of death: Apparently December 12, 1781, inquisition December 22, 1781

Coroner: William Beatty

Cause of death: Froze to death.

Jury: Peter Burkhart, Mark Harmon, John Gump, John Weller, Jacob Weller, Henry Ambrose, Balser Simon, Frederick Simon, Casper Rine, Robert Anderson, Henry Geisey and Peter Young, all residents of Frederick Co.

Comments: Matthias Young had been "on guard" in Frederick Town. On the way home, he stopped at Ambrosey's place [not clear if this was a tavern or a private residence, also menioned was Ambrosey's Mill, refer to index], and "drank himself nearly drunk". Young left there and was found a mile and a half away, frozen to death. It was thought that the deceased lay down on the way home and froze. [Folder 40298-4]

Deceased: Negro July

Date of death: Night of November 13, 1782, inquisition November 15, 1782

Coroner: Col. William Beatty

Cause of death: Died of natural causes after an illness.

Jury: Christian Weaver, Jacob Schifler, Henry Bair, [crossed out Charles Sholl], Jacob Baltzell, George Bair, [crossed out Christian Sheiner], Christian Shull, Jacob Missell, John Gumbare, Jr., [crossed out Frederick Byerly and John Heaver], David Lowery, John Bruner, Michael Baltzell, Adam Bentz, Jacob Houcks, and John Huffman, all residents of Frederick Co.

Comments: July died in the Public Gaol of Frederick Co. He was described as having been in a poor state of health for some time. No mention that July was a slave, or if he was, who his owner was. [Folder 40298-5]

Deceased: John Engler
Date of death: Morning of December 17, 1782, inquisition December 17, 1782
Coroner: Col. William Beatty
Cause of death: Natural causes
Jury: Abraham Faw, George Bair, William Dern, William Rice, Jacob Shifler, Jacob Boyer, Jr., Andrew Miller, John Gumbare, Jr., Jacob Boyer, Sr., Conrad Grosh, Christian Shull, Adam Bentz, [crossed out Jacob Baltzell, Michael Baltzell and Adam Gross], Philip Shade, Jacob Shellman, Frederick Shull, and Stephen Brunner, all residents of Frederick Co.
Comments: John Engler died in the Public Gaol of Frederick Co. after having been sickly for a period of time. [Folder 40298-5]

Deceased: Jacob Frankson/ Jacob Sonoffrank [not sure what the name of the deceased was, the summary on the back of the inquisition reads "Sonoffranck" written as one word; the first mention of the deceased in the inquisition read "Jacob Frankson" with Frankson crossed out, and rewritten as "Son of frank" in three words, as if Jacob was the son of a man named Frank. Throughout the inquisition, the deceased is refered to as "Jacob Son of frank" written in three words, and with "frank" not capitalized. There is no mention in the inquisition that Jacob was a child.]
Date of death: Apparently March 13, 1783, inquisition March 13, 1783
Coroner: Leonard Smith
Cause of death: Drowned
Jury: Thos. Frazier, Jno. Beltz, Frederick Zickers ?, Benjamin Downes, James Sergent, Jr., Conrad Kiser, James Waimer ?, John Frasier, Leon Tanner, Peter Wolken ?, Eliphaz Douglas, and Johannes J----.
Comments: The deceased and others were crossing a bridge over "Kittockting Creek" when the deceased fell off the bridge and drowned. [Folder 40298-6]

Deceased: Philip Lease
Date of death: About 8 PM April 8, 1783, inquisition April 9, 1783

Coroner: William Beatty
Cause of death: Act of God.
Jury: John Carter, Jacob Collins, Solomon Bentley, John Smith, Lackey
Flanagan, Paul Clapsadel, William Smith, John Manchey, George Adam
Kelleberger, Benjamin Barnhart, John Delaplane, John Heartsook, John Creable,
and Abraham Miller, all residents of Frederick Co.
Comments: Inquisition taken at the house of John Creable in Frederick Co.
Philip Lease and Nicholas Dehoff were walking on the main road, on their return
trip from Virginia. Lease had been in "perfect health". At the time of his death,
Lease took a "mouthfull of bread and meat" while walking along, then fell over
dead. [Folder 40298-6]

Deceased: Negro Paul
Date of death: Not stated, inquisition on March 14, 1783
Coroner: Leonard Smith
Cause of death: Not stated.
Jury: Thos. Frazier, James Sargent, Jr., Jonathan Frazier, John Frasier, John
Sargent, Christopher Hutchins ?, Thos. Harmon, Jos. Smith, Benedict Jamison,
Simon Allspach, Benjamin Peake, and Arthur Grimes.
Comments: Paul was found dead in the woods, partly eaten by hogs. Paul had
been free for many years prior to his death; his former owner was Mrs. Butler.
The body of the deceased was found on land owned by Leonard Smith, Coroner.
There was no explanation as to why Paul's body would have been on Leonard
Smith's land. [Folder 40298-6]

Deceased: Jacob Cook [coroner states that deceased had alias: Jacob Coaghe; in
another place, the coroner states that the deceased had an alias that was spelled
Jacob Coache]
Date of death: Not stated, inquisition March 20, 1783
Coroner: Col. William Beatty
Cause of death: Drowned
Jury: William Head, Jacob Frock, John Price, Ephraim Ridge, Richard Wood,
Valentine Creager, Benjamin Ridge, William Ridge, Richard Head, Zach.
Miller, Peter Shook, Thomas Brawner, Christian Cassel, George Clem, and
Jacob Catten, all residents of Frederick Co.
Comments: Inquisition held at the plantation of Peter Troutman, near Fishing
Creek in Frederick Co. The deceased was aged 7 years, 5 months and 18 days at
the time of his death; he drowned after falling from a log he was using to cross
Fishing Creek. [Folder 40298-6]

80

Deceased: Negro Bosen
Date of death: Night of January 1, 1783, inquisition January 2, 1783
Coroner: William Beatty
Cause of death: Natural Causes
Jury: Edward Salmon, Jacob Schisler, Jacob Snider, Henry Lamburgh, Jno.
Booker, Valentine Bentz, Jno. Cronise, Philip Talbart, Philip Smith, Jacob
Zimmerman, Jacob Snoudegle, George Getzendanner, John Hoffman, Andrew
Low, Christian Rhode, and Peter Meem, all residents of Frederick Co.
Comments: Bosen was a male, aged about 32 years at the time of his death in the
Public Gaol of Frederick Co. The deceased was described as having been in
sickly health prior to his death. [Folder 40298-6]

Deceased: Captain Joachim Kim
Date of death: April 13, 1783, inquisition April 13, 1783
Coroner: William Beatty
Cause of death: Suicide by cutting his throat "in a state of insanity". Instruments
used to cut throat were a razor and a pen knife; value of instruments was fifteen
pounds of tobacco. Size of cut was three inches long and two inches wide.
Jury: Abraham Faw, Jacob Trout, Valentine Shreiner, Joseph Cromwell, George
Dent, Matthias Bartgis, Ulrick Ming [juror signed "Wallory Ming"], John
Gamber, Jr., Benjamin Johnson, William Ritchie, John Adlum, Christian
Weaver, Peter Grosh, Nicholas Tice, and Jacob Bayer, Jr., all residents of
Frederick Co.
Comments: Capt. Joachim Kim had been taken prisoner of war, captured under
Lord Cornwallis on April 13, 1783. While alone in "a certain room of McDaniel
Hower's house", Capt. Kim used a razor and a pen knife to cut his throat. The
deceased lived for about one hour after cutting his throat. [Folder 40298-6]

Deceased: Unnamed Negro man who was described as a recently captured
runaway
Date of death: Not stated, inquisition May 10, 1783
Coroner: William Beatty
Cause of death: Drowned
Jury: Abraham Haff, Isaac Keepers, James McCardel, Gilbert Rudoff, John
Fower, William Pope, Robert Hammitt, Samuel Linton, Sr, [crossed out Robert
Adderton], William McCay, Thomas Mount, John Dawson, William Dawson,
Benjamin Dawson, Richard Sheckells, and Daniel Grim, all residents of
Frederick Co.
Comments: Negro man had been "taken up" on March 20, 1783. On the day of
his death, he was tied up, and was boarded on the "Manocacy Ferry". The water
was about 3 feet 9 inches deep and was described as muddy. The man, who was

described as "not having the fear of God before his eyes," threw himself overboard. His hands were tied and he sunk in the water and drowned. [Folder 40298-7]

Deceased: Christian Haas
Date of death: May 17, 1783, inquisition May 24, 1783
Coroner: Charles Warfield, Esq.
Cause of death: Suicide by cutting his throat with a razor.
Jury: John Welch, Peter Schitz, George Glass, Phillip Beyer, Adam Lemmon, Conrad Dudderer, Peter Kemp, Joseph Greenwood, Emanuel Brower, Thomas Stevenson, Nicholas Unstatt and Jacob Stripe, all residents of the state of Maryland.
Comments: Inquisition taken in Burnt House Woods Hundred. Christian Haas was described as being "a lunatick and a person of insane mind" since May 3, 1783. Haas went into the woods near Sams Creek and cut his throat. [Folder 40298-7]

Deceased: Elizabeth Snoke/ Elizabeth Snook/ Elizabeth Snokes
Date of death: Evening of May 27, 1783, inquisition May 28, 1783
Coroner: William Beatty
Cause of death: Died of injuries sustained when her horse fell while she was riding.
Jury: Valentine Creager, Charles Hedges, Adam Link, Jr. [not "Lick"], Peter Lick [not "Link"], Bastian Winebruner, Thomas Brawner, John Price, Isaac Miller, Peter Troutman, Philip Price, Henry Lyde, Jacob Culler, William Head, Richard Head, and Thomas Flemming, all residents of Frederick Co.
Comments: Inquisition held at the home of Adam Snokes [Adam Snokes with an "s"]. Accident occurred while deceased was on her way home. She was riding her horse on the main road, near the plantation of William Becket Head. The accident occured while Mr. Head was watching. The horse "was seen to blunder and fall down." Mr. Head ran to assist Elizabeth Snokes, who when asked if she was injured, "clapt her hand upon her breast and said 'yes'". Elizabeth Snokes died after about a half hour. [Folder 40298-7]

Deceased: Andrew Nairey
Date of death: Apparently October 14,1783, inquisition October 14, 1783
Coroner: William Beatty
Cause of death: Natural causes. Deceased had recently been "sickly".
Jury: Andrew Miller, George Burkhartt, Leonard Lantz, Jacob Bayer, Daniel Cassell, Nicholas Paul [crossed out "Frederick", apparently coroner initially wrote Frederick Paul], [crossed out Andrew Boyd], Jacob Gronert, Thomas

Ogle, Jacob Baltzell, John Gaver, Christopher Snyder, Ruperd Ontz [juror signed Robt. Owen], John Hoover, David Mantz and Frederick Scholl, all residents of Frederick Co.
Comments: Inquisition held at the Public Gaol of Frederick Co. [Folder 40298-7]

Deceased: Margaret Alspaugh
Date of death: Morning of August 11, 1783, inquisiton August 11, 1783
Coroner: William Beatty
Cause of death: Natural causes
Jury: Philip Berger, Frederick Keefer, Jacob Hoffman, Charles Schell, John Hoover, Frederick Schell, David Mantz, Jacob Gamber, Matthias Houcks, Philip Riser, Daniel Cassell, William House [House written by coroner, signature of surname signed by juror hard to read but does not look like "House", looks like "Lantz"], William Markell, Jacob Baltzell, George Gantz, and Frederick Bireley, all residents of Frederick Co.
Comments: Inquisition taken at the Public Gaol of Frederick Co. Prior to her death, deceased had been "for some time sickly and much disposed". [Folder 40298-7]

Deceased: Lewis Poole
Date of death: Found dead on November 17, 1783, inquisition November 17, 1783
Coroner: John McAlister, Justice of the Peace
Cause of death: Died of "cold and fatigue".
Jury: James Morrison, Peter Troxall, John Troxall, Robert Roberts, Thomas Richford, Patrick Rogers, Abraham Boone, George Smith, Jacob Smith, Aron Rowe, William Murdock and David Tanner, all residents of Toms Creek Hundred, Frederick Co.
Comments: Inquisition taken in Toms Creek Hundred. Body of deceased found at the end of John Witers lane. [Folder 40298-7]

Deceased: Not able to be identified
Date of death: Not known, inquisition September 22, 1784
Coroner: Leonard Smith
Cause of death: Unknown
Jury: Melchor Tabler, Christian Aunne, Edward Phillips (?), Wm. Gilpen, Wilhelm Tabler, Francis Hoffman, Joshuay Burton, Philip Nicholas --- [last name illegible], Christopher Hoff, Sr., next name illegible, Henrich Tullice, and Peter Talber.
Comments: "Part of a body and bones" was found and examined. Body found in

the mountains in a rocky area. [Folder 40298-8]

Deceased: Joseph Ipe/ Joseph Ipes
Date of death: January 2, 1784, inquisition January 12, 1784
Coroner: William Beatty
Cause of death: Struck in the head.
Jury: Basil Dorsey, Nathan Maynard, Jacob Koontz, Eli Hobbs, William Kean, Peter Cutsarah, David Arnold, John Sellman, Joseph Darby, Peter Arnold, Beale Babs, Charles Chainey, Gerrard Davis, John Compton, Jared Davis and Thomas Porter, all residents of Frederick Co.
Comments: Inquisition taken at William Harris' residence. On January 2, 1784, the deceased was at the home of Jacob Ake. It was reported that "there was until the evening drinking of whiskey". There was a large bruise on the crown of the deceased's head which was believed to be the cause of death; the bruise was determined to have been caused by Jacob Ake. Emeli Ake provided testimony. Joseph Ipe lived for twenty four hours from that evening before he died. [Folder 40298-8]

Deceased: George Wright
Date of death: Apparently July 4, 1784, inquisition July 4, 1784
Coroner: Jacob Young, Esq. who was "a justice assigned to keep the peace", coroner was "absent" on July 4, 1784
Cause of death: Small pox
Jury: Nicholas Tice, Adam Jacobs, Frederick Hutin, Antoin Stoh ?, Daniel Hauer, Jacob Hoffman, Sebastian Missear, Wollory Ming, Joseph Morris, Jacob Kendle, Charles Schell, Andreas Boyd, Nicholas White, Abraham Tilber ?, Conrad Boltz.
Comments: Died in the Public Gaol of Frederick Co. [Folder 40298-8]

Deceased: George Shaver
Date of death: March 16, 1784, inquisition March 16, 1784
Coroner: Leonard Smith
Cause of death: Drowned
Jury: Heinrich Shradory ? [same as Ludwig], John Niswanger, George Foxman, Samuel Taregksinger, Charles Beggarly, Matthias Woltzin, Valentine Ebert, James Weekly, Y----- Zingern, Ludwig Shradory ? [same as Henrich], George Blessing, and Jacob Cline.
Comments: George Shaver drowned when he accidentally fell into Kittocton Creek. [Folder 40298-8]

Deceased: William Lowe
Date of death: August 24, 1784, inquisition August 24, 1784
Coroner: William Beatty
Cause of death: Flu and fever, ruled natural causes.
Jury: Nicholas Tice, Henry Garnhard, Jacob Boyer, Jr., Andrew Low, Adam Grosh, Jacob Ramsburg, George Dent, David Mantz, Daniel Cassell, Leonard Lantz, Richard Sheckells, David Lowry, Lawrence Brengle, Michael Kirschner [possibly "Jr.", writing was continued on the next line and it looks like "Jr." was intended for Kirschner, juror did not sign "Jr." after his name], and Jacob Kendle, all residents of Frederick Co.
Comments: Inquisition held at the Public Gaol of Frederick Co. where Lowe died. [Folder 40298-8]

Deceased: Henry Funk
Date of death: Not stated, inquisition December 31, 1784
Coroner: William Beatty
Cause of death: Accidentally killed by falling tree.
Jury: Peter Shafer, Jacob Staley, John Houck, Matthias Buckey, Adam Beam, Youcham Strever, Henry Staley, Jacob Staley, Melchor Staley, George Shafer, Philip Anglelberger, George Free, and Jacob Mummye, all residents of Frederick Co.
Comments: Inquisition taken at the house of the deceased. Henry Funk was aged sixty years at the time of his death. Accident occurred while Funk was cutting fire wood by himself. [Folder 40298-9]

Deceased: Not known
Date of death: Not stated, inquisition July 4, 1784
Coroner: John McAlister, Justice of the Peace
Cause of death: Murdered
Jury: Henry Spalding, John Mefford, George Crabbs, David McKaleb, William Currans, James Armstrong, Michael Lutz, Philip Six, John Smith, John Calf, Jacob Shroyer, and William Lower, all residents of Toms Creek Hundred, Frederick Co.
Comments: Inquisition was held in Toms Creek Hundred. Deceased was described as a young child whose gender was not stated. The child's body showed marks of violence, so it was believed that the child had been murdered. The body of the deceased had been thrown into the Monocacy Creek. The suspect for the murder was thought to be the mother of the child, either Mrs. Clark or Mrs. Walker. [Another report was on file also. Differences in the report were: Christian Crabbs was crossed out as a juror; the name of juror George Crabbs had originally been written George Mefford; the name of juror John Calf

had originally been written William Calf; the name of William Lower looks more like William Sower in this report.] [Folder 40298-9]

Deceased: John Gilliland
Date of death: Apparently October 23,1784, inquisition October 23, 1784
Coroner: John McAlister, Justice of the Peace
Cause of death: Drowned
Jury: Thos. Samuel Poole, Henry Spalding, Wm. Shields, Sr., Nathaniel Patterson, Wm. Shields, Jr., Christian Smith, George Smith Sr., George Hockensmith, Jacob Hockensmith, Conrod Hockensmith, Jr., Lina (?) Griffin, Uria Gates, and Samuel Shields.
Comments: Body of the deceased was found on the mill race of Jacob Hockensmith in Toms Creek Hundred, by John McAlister, Justice of the Peace. [Folder 40298-9]

Deceased: Christena Pebble/ Christiana Pebble, Peter Pebble, Elizabeth Pebble, Philip Pebble (child), Abram Pebble
Dates of death: Apparently May 7, 1785, inquisition May 7, 1785
Coroner: John McAlister, Justice of the Peace
Cause of death: All five persons were murdered.
Jury: Joseph McKaleb, Thos. Sam. Pole, George Goble, John Robertson, Jon Crapster, John Hartman, Peter Mercer, Nicholas Fringer, James Townsley, Philip Evelin [in another report, the coroner wrote Philip Babelon, but it appears to be the same person, there were no signatures of the jurors in these two reports], Michael Haynes, John Roberts, Hugh Thompson, and George Winters.
Comments: Murderer was Philip Pebble, husband of Christena Pebble, and father of Peter Pebble, Elizabeth Pebble, Philip Pebble and Abram Pebble. Christena Pebble was killed by one or more blows above the right eye and behind the right ear with an axe. The oldest son, Peter Pebble, was killed by a blow above his left ear. The second child, Elizabeth Pebble, was killed by a wound to the left side of her head. The third child, Philip Pebble, was killed by a blow to the right side of the head above the ear. The fourth child, Abram Pebble, who apparently was an infant, "a sucking child", was killed by a wound to the forehead. All wounds were made with the same axe, which was valued at four shillings. The children were specifically stated to be the children of Philip and Christena Pebble; the above order of the children appears to be their birth order. Philip Pebble, the father, cut his throat with a pen knife valued at six pence. On May 7, 1785, Dr. John Buchannan examined the body of Mr. Pebble, which was found at his bedside still alive. The doctor stated that Mr. Pebble's wounds were "mortal" and that he would not live long. [Folder 40298-10]

Deceased: Philip Pebble [compare list of jurors to those in the Levy List]
Date of death: May 12, 1785, inquistition May 13, 1785
Coroner: William Beatty
Cause of death: Committed suicide by cutting throat with a razor and a pen knife.
Jury: John Adlum, Nicholas Tice, Jacob Bayer, Sr., Michael Bayer, [crossed out Jacob Hoffman], Matthias Bartgiss, Martin Waltz, Woodward Evitt, Philip Shade, Henry Ziegler, Benjamin Ogle, Thomas Knox, and Christian Shoup, all residents of Frederick Co.
Comments: Inquisition taken at the Gaol of Frederick Co. Pebble had cut his throat on May 7, 1785 between 5 AM and 7 AM at the home of his mother, which was located about 8 miles from Taneytown. The cut in his throat was three inches long and two inches deep. Pebble was taken to the gaol where he died between the hours of twelve and one on the night of the twelfth. The report states that Pebble was "a person of a wicked and evil mind, not at all regarding or fearing the punishment due to such enormous crimes but being moved and seduced by the instigation of the Devil". [Folder 40298-10]

Deceased: Sam, a Negro infant who was the property of Henry Six
Date of death: Not stated, inquisition August 24, 1785
Coroner: William Beatty
Cause of death: Accident.
Jury: Azel Waters, John Cookerly, George Birely, Jacob Ovalman, Henry Ovalman, George Boner, Tice Smith, William Ott, Conrad Cline, Herbert Hines, John Ivans, John Evans [different man than Ivans], John Smith and Peter Kempe, all residents of Frederick Co.
Comments: Sam was about five months old. The child was tied in a chair, and was crying. Henry Six moved the chair in an effort to quiet the child, but the chair fell over. The child who was tied into the chair landed on his face, and died instantly from the fall. [Folder 40298-10]

Deceased: John Crockett Dorsey
Date of death: Between 4 and 5 PM October 11, 1785, inquisition October 11, 1785
Coroner: William Beatty
Cause of death: Sickness
Jury: Henry Garnhart, Henry Winemiller, Jacob Gamber, Philip Shade, Jacob Hoffman, Daniel Cassell, Isaac Mantz, William House written by coroner but William Lantz signed by juror, Jacob Bayer, Jr. Michael Hissler, Wm. Cook, Charles Shell, and Woodward Evitt, all residents of Frederick Co.
Comments: Inquistition taken at the Gaol of Frederick Co. where Dorsey had been confined for debt. Dorsey had been sick for some time prior to his death.

[Folder 40298-10]

Deceased: Jacob Dungan
Date of death: March 27, 1785, inquisition March 30, 1785
Coroner: John McAlister, Justice of the Peace
Cause of death: Suicide by hanging with a rope valued at four pence.
Jury: Joseph McKaleb, Hugh Thompson, George Goble, Thos. Barr, Christily
Dehoff, Adam Black, Jacob Piper, Conrod Lees, Philip Joyner, William Stenson,
Samuel Stenson, Thos. Parkenson, and Michael Null, all residents of Piney
Creek Hundred, Frederick Co.
Comments: Inquisition taken at Piney Creek Hundred, Frederick Co.,MD.
Dungan hanged himself on a small white oak sapling at the end of John Reed's
lane. [Folder 40298-11]

Deceased: Jacob, a Negro [compare list of jurors to those in the Levy List]
Date of death: Not stated, inquisiton March 27, 1785
Coroner: William Beatty
Cause of death: Froze to death.
Jury: Major Abraham Haff, Nicholas Hobbs, Samuel Cock, Joseph Hobbs,
Nathan Maynard, John Mackelfish, Jr., Ludwig Bricker, Nathaniel Burket,
Redmond McDonel, Benjamin Becraft, Caleb Harn, Elijah Harn, and John
Dorsey son of Edward, all residents of Frederick Co.
Comments: Jacob was the property of John Dorsey of John. Inquisition taken at
plantation of Richard Laurence in Frederick Co. Jacob had run away the prior
Wednesday and died of exposure to the cold while hiding out in the woods.
[Folder 40298-11]

Deceased: Thomas Barlow
Date of death: Not stated, inquisition January 31, 1785
Coroner: John McAlister, Justice of the Peace
Cause of death: Suicide by cutting his throat.
Jury: Henry Stevenson, Price Lamb, William Pebble, John Coe, Jesse Coe,
Henry Anstot, Thomas Parkenson, Nicholas Dehoff, Edward Parkenson,
Valentine Bost, John Bargue, John Dehoff, Philip Dehoff, and George
Foglesong, all residents of Frederick Co. All men were noted as being residents
of the same hundred, but the place where the name of the hundred was to be
filled in was left blank.
Comments: Body of Barlow found in his room. Barlow used a pen knife worth
10 pence to cut his throat. [Folder 40298-11]

Deceased: Michael Fitzgerald [compare list of jurors to those in the Levy List]
Date of death: The prior night, which was the last day of February 1785,
inquisition March 1, 1785
Coroner: William Beatty
Cause of death: Act of God.
Jury: Major Abraham Haff, Samuel Cock, Abraham Cassell, Richard Gore, John
Wagoner, Jr., Charles King, John Pagent, Conrad Pool, Thomas Walford, Perry
Obian [O'Brian], James Newport, John Miller, Jacob Lease and Abraham Eador,
all residents of Frederick Co.
Comments: Inquisition taken at the home of George Adams near Monocacy
Creek. Fitzgerald had been sick for five or six days prior to his death. On the
night of his death, Fitzgerald was described as being "much out of his senses"
when he wandered about a half mile from his home. John Stoner, Jr. found
Fitzgerald sitting in the snow at about 8 PM that night; Fitzgerald was described
as being "much in the liquor". Stoner attempted to help Fitzgerald to his home,
but after going a short distance, Fitzgerald complained that he was very sick.
Stoner laid Fitzgerald down and went to get John Craps to assist him in helping
Fitzgerald. When Craps arrived, he and Stoner took Fitzgerald a short distance
when he "seemed to draw his breath short", so they laid him down and he
immediately expired. [Folder 40298-11]

Deceased: Catherine Miller's infant [compare list of jurors to those in the Levy
List]
Date of death: Not stated, inquisition February 13, 1786
Coroner: William Beatty
Cause of death: Apparently stillborn.
Jury: Samuel Cock, Alex Ogle, Philip Christ, John Heffner, Frederick Hoffman,
Henry Jackson, Jacob Cattern, Joseph Chane, Jacob Lamon, Henry Sellers,
Henry Pitsel, Michael Crist and George Myers, all residents of Frederick Co.
Comments: The deceased was found dead at the plantation of Philip Price in
Frederick Co. The mother delivered the child by herself; she claimed that the
child was stillborn. After the birth, the mother hid the body of the infant. The
jury felt that the assistance of a midwife could have saved the child, and that the
mother's "wicked and premeditated desire" was the cause of the child's death.
[Folder 40298-12]

Deceased: Name not known, a man [compare list of jurors to those in the Levy
List]
Date of death: Not stated, inquisition May 30, 1786
Coroner: William Beatty
Cause of death: Drowned

Jury: Capt. Edward Dyer, Jacob Lease, John Silver, James Newport, James Silver, Christian Alinger, Charles Button, Christian Everts, George Wentz, William Umbach, George Everts, Samuel Flemming, and Henry Ramsburgh, all residents of Frederick Co.

Comments: The deceased was a stranger who was travelling toward Pennsylania; he came to a branch that crossed the main road at the planatation of Lewis Duvall. The branch was described as "deep with the back water of Monocacy." Valentine Weaver was riding his horse across the same branch at the time, and the deceased asked him for a ride across. Both Weaver and the deceased fell off the horse and into the water; Weaver made it to shore but the deceased drowned. [Folder 40298-12]

Deceased: Josiah Miller [compare list of jurors to those in the Levy List]
Date of death: Between October 29 and November 2, 1785, inquisition November 3, 1785
Coroner: William Beatty
Cause of death: Liquor poisoning
Jury: Obednigo Hyatt, Thomas Reynolds, Abner Bentley, John Shumaker, William Stokes, John McKeney, Adam Strine, Conrad Most, Martin Earhart, Adam Rush, Jacob Fox and John Shockney, all residents of Frederick Co.
Comments: Miller was described as "being a person much given to strong liker [liquor] and evil minded not at all regarding or fearing the punishment due to such crimes, but being moved and seduced by the instigation of the Devil" when he took a keg containing one gallon of "the first shot of peach brandy" from the stillhouse of George Hamilton or George Hausilton [George Hazelton?] on Saturday, October 29, 1785. On Sunday morning, October 30, 1785, Miller was seen in the woods "lying drunk" and he was found dead there on November 2, 1785. [Folder 40298-12]

Deceased: Jack, a Negro man [compare list of jurors to those in the Levy List]
Date of death: June 11, 1786, inquisition June 12, 1786
Coroner: William Beatty
Cause of death: Drowned
Jury: Joseph Wood, Levi Bentley, Benjamin Barnhart, Zachariah Albaugh, David Cumming, Luke Barnard, Joseph Milton, Jacob Cookerley, Anglebert Hartsook, Charles Clance, John Ream, and Balser Ream, all residents of Frederick Co.
Comments: Owner of Jack was William Renner. Jack was swimming in Col. Woods' mill stream when he drowned. The water was 10-12 feet deep. [Folder 40298-12]

Deceased: Susanah Wilson [compare list of jurors to those in the Levy List]
Date of death: Wednesday, May 30, 1786, inquisition June 6, 1786
Coroner: Jacob Young, Esq.
Cause of death: Drowned in Monocacy River.
Jury: Richard Smith, Capt. Michael Bayer, Capt. Jon. Morris, George Bare,
Capt. L. Williams, Capt. Geo. Burkhard, Jno. Gebhart, Henry Garnhard, Isaac
Mantz, George Kitzendaner, Jacob Steiner, Jr., Samuel Hime, Jas. Smith, Jacob
Schisler, Christian Crist, Jacob Baltzell, Saml. Miller, Danl. Lochn, George
Kramer, Michael Kramer, Jacob Torff, and Frederick Rial, all residents of
Frederick Co. [Folder 40298-12]

Deceased: Arron Singleton [compare list of jurors to those in the Levy List]
Date of death: July 15, 1786, inquisition July 16, 1786
Coroner: Henry Darnall
Cause of death: Beaten to death by Elias Harding with a wooden club.
Jury: John Darnall, Ignatius Davis, Joseph Smith, John Buckey, Balser Cramer,
George Cramer, James Turtle Farthing, John Richardson, Henry Brandenburg,
Thomas Dawson, Francis Gilbert, and Adam Cramer, all residents of Frederick
Co.
Comments: Inquisition taken at the home of the late Arron Singleton. Harding
was described as "Elias Harding late of the county [Frederick] aforesaid" and as
being a laborer. Elias Harding was described as not "having the fear of God
before his eyes but being moved and seduced by the instigation of the Devil".
The assault occured between the hours of 11 AM and 2 PM on July 15, 1786.
July 25, 1786 before Henry Darnall, bond made for Elias Harding. Elias Harding
to pay 200 pounds current money, William Harding to pay 100 pounds current
money, and Zepiniah Harding to also pay 100 pounds current money. Elias
Harding to appear before the court in Frederick Town on the third Tuesday in
August, 1786. Dr. John Christian Massing, aged about 28 years, stated that on
Saturday, July 15, 1786, he attended the said Arron Singleton. It was the opinion
of the doctor that Singleton died from a wound to his left temple in which his
skull was fractured, and that the wound was caused by a club. Statement of
Massing taken by Henry Darnall. Deposition of William Tannihill, aged about
19 years, taken by Henry Darnall [date of deposition not stated]: William
Tannihill and Arron Singleton were working in the field when Elias Harding and
Singleton had words which led to a fight. Tannihill broke up the fight and held
Harding, while a negro was to hold Singleton. It was mentioned that other
negroes were also present. Singleton ran about 80 yards and got his reaphook
and threatened Harding in a violent manner, but Tannihill's impression was that
Singleton was just trying to scare Harding and had no intention of injuring him.
Harding got a club, and for a time stood with Tannihill between him and

Singleton. Tannihill stated that the Harding and Singleton seemed to be
reconciled so he walked away, then heard a blow and saw Singleton fall.
Singleton died about 11 hours later. Harding gave the club to a negro and told
him to burn it which he did. [Folder 40298-13]

Deceased: Mary, a Negro woman [compare list of jurors to those in the Levy
List]
Date of death: June 12, 1787, inquisition June 13, 1787
Coroner: William Beatty
Cause of death: Murdered by Steven, a Negro man.
Jury: Jeremiah Covell, Jacob Lease, John Ward, Jonathan Covell, William
Stevens, William Wood, William Cox, John Kirby, William James, Edward
Barnes, Christian Museater, John Barnes and Plummer Iams, all residents of
Frederick Co.
Comments: Mary and Steven were the property of Ormond Hamon. Inquisition
taken at the plantation of Ormond Hamon, in Frederick Co. Steven did not have
"the fear of God before his eyes but moved and led by the instigation of the
Devil with force and armes" and did "cast and throw and beat out her brains".
Steven then ran away and was at the time of the inquisition missing. [Folder
40298-14]

Deceased: Clarissa, a Negro woman [compare list of jurors to those in the Levy
List]
Date of death: Not stated, inquisition November 12, 1787
Coroner: William Beatty
Cause of death: Head injury.
Jury: Jacob Young, Edward Anderson, Henry Brother, Henry Garnhard, George
Schley, William Cook, Jacob Steiner, Jr., Christian Baker, Michael Baltzell,
John Buckias, Samuel Stalians, and George Beare, all residents of Frederick Co.
Comments: Clarissa and a negro man named Hiaro had words, and he hit her in
the back of the head. The blow to Clarissa's head was ruled to be the cause of her
death, but her death was also ruled accidental. Hiaro confessed to Mrs. Gantz
that he hit Clarissa. No statement of who owned Clarissa and Hiaro. [Folder
40298-14]

Deceased: Jacob, a Negro man [compare list of jurors to those in the Levy List]
Date of death: Not stated, inquisition April 5, 1787
Coroner: William Beatty
Cause of death: Fell down.
Jury: Gary Harding, Nicolas Dawson, John Jacobs, William Jacobs, John
Johnson, Joseph Jacobs, William Marshal, Jacob Bayer, Jr., Edward Bennett,

Richard Freeman, William Wan and Levi Hughes, all residents of Frederick Co. Comments: Jacob was the property of John Chisholm. Inquisition was held at the plantation of Gary Harding. The body of the deceased was lying near the main road at the time of the inquisition. Jacob was described as being very old and feeble. He left his master's house and went to Joseph Jacobs's house, then left there and was found dead on the road, face down. It was supposed that he stumbled and fell, but was too feeble to get up, so he laid there until he died. [Folder 40298-14]

Deceased: Laurence Laighie/ Laurence Lakea [compare list of jurors and spelling of deceased's name to that in the Levy List]
Date of death: February 3, 1787, inquisition February 4, 1787
Coroner: William Beatty
Cause of death: Fell off his horse and froze to death.
Jury: Major Abraham Haff, George Adams, John Mills, Sr., William Leese, Caspar Keller, Robert Haff, Conrad Pool, Charles King, James Hooper, Adam Snook, Capt. Nathaniel Henry, George Hill, Samuel Stallions, and John Miller, all residents of Frederick Co.
Comments: The night before, the deceased had been at the home of Middleton Smith. He left Smith's home in good health to travel home on the main road, but fell off his horse on the way. It was very cold that night and it was determined that he died from the cold. [Folder 40298-14]

Deceased: Catharine Harbaugh [compare list of jurors to those in the Levy List]
Date of death: Not stated, inquisition September 22, 1786
Coroner: William Beatty
Cause of death: Accidentally shot.
Jury: Jacob Harbaugh, Sr., John Weller, Jacob Weller, John Kamp, Laurence Creager, John Williar, Philip Williar, Peter Williar, Capt. Daniel Smith, Martin Mixal, Ludwick Harbaugh and Christian Smith, all residents of Frederick Co.
Comments: Inquisition at house of John Harbaugh, father of the deceased. Catharine had been missing for two hours. After a search, her body was found in the barn with a wound in her back near her heart. The inquisition determined that a Negro boy, Tom, age 8, had been playing with a loaded gun in the barn when he accidentally shot Catharine. [Folder 40298-14]

Deceased: Mary Abell [compare list of jurors to those in the Levy List]
Date of death: April 3, 1787, inquisition April 4, 1787
Coroner: William Beatty
Cause of death: Beaten to death.
Jury: Jacob Young, William Thomas, Benjamin Ogle, Abraham Faw, George

Burkhart, Nicholas Tice, John Adlum, John Beatty, Nicholas White, John Jacob Schley, John McPherson, John Gumbear, Jr., Michael Raymer, Thomas Price, Jonathan Morris and Jacob Bayer, Jr., all residents of Frederick Co.

Comments: Inquisition held in Frederick Town at the house of John Abell, husband of the deceased Mary Abell. Mary Abell died at her house after being beaten with a hickory stick by her husband. John Abell was described as "not having the fear of God before his eyes but moved and led by the instigation of the Devil." [Folder 40298-14]

Deceased: Infant of Mary Welsh [compare list of jurors to those in the Levy List]
Date of death: Apparently December 15, 1787, inquisition December 16, 1787
Coroner: William Beatty
Cause of death: Killed by Mary Welsh.
Jury: Richard Smith, Thomas Darnall, William Thomas, Thomas Sprig, Mark Brafield, Thomas Grover, Balser Crum, Peter Camp, Joseph Lock, Joseph Beall, William Tannihill, John Dawson, and William Dawson, all residents of Frederick Co.
Comments: The inquisition was apparently held at the plantation of Mrs. Scaggs whose dog found the partial body of the infant. Mary Welsh had come to the house of Mrs. Scaggs on the evening of December 15, 1787, then at some time in the night Welsh went outside and delivered the infant by herself. It was then determined that Welsh killed the infant in the woods and concealed its body. [Folder 40298-15]

Deceased: Ann Nell [compare list of jurors to those in the Levy List]
Date of death: June 16, 1787, inquisition June 17, 1787
Coroner: John Gwinn, Esq., Justice of the Peace
Cause of death: Suicide by hanging with a hemp cord valued at two pence.
Jury: Joseph McKaleb, John Hughes, William Cary, John Slick, Nicholas Fringer, John Trucks, George Trucks, Eli Bentley, Jacob Little, Adam Good, Jacob Rudisill, John McKaleb, George Kelly, Jacob Myers, Joseph Little, Jonathan Cochran, John Trucks, Valentine Null and John Crouse, all residents of Frederick Co.
Comments: Ann Nell hung herself on a peach tree in a rye field at the dwelling house of Philip Nell. The deceased was described as "not having the fear of God before her eyes, but being seduced and moved by the instigation of the Devil." [Folder 40298-15]

Deceased: George Harbaugh, Sr.
Date of death: Not stated, inquisition February 25, 1787

Coroner: William Beatty
Cause of death: Drowned.
Jury: Daniel Smith, Yelles Stouffer, Daniel Delozier, Conrad Eyler, Frederick Eyler, Christian Smith, Peter Flickinger, Martin Mixal, Patrick Mowney, Daniel Fry, John Kamp, Jonathan Fry, and Leonard Moser, all residents of Frederick Co.
Comments: Inquisition held at the house of George Harbaugh, Sr. On Wednesday, George Harbaugh, Sr. left home and went to Pennsylvania. On the return trip, he stayed at the home of Casper Kline. On Saturday morning, Harbaugh complained that his neck was bothering him. Harbaugh left Kline's that morning and was seen riding in the direction of his home. Later that day he was found drowned in a shallow branch. It was supposed that he fell off his horse while he was drinking, but was unable to get up because he was a heavy and very feeble man. It was reported that he had his hat in one hand and his stick in the other hand when his body was found. [Folder 40298-15]

Deceased: John Stull [compare list of jurors to those in the Levy List]
Date of death: August 10, 1788, inquistion August 11, 1788
Coroner: William Beatty
Cause of death: Natural causes.
Jury: Joseph Hobbs, Robert Gassaway, Azel Waters, Andrew Adams, Joseph Ogle, Henry Wickham, Joseph Brown, [crossed out George Devilbiss], John Cambell, Samuel Baker, John Christ, John Humer, and Charles Dorsey, all residents of Frederick Co.
Comments: John Stull walked out into his tobacco field at about 11 AM on August 10, 1788. He was found dead between 4 and 5 PM that same day. He was thought to have had an apoplectic seizure. [Folder 40298-16]

Deceased: Abraham Harvey [compare list of jurors to those in the Levy List]
Date of death: Not stated, inquisition December 31, 1787
Coroner: Leonard Smith
Cause of death: Unknown.
Jury: Joseph Belt, Jos. West, John Hillery, Benj. Jamison, Benj. Smith, Isaac Williams, David Thomas or Daniel Thomas, Conrad Christ ?, Frederick Heeter, Elimelach Gant or Elimelach Gantz, Henry Falcon, and Patrick Gormer.
Comments: The deceased was a servant of Thomas West. Harvey was found dead in his bed with no marks of violence. [Folder 40298-16]

Deceased: Joseph Graham [compare list of jurors to those in the Levy List]
Date of death: Between 8 and 10 PM July 30, 1788, inquisition July 31, 1788
Coroner: William Beatty

Cause of death: Fell while intoxicated.
Jury: Jacob Young, Esq., John Beatty, Jonathan Morris, William Thomas [it was noted that William Thomas was an inspector], William Ritchie, Benjamin Ogle, Jacob Rohr, Jacob Schisler, Philip Rohr, [crossed out Thomas Getzendanner], John D. Cary, Henry Garnhart, David Morris, James Clark and Abner Ritchie, all residents of Frederick Co.
Comments: Inquisition taken at Frederick Town. Graham was "intoxicated and drunken with liquor" when he attempted to climb a hill. The deceased fell into a creek at the bottom of the hill where he died. The report does not state that Graham drowned. [Folder 40298-16]

Deceased: Dominick Bradley
Date of death: Evening of August 16, 1788, inquisition August 17, 1788
Coroner: William Beatty
Cause of death: Accident.
Jury: John McGary, Robert Dean, Henry Leverit, Luke Mudd, Daniel Smith, Joseph Ramsey, Thomas Patterson, Conrad Matthews, James Cooper, Charles Edelen, Daniel McCormack, and Archey Cooper, all residents of Frederick Co.
Comments: Inquisition at the house of Philip Matthews. Bradley was lying under a wagon when it fell on him and "did smash his head to peaces [pieces]." [Folder 40298-16]

Deceased: Edward Bair [compare list of jurors to those in the Levy List]
Date of death: August 12, 1788, inquisition August 16, 1788
Coroner: Henry Darnall
Cause of death: Drowned
Jury: William Murdock Hall, Balser Cramer, George Cramer, John Richardson, John Buckey, George Buckey, John Brafield, Edward Crab, Walter Hagon, Edward Rose, Adolph Everhart, Christopher Brun, John Maclean, Charles Bable [juror signed Charles Poble], Charles Knup [juror's signature looks like Carl Knoff], John Hadon, John Ragon, John Davis, Charles Philpot Taylor, Thomas Mount, Christopher Tripple, Henry Vent, Joseph Waggoner and Anthony Hines [juror's signature looks like Antoin Fritz, not Hines], all residents of Frederick Co.
Comments: Inquisition taken at Monocacy River in Frederick Co. It was determined that the deceased accidentally drowned while trying to cross the river. A line that read "intoxicated with liquor" was crossed out in the report. [Folder 40298-16]

Deceased: Philip Shaff [compare list of jurors to those in the Levy List]
Date of death: Not stated, inquisitiion February 6, 1788

Coroner: Leonard Smith

Cause of death: Froze to death.

Jury: Elias Harding, Herman Conrad, Teator Gorvick, Conrad Yesterday, William B. Lamar, Daniel Weaver, Jno. Long, Geo. Blessing, Frederick Kershner, Ludwick Yesterday, and Francis Yesterday.

Comments: There were no marks of violence found on the body. [Folder 40298-16]


Deceased: Not known, infant aged about 2 days [compare list of jurors to those in the Levy List]

Date of death: Not stated, inquisition August 8, 1788

Coroner: Leonard Smith

Cause of death: Not determined.

Jury: Benj. Jamison, Elias Wilyard, Peter Nave, Geo. Pom, Adam Knouff, Jacob Durckel, Geo. Cash or Geo. Cost, Philip Finck, Valentine Mirker, Jacob Shane, Arron Fandin, and Johannes Schilling.

Comments: Body was found in a branch of water. [Folder 40298-16]


Deceased: Susan Zimmerman [compare list of jurors to those in the Levy List]

Date of death: August 17, 1789, inquisition August 18, 1789

Coroner: William Beatty

Cause of death: Drowned.

Jury: Ludwick Kemp, Alexander Wilson, Michael Tressler, George Toup, [crossed out George Zimmerman, Sr.], George Zimmerman, Jr., Godfrey Brien, Michael Shots [juror signed Michael Schatz], Steven Bruner, Philip Shots [juror signed Philip Shots], David Shots [juror signed David Shots], Jacob Kiteshu, and John Baysole, all residents of Frederick Co.

Comments: Inquisition taken at the house of John Zimmerman. Deceased was aged three years and one month at the time of her death. She had been left alone around 4 PM and was found drowned in the spring at about 5 PM. [Folder 40298-17]


Deceased: John Ryan [compare list of jurors to those in the Levy List]

Date of death: March 2, 1789, inquisition March 5, 1789

Coroner: John Gwinn, Justice of the Peace of Frederick Co.

Cause of death: Died of injuries to the head and breast after being beaten.

Jury: Ralph Crabbs, Joseph Little, George Trucks, Barnaby McSherry, Samuel Perry, Michael McGuire, Jr., Christopher Erb, Jacob Yingling, Peter Baum, Jonathan Haun, Henry O'Hara, Philip Slaughenhoup, Wendle Erbaugh, Felix Frogenfelter, Jacob Sherman, Jr., Laurence Erbaugh, John Baker, and Frederick Yingling, all residents of Frederick Co.

Comments: On the evening of February 24, 1789, John Ryan and Michael Quinner, Jr., were at the home of Philip Naile. Quinner was described as "not having the fear of God before his eyes, but being moved and seduced by the instigation of the Devil" when he beat Ryan, causing mortal injuries to the head and breast of Ryan. Ryan languished at the home of Philip Naile until his death on March 2, 1789. John Quinner was also present at the house of Philip Naile when the assault occured on Ryan; he was said to have encouraged the actions of Michael Quinner, Jr. At the time of the inquisition it was noted that Michael Quinner, Jr. and John Quinner had no known chattels and goods, and that they had "fled or removed themselves to some place or places unknown." [Folder 40298-17]

Deceased: --- Red [compare list of jurors to those in the Levy List]
Date of death: Not stated, inquisition March -- 1789
Coroner: Leonard Smith
Cause of death: Fell.
Jury: Jos. West, Thomas W. West, Benjamin West, Geo. Hickrey, Geo. Poe, Michael Redemon, John Niswan, Sr., Conrad Kisor, Johannes [last name ?], Harmon Conrad, Frederick Uhl, and Samson Smith.
Comments: Report was falling apart and pieces were missing. [Folder 40298-17]

## ORDINARY KEEPERS AND ROAD OVERSEERS

*Filed under "Frederick County Court: Grand Jury Papers 1784-1847" Maryland Archives MdHR 40,297-1/19 location 1/41/7/34 C-792*

List of Ordinary Keepers Licensed at August Court 1784
Andw. Adams, Geo. Adams, Valentine Adams, John Balsor, William Bentley, Samuel Boggass, Mercy Bonham, Henry Brothers, Valentine Brunor, John Buckey, George Burkitt, Sen., John Cookerly, Robert Dean, Conrad Duttero, Guy Elder, Adam Good, Jacob Grove, Balsor Heck, Nicholas Hildebrand, Philip Hines, William Hobbs, George Hockersmith, Edward Hodgkins, David Hyme, Adam Iseminger, John Keney, David Kephart, Andrew Keplor, Henry Landis, John Laney, Peter Leepley, Joseph McKillup, Jacob Mettert, Jacob Miller, Jonathan Morris, Peter Morser, Benjamin Musgrove, Robert Owen, Nicholas Powell, William Renner, Tobias Risener, Rudolph Roar, George Jacob Schley, Jacob Shearman, George Snyder, Frederick Stemple, Jeremiah Steward, Leond. Storm, Joseph Swearingan, Robert Talbutt, John Teterley, Isaac Wayne, John Wright, Christian Yesterday, and Henry Zealor.
By William Ritchie, Clerk

98

List of Ordinary Keepers Licensed at August Court 1785
Andrew Adams, George Adams, Valentine Adams, Wm. Albaugh of Jno., John
Balser, William Bentley, Samuel Boggass, Mercy Bonham, Catherine Boyer,
Henry Brothers, John Buckey, John Cookerly, Robert Dean, Daniel Dingle, Guy
Elder, Mathew Gault, Jacob Grove, Martin Hanes, Nicholas Hildebrand,
William Hobbs, George Hockersmith, David Hyme, Adam Isominger, Benjamin
Jones, John Keeney, Henry Kemhart, David Kephart, Valentine Ker, Andrew
Kessler, Charles King, John Lanos or John Lanor, Peter Leeply, John Leyster,
Joseph McKillup, Jacob Meddart, Jacob Miller, Jonathan Mooris, Peter Morser,
Benjamin Musgrove, Robert Owen, William Renner, Rudolph Roahr, John
Roberts, Tobias Rudecill, Geo. Jacob Schley, Jacob Shearman, George Snider,
Frederick Stemple, Leonard Storm, Thomas Swearingen, Robert Talbutt, John
Teterly, John Thompson, John Welty, Henry White, Christian Yesterday, and
Henry Zealer.

List of Ordinary Keepers Licensed at November Court 1785
George Boner, George Burckhartt, William Davey, Jacob Gitzadanner, John
Haley, Balser Heck, Edward Hodgekiss, Casper Keller, John Mefford, Thomas
Ogle, Christian Prengle, Adam Ramsower, and John Waggoner.

List of Ordinary Keepers Licensed at March Court 1786
Conrad Becker, Abner Bentley, Philip Fine, Martin Fletcher, Thomas Hagarty,
John Rogers, and Solomon Sodshaw.

Licenses granted "At the adjourned court 10th April" [1786]
Jacob Fleatzer, Biggar Head, Charles King, Rebeckah Owen, and Valentine
Shreiner.
By Wm. Ritchie, Clerk

List of Ordinaries licensed by Frederick County Court March 1798
Henry Baer, Eli Bentley, Frederick Betz, John Biggs, Henry Boteler, Christian
Bower, Henry Brother, Valentine Brother, Emanuel Brower, Jr., Henry Brown,
John Bucky, Christian Caufman, Josiah Clements, Frederick Colliberger, John
Cookerly, Henry Coppersmith, Jacob Cover, George Creager, Balser Earbaugh,
Christian Easterday, Leonard Eichelberger, John Erb, Andrew Etzler, Frederick
Fox, Jacob Gamber, Henry Garnhart, Bernard Gilbert, Christian Gitzendanner,
Jacob Goodland, Adam Goyer, Rachel Grove, Christian Haas, Hugh Hagan,
John Stephen Hall, William Hobbs of Sam., Jacob Holtzman, Jacob Houx [might
mean Houcks ?] or Jacob House, Anthony Angel Josse ? [not "Jesse"], Adam
Keller, Andrew Kessler, Jacob Kiler, Catherine Kimbel, Francis Klinchart,
David Levy, Jr., Ignatius Livers, Philip Loyer, John Lyster, William Markel,

Jacob Martin, Archibald McAvicker?, Jacob Meddert, Jonathan Mooris, Peter Morser, Henry Motter, Philip Nichodemus, Samuel Pennybaker, John Peter, Patrick Reed, William Rice, Henry Schell, George Jacob Schley, Gassaway Sellman, Jacob Shearman, John Shiss, Henry Shriner, Andrew Shriver, George Smith, George Smith [again], Jacob Smith, Elizabeth Snyder, George Snyder, Benjamin Stallings, Frederick Stemple, Elias Thrasher, Ludwick Wampler, John Werner, John Whiteneck, Jesse Wright, and Henry Winroad.

Ordinary licenses granted November Term 1798
Jacob Angell, George Beckinbaugh, Daniel Cover, Henry Crouise, Richard Ensey, William Greenamyer, Elias Groshong, Peter Grove, Jacob Hockensmith, Catherine Kimbel crossed out, George Lease, Joseph Little, Frederick Loy, Philip Luckett, Maj. Jacob Miller, James Moorison, William Ogle, Peter Orndorff, James Rice, Paul Trit, John Ungeser, and Edward Wheatcroft.

List of retailers of liquors licensed by Frederick County Court March Term 1798
Thomas Adlesperger, Frederick M. Ameling ?, Christopher Burckhart, Jr., William Burges, Henry Burkhart, Robert John Conn, Abraham Crapster, John Dagan, Daniel Dorsey, David Fischer, Jacob Geisenderfer, Thomas Gibson, John Hammond, Nathan Hammond, Jr., Joshua Harley, John Higdon, Philip Hines, John Hoffman, James Hughes, William Lambky, Joseph Little, William Lowe, Samuel N. Luckett, John Lyster, Francis Mantz, Patrick McGill, James McHaffie, John McKaleb, Philip Nichodemus, Benjamin Ogle, Charles Schell, Philip Sengstack, James Smith, Lawrence Switezer, Joab Waters, and John Yengling.

Retailers licenses granted November Term 1798
John Lawrence Dorsey, William Greenamyer, Vachel Hammond, Casper Hevring?, Richard Mills, Christopher Owings, George Ramsburg, William Springer, and Andrew Thompson.

List of ordinaries licensed in the recess of court by the Justices of Frederick County Court
John Holtzman February 11, 1799 (only one)

List [of] "retailers liquors" licensed in the recess of court by the justices thereof
John Kean December 12, 1798
Elisha Faulkner December 21, 1798
Woodward Evitt December 22, 1798

Francis Clarke December 24, 1798
Valentine Bruner February 11, 1799

Retailers Licenses granted
Lewis Browning September 17, 1798 to retail until November Term 1798 by R.
Potts, Esq., Chief Justice
By Wm. Ritchie, Clerk Frederick County Court

## ROAD OVERSEERS

This document contains a list of overseers who were appointed to monitor the roads in an assigned territory. Beside each territory description, an overseer's name had been noted, and another overseer's name had been crossed out. It appears that the crossed out names were those of the original overseers who had served during the prior year. The document was originally written in November 1783 to name the overseers for 1784, and the handwriting and the ink of the names that were crossed out matches that of the original document. It appears that the crossed out name is that of the overseer for 1784, while the other overseer served in a later term, perhaps 1785. Apparently when the overseers were named for a new term, the clerk crossed out the name from the prior year and wrote in the new name to avoid rewriting the entire document. The crossed out names are in many cases difficult to read.

Format: Area for which overseer was responsible; Crossed out name of original overseer; Overseer who served a subsequent term.

"The following are the public and main roads ascertained by the Justices of Frederick County November Court 1783. And the persons whose names are thereto annexed were by the same court appointed overseers thereof for the ensuing year, agreeable to the Acts of Assembly in such case made."

1) From Linganore Chappell to the west side of Sams Creek; Simon Meredith; Henry Crowell.
2) From the east side of Sams Creek to the extent of the county; John Gist; Henry Nichodemas.
3) From Linganore Ford to Col. Thomas Dorsey's Quarter; Edward Dorsey both terms.
4) From the upper part of Col. Thomas Dorsey's Quarter to the extent of the county; Henry Poole both terms.
5) From the Chappell Quarter to the east side of the Spring Branch that crosses

the main road in David Plain's plantation; David Plain; Peter Becraft.

6) From the branch on the west of Colliberger's Tavern till it intersects the Annapolis road leading to Frederick Town by Geo. Adams' Tavern; William Dorsey; Peter Fine.

7) From the fork of the road below Colliberger's Tavern to Israels Creek by Creager's; William Smith; Michael Creager.

8) From Frederick Town to Ruess Ford on Monocasy and the fording place. From the fork of the same road near town to Morris' Fulling Mill, and from Frederick Town to Johnson's Mill on Monocasy; Christian F--- [can't read]; Bened. Stoner.

9) The road from the west side of Monacasy at Marshall's Ford to the bridge at Jacob Harmon's on Bennett's Creek; Zachariah Lin--; Henry Smith.

10) From the bridge at Harmon's to the county line; Thomas Baldwin; John Hinton.

11) From Ballanger's Creek to Jonathan Thomas'; Ignatius Davis; John Darnall.

12) From Sleagle Tavern to the top of the mountain; George Youst; Joseph Hill.

13) From the new road that leads from the top of the mountain where George Matthews lived to Ballanger's Branch; Lewis Kemp; Ludwick Kemp.

14) From the west bank of Monocasy Ferry at Adam's Ferry to where the Baltimore Road leaves [the] same and the fording place on Israel's Creek by James Beatty's; Jacob Lease; James Beatty.

15) From McAlister's Mill [to] the main road to Christian Yesterday's; John Hillery both terms.

16) From the road that leads out of the main road by Peter Bainbridge's to the top of South Mountain; Valentine Lingenfelter; Thos. Gilbert.

17) From Geo. Adams' to the cross roads at Andrew Adams' and from the east side of the glade near Christn. Smith's to the east side of Israel's Creek; John Grapps both terms.

18) From the cross roads at And. Adams' to Smith's Branch and from the east side of the glade near John Barrick's until it intersects the road from Bigg's Ford to Israel's Creek; Peter Barrick; Michl. Riddlemoser.

19) From Solomon Ferree's crossing [of] Little Pipe Creek at the new bridge to the middle of Great Pipe Creek and from said road near the Little Pipe Creek to intersect the road from Great Pipe Creek to Baltimore and from Pipe Creek by Frederick Dern's Mill til it intersects the York Road; Danl. Fundibergh; Geo. Boner.

20) From Smith's Branch to John Cookerly's and from Col. Woods' Mill [to] the new road until it intersects the road that goes from Smith's Branch to John Cookerly's; John Phillips; Philip Hufford.

21) From Knouff's Ford on Monocasy to the middle of Great Pipe Creek below the bridge and from Wilson's Ford on Monocasy until it intersects the road

from Monocasy to Pipe Creek, and from the Tobacco Box Branch where the main road crosses, that leads from Casper Smith's to Col. Bruce's Mill to the south side of Great Pipe Creek at Dern's Mill; John Ridgely, Esq.; James Petit.

22) From Bigg's Ford on Mococasy to the east side of the glade. From the branch by Geo. Sexton's to Bigg's Ford. From the east side of Monocasy at Alexd. Ogle's Ford to the east side of the glade by John Barrick's, and from the end of Casper Devilbiss' and Simon Shover's lane to the end of the lane of William Smith son of William; John Crane; James Hale.

23) From Jacob Moiley's to Toms Creek and from Hampton Furnace to Wilson's Ford on Monocasy; Sam Carrick only name present, apparently served both terms.

24) From Toms Creek to the Province Line. From the Province Line to Rouse's Ford on Monocasy and to the center of the bridge near said ford, and from the Province Line near John Young's plantation by Hockersmith's Mill to Trout's Ford on Monocasy; James Allison; James Park.

25) From Ambrosey's Mill to Miller's Mill. From the mountain to Captain's Creek and from Nicholas Leatherman's til it intersects the road to Cassell's Mill; James Ogle; Henry Ferro.

26) From Cassell's Mill [to] the main road that leads to Frederick Town til the road turns out to Bigg's Ford on Monocasy. From Ogle's Mill to the Shallow Ford on Monocasy and from the fork of the road near Stephen Julien's to Fishing Creek; Philip Christ; Peter Houck.

27) From the fork of the road at Schnertzell's building erected by Dulany to the top of the Ketoctin Mountain; Peter Swilley; Val. Brunner.

28) From Frederick Town to James Marshall's Branch, from then to the main road that leads to Kemp's Mill by Pierpoint's Smith Shop, and from Frederick Town to Kennedy's Ford on Monocasy; Christian ? Hildrebrand; Jno. Dawson.

29) From Frederick Town to the east side of Adam's and to Bigg's Ford on Monocasy; Jacob Humbart; Saml. Flemming.

30) All the streets and alleys in Frederick Town, and the several fording places in the Town Creek, which lie to the east of the center or middle of Market Street; Danl. Gaver; Henry Winemiller.

31) All the streets and alleys in Frederick Town and the several fording places in the Town Creek, which lie to the west of the center or middle of Market Street; Christn. Prengle; David Harvey.

32) From Michael Waggoner's through Winchester Town to the Baltimore County Line; Philip Logston; Wm. Dublin.

33) From Ruess' Ford on Monocasy [to] the new road to the branch at John Mobberly's; Geo. Cling ?; Wm. Turner.

34) From John Mobberly's Branch [to] the new road to where it intersects the old road near Wm. Hobbs'; Danl. Smith written in originally and crossed out in error (apparently intended for #35 below) to write in Leond. Hobbs; Jno. McElfresh, Jr.

35) From the east side of the mountain to Casper Smith's and to the extent of the county; Danl. Smith; Christ. Herbaugh.

36) From Erb's Mill to Winchester Town; Jacob Forman both terms.

37) From the top of the Ketoctin Mountain and under the north side of the same til it intersects at [the] path that leads from James Hook's to the main road leading by Nathan Magruder's leading to Winchester in Virginia; Richd. Andrum; Snowden Hook.

38) From Rouse's Ford on Monocacy, and from the center of the bridge near said ford, through Taney Town to Pipe Creek at the mouth of the Meadow Branch and from John Mefford's into the same road; John Robinson both terms.

39) From the mouth of Monocasy to Jonathan Fromass'. From Griffith's old place to Powell's Ford on Patonmack [Potomac] River, and from the Widow Barker's to the Middle Ford of Monocasy; Richd. Davis both terms.

40) From the top of the Ketoctin Mountain, the new road by Van Swearingen's Tavern to the bridge on Ketoctin Creek; Conrad C---; Van Swearingen.

41) From William Bentley's crossing [at] Israel's Creek to a branch of Saw Creek near Andw. Michaell's plantation, and from said road near Garver's plantation to Col. Woods' Mill, and from said mill to intersect the road from Bentley's to Baltimore on the hill near Christian Shutter's plantation; Jacob Miller; Jno. Heartsooch.

42) From the west side of the branch near Andrew Michaell's plantation to intersect the road by John Carmack's plantation; George Hunter; Jno. Maynard.

43) From Jacob Moiley's Run to Captain's Creek, and the new road that comes from Captain's Creek to Monocacy, and the road from Bayerley's Mill to William Elder's, and the road from Charles Elder's to Ambrosey's Mill; Henry Crine or Henry Criner; Jacob Crist.

44) From the York Road near Great Pipe Creek, to the west [at] Cabbin Branch; Wm. Ebernathy ?; Joseph Wright.

45) From the top of the South Mountain [to] the new road that leads from Beall and Compy's Forge to the top of Ketoctin Mountain "from a little Daniel Miller's" on Ketoctin Creek to cross said creek, from thence on the south side of Klein's plantation round Knouff's plantation to George Shaaff's and from thence to Jacob Silar's; Thos. Harrison; Peter Gaver.

46) From the mouth of the Bear Branch to intersect the road from Trucks' to Baltimore; Gasper St---; another name crossed out is unreadable; Michael Fouts.

47) From Cabbin Branch, over said branch to Michael Waggoner's; A-- Myer; Philip Angler ?.

48) From Erb's Mill to the Pennsylvania Line; Christ. Erb; Peter Bankard.

49) From Stouder's Ford on Monocacy to William Bentley's; John Stouder; Joseph Hobbs.

50) From Fishing Creek to Hunting Creek, and from Robert Woods' Mill where the new road intersects the main road leading from Ambrosey's Mill to Cassell's Mill; Peter Troutman; George Domer.

51) From Hunting Creek to Captain's Creek, and from Stouder's Ford on Monocacy to Robert Wood's Mill; Danl. Prutzman; Jno. Spoon.

52) From John Cookerly's to the Widow Berrier's; Joshua Dilleplayn; John Keney.

53) From Great Pipe Creek to Taney Town; Jacob Stemple ?; Martin Adams.

54) From Ketoctin Furnace to Cassell's Mill, the road laid off by a late order of court; John Shideare or John Skideare [barely readable]; Philip Morningstar.

55) From Christian Yesterday's to the top of the Ketoctin Mountain where Nathan Magruder lives, and the new road leading from Beall and Compy's Forge from Ketoctin Creek to the top of the Ketoctin Mountain; Balser Duttero; Saml. Phillips.

56) From the east side of the Spring Branch that crosses the main road in David Plain's plantation to the branch on the south west side of John Colliberger's Tavern; Jacob Ockerman; Benj. Musgrove.

57) From Taney Town through Wm. Harris' plantation to Piney Ford bridge and from thence to the temporary line; James Ryley only name present, apparently served both terms.

58) From the temporary line above Richard Hill's into the road from Monocacy to Taney Town; Alexd. McAlister only name present, apparently served both terms.

59) From Ketoctin Bridge to the top of the South Mountain on the road leading to Sharpsburgh; Jacob Kefhauer ?; Adam Smelzer.

60) From Griffith's old place to the top of the Ketoctin Mountain near James Hook's plantation; Arthur Nelson only name present, apparently served both terms.

61) From the fork of the road where the Sharpsburgh road leads out of Braddock's road to the top of the South Mountain, being the direct road from Frederick Town passing Robert Turner's old place to Fort Frederick; Adam Knouff; Jacob Smith.

62) From the Poor House passing Schnertzell's building erected by Dulany to Ballanger's Creek; Martin Shoup; Lawr. Hyme.

63) From Frederick Town to Peter Brunner's, and from Town, the new road by Henry Shaver's to Peter Shaver's hemp and oil mills; Christ. Myers only

name present, apparently served both terms.

64) From John Groff's Mill til it intersects the main road leading from Maroh Creek to Balto. Town at Mich. Dern's or Mich. Derr's farm, one mile below Piney Creek, and also from the said mill until it intersects the main road aforesaid at Jo Myer's [just Jo Myer's with no period after Jo] farm, about three miles below Pipe Creek, opened by a late act of assembly; Wm. Ritchie, Clerk; Mich. McGuire, Jr.

65) From the fork of the road near Hine's Tavern to Linganore Ford at Keller's Mill; John Larkin only name present, apparently served both terms.

Written by William Ritchie, Clerk.

## LEVY LIST 1785-1790

*Maryland Archives C818-1 1/54/10/5*

November Court 1784
Grand Jurors:Thomas Schley, Senr., Joshua Howard, Amos Davis, Joseph Wood, Junr., William Albaugh, Basil Beall, Christopher Stull, Nicholas White, Benjamin Ogle, Jacob Bayer, Samuel Lilly, George Bare, Benjamin Eastburn, Henry Coleman, Jonathan Wood, Lucas Fleck, John Biggs, and Basil Wood.

Petit Jurors: Samuel Fleming, Charles Beall, Samuel Linton, Joseph Beall, Francis Thomas, John Haymond Jones, Mountjoy Bayly, John Gaver, Abraham Lemaster, Thomas Darnall, Peter Burckhartt, Alexander Warfield, Joseph Ogle, Peter Shover, Thomas Flemming, Michael Wilson, Joseph Wilson, William Dern, William Davey, Adam Bayer, George Burckhartt, Junr., George Trucks, John Lane, George Schnertzell, Nicholas Tice, Joseph Smith, Michael Troutman, Philip Rodenpeelor, Joseph Swearingen, Christian Smith, George Ott, John Stone, Jacob Herman, Michael Null, William Eastup, Elias Magers, John Snowfer, Conrad Grosh, Abraham Faw, John Beatty, Samuel Cock, George Burckhartt, Senr., Capt. Michael Bayer, John Shellman, Senr.

November Court 1784 Payments:
* George Hawk for nursing and burial charges of William McGlauchlin, an invalid soldier.
* Valentine Metzgar for nursing and burial charges of John Stout, a poor person.
* Catherine Falk for nursing and burial charges of Francis Dewess, a poor person. Account filed June 16 ?; thereafter to be credited Henry McCleary.
* William Elder for 2 old wolves' heads.

* Jacob Lochman for 1 old wolf's head.

March Court 1785
Grand Jurors: Thomas Schley, Senr., Michael McGuire, John Jones, Junr., Henry Coleman, Henry Feaster, John Ferguson, Jacob Cassell, John Werner, Basil Beall, Samuel Thomas, Isaac Wilson, Michael Troutman, George Werner, Samuel Linton, William Albaugh, John Climson.

Petit Jurors: Charles Beall, George Trux, Henry Six, Garey Harding, John Jacobs, Benedict Jameson, Daniel Hook, William Durbin, John Compton, Nicholas Dawson, Edward Boteler, James Samuel Hook, Nicholas Tice, Amos Davis, Christopher Burckhartt, Michael Null, Jacob Crist, Christian Shryock, Bostian Myers, William Dern, Thomas Patterson, Lucas Fleck, Frederick Dern, William Duvall, Ralph Hilleary, Andrew Lowe, Samuel Fleming, John Laney, Thomas Darnall, Robert Fleming, Benjamin Eastburn, Abraham Lemaster, Francis Thomas, William Murdock Hall, John Eckus, Joseph Wilson, John Hammond, Michael Heffner, George Heffner, Peter Mantz, George Dent, Alexander Warfield, George Bare, Luke Mudd, Joseph Ogle, and Adam Bayer.

March Court 1785 Payments:
* George Bair for nursing and burial charges of Joseph Todd, a pauper.
* Jacob Meddert for necessaries furnished to Wm. McLaughlin during his sickness.
* Francis Croyley a witness for the State vs. Jno. Smith. Smith convicted of stealing at November Court 1784.
* Elizabeth Pritchett a witness for the State vs. George Adams. Case discharged.
* Richard Linnic a witness for the State vs. Wm. Williams. Case discharged.
* Mssrs. Young and Scott for John Lipps, witness in the State vs. Michl. Custard. [not clear if Lipps was the witness and Young and Scott received payment for his services on his behalf, or if all three served as witnesses]

August Court 1785
Grand Jurors: Abraham Faw, William Purdy, Samuel Linton, Samuel Pevry, Francis Thomas, John Stone, Richard Ridgely, Andrew Hawn, William Eastup, William Albaugh, Philip Smith, Nathaniel Porter, Francis Mantz, Nicholas Tice, Henry Koontz, George Bare and Jacob Bayer, Senr.

Petit Jurors: Joseph Beall, Elisha Beall, Roger Brooke, John Burton, John Carn, Henry Six, Abraham Lemaster, Joseph Swearingen, Samuel Thomas, Nicholas Dawson, Michael McGuire, Jacob Wampler, Richard Smith, James Hook, Junr., Jacob Gumbare, Hugh Flannigan, Peter Shover, Azel Waters, James Smith,

Mathias Dadisman, Henry Feaster, Senr., Philip Rodenpeeler, John Jacobs, George Boner, James Beatty, Luke Mudd, William Shields, and John McPherson.

August Court 1785 Payments:
* Peter Stilley and Richard Harrison, witnesses for the State vs. Jno. Balsor. Outcome: "quashed."
* Wm. Ferrenee ? a witness for the State vs. Balsor. Outcome: "quashed."
* Henry Brimm for attending the Bar as Constable, and for suppressing the irregular meeting of Negroes.
* William Miller for attending the Bar as Constable.
* Col. Wm. Beatty for attending the gaol for release of insolvent debtors.
* Col. Wm. Beatty for holding inquests on dead bodies as coroner.
* Thos. Ogle for 1 old wolf's head. Certificate to Wm. Pebble dated January 7, 1783.
* Conrad Doll for making a coffin for Philip Pebble.
* Henry McCleary paid.
* John Hutton paid.
* Henry Zealer paid.
* Capt. Jno. Morris for 13 days court sitting at his house.
* Wm. Magruder for 1 old wolf's head.
* Richard Potts, Esq. paid.
* Wm. Ritchie paid.
* Abner Ritchie paid. [crossed out]
* Geo. Scott, Esq. for attending the gaol for the release of insolvent debtors.
* Jacob Young, Esq. for attending the election at the gaol for release of insolvent debtors.
* Wm. M. Beall, Esq. for attending the release of insolvent debtors.
* John Ross Key, Esq. for attending about Great Pipe Creek Bridge.
* Abner Ritchie paid.
* Richard Ancrom, Junr. for 1 old wolf's head; certificate assigned to Wm. Thomas of Hugh.
* John Harrison, Esq. for attendance on the releasement of insolvent debtors and election.
* Yost Blickenstaff for 4 young wolves' heads; assigned to Geo. Murdock, Esq.
* Joseph Murray for 11 young wolves' heads; assigned to Geo. Murdock.
* Joseph Murray for 4 young wolves' heads; to be credited to Geo. Murdock, Esq.
* John Shelman for taking care of Scales, Weights and Measures.

Justices' Attendance in County Court:
Upton Sheredine, Esq.: Nov 1784, Aug 1785
Wm. Beatty, Esq.: Nov 1784, Mar 1785, Aug 1785
Jacob Young, Esq.: Nov 1784, Mar 1785, Aug 1785
James Johnson, Esq.: Nov 1784, Mar 1785, Aug 1785
Wm. M. Beall, Esq.: Nov 1784, Mar 1785, Aug 1785
Wm. Luckett, Esq.: Nov 1784, Mar 1785, Aug 1785
Joseph Wood, Esq.: Nov 1784, Mar 1785, Aug 1785
Jno. McAllister, Esq.: Mar 1785, Aug 1785
Jno. R. Key, Esq.: Mar 1785, Aug 1785
George Scott, Esq.: Nov 1784, Mar 1785, Aug 1785
Wm. Magruder, Esq.: Nov 1784, Mar 1785, Aug 1785
Charles Warfield, Esq.: Nov 1784, Mar 1785, Aug 1785
Henry Darnall, Esq.: Nov 1784, Aug 1785
John Harrison, Esq.: Mar 1785
Geo. Murdock, Esq.: Nov 1784, Mar 1785, Aug 1785
Jno. Gwinn, Jr., Esq.: Mar 1785, Aug 1785

Justices' Attendance in Orphans Court: [probably August Court 1785]
Upton Sheredine, Esq. 4 days
William Beatty, Esq. 7 days
Wm. M. Beall, Esq. 8 days
George Scott, Esq., 6 days
John Harrison, Esq. 6 days

August Court 1785: Payment to those who served as jurors of inquest on the body of Negro Jacob:
Maj. Abraham Haff, Nicholas Hobbs, Samuel Cock, Joseph Hobbs, Nathan Maynard, John Mackelfish, Junr., Lodowick Bricker, Nathaniel Burckhartt, Redmond McDonald, Benjamin Becraft, Caleb Harn, Elijah Harn, and John Dorsey of Edward. [compare list of jurors to those in the Coroner's Inquest]

August Court 1785: Payment to those who served as jurors of inquest in the body of Michael Fitzgerald:
Maj. Abrahm Haff, Samuel Cock, Richard Gore, Abraham Cassel, Jacob Leaser, John Waggoner, Junr., Tevry O'Brian, Charles King, John Bagent, Conrad Pool, Abraham Eador, Thomas Walford, James Newport, and John Miller. [compare list of jurors to those in the Coroner's Inquest]

August Court 1785: Payment to those who served as jurors of inquest on the body of Philip Pebble:

Nicholas Tice, Jacob Bayer, Senr., Michael Bayer, Mathias Bartgis, Martin Waltz, Woodward Evitt, Philip Shade, Henry Zealer, Benjamin Ogle, Thomas Knox, and Christian Shoup. [compare list of jurors to those in the Coroner's Inquest]

August Court 1785 Payments:
* George Murdock, Esq. for attending the releasement of insolvent debtors, attending about the court house, and for serving 1 year in office as the Register of Wills.
* Balance due to Doctor Fisher.
* Jno. McAllister for acting as coroner.

September 1, 1785: The tax collector was authorized to collect, from those who owned property in Frederick County, five shillings for each hundred pounds of property owned. Signed: Upton Sheredine, Jacob Young, Wm. Beatty, W. M. Beall, John McAlister, Geo. Murdock, and John Ross Key.

September 3, 1785: Richard Butler was at the office of Doctor Fisher.

November Court 1785:
Grand Jurors: Patrick S. Smith, Nicholas Tice, Samuel Thomas, Ephraim Howard, Jonathan Wood, John Burton, Henry Coleman, Peter Mantz, Thomas Thrasher, Adam Bayer, Jacob Trout, William Dern, George Bair, Michael Troutman, John Divilbiss, Leonard Storm, Thomas Castle, and Richard Smith.

Petit Jurors: Joseph West, William Crum, John Ramsbergh, Charles Beall, Thomas Noland, Nathaniel Norris, Jacob Appler, John Jacobs, Lucas Fleck, Nicholas Dawson, Abraham Lemaster, Francis Thomas, Joseph Beall, Joseph Wilson, Michael McGuire, Jun., Michael Crist, Joseph Taney, John Gump, Alexander Warfield, John McPherson, Daniel Smith, John Stalcup and Daniel Dorsey.

March Court 1786
Grand Jurors: Basil Beall, William Albaugh, Michael Null, Thomas Harris, Abraham Poore, Henry Feaster, Nathan Maynard, Henry Hann, John Gump, Thomas Castle, Michael Troutman, John Burton, Jacob Burton, Thomas Maynard, Junr., George Bare, Christian Smith, and Richard Lilley.

Petit Jurors: Conrad Duttero, Joseph Wood (Linganore), John Martin Derr, William Dern, Thomas Fleming, Peter Troutman, Thomas Durbin, Hugh Thompson, John Ramsbergh, William Thomas of Hugh, James Smith, Basil

110

Israel, Jeremiah Belt, John Shellman, Samuel Linton, Ralph Hilleary, Isaac
Wilson, Elisha Beall, Andrew Lowe, Leonard Lontz, John Ferguson, Nicholas
Tice, Joseph Smith, Abraham Lemaster, Francis Thomas, Azel Waters, John
Jacobs, James Samuel Hook, Daniel Hook, Philip Noller, John Cumpton and
William Emmitt.

#### August Court 1786
Grand Jurors: Nicholas Tice, William Thomas of Hugh, George Bair, Amos
Davis, John Hammond, Henry Maynard, Henry Wood, Henry Warfield, George
Hammond, William Albaugh, Charles Simpson, Abraham Pore, Philip Nollert,
James Wells, Michael McGuire and Benjamin Musgrove.

Petit Jurors: Ralph Hilleary, William Purdey, Isaac Wilson, crossed out Richard
Coale, Christian Smith, Adam Good, Michael Null, Joseph Taney, Roger
Brooke, George Trux, Peter Beard, Samuel Linton, Basil Beall, Thomas
Dawson, Samuel Cock, Peter Troutman, Elijah Beatty, John Ramsbergh, Jacob
Crist, William Emmitt, Joseph Wilson, Luke Mudd, Joseph Smith, Garey
Harding, Daniel Hook, Adam Creager, James Hughes, Peter Shover, Joseph
Beall, Charles Gartrill, James Simmons, James Samuel Hook, John Compton,
John Shellman, George Bare, John Bruner (merchant), and William Thomas of
Hugh.

November Court 1785 Payments:
* John Shellman for taking care of Scales, Weights and Measures.
* Joshua Kirbey a witness for the State vs. Elizabeth Duffield. Outcome:
  Acquitted.
* Henry Forney a witness for the State vs. Robt. Brown. Outcome: Condemned.

March Court 1786 Payments:
* Daniel Smith, Constable, for attending the Bar of the Court.
* To Samuel Fasant, Daniel Chadd, David Walter, Philip Hubberd, and Nathan
  Estep witnesses for the State vs. Frederick Hizor. Outcome: Acquitted.
* Susanna Price and Mary Smith, witnesses for the State vs. Catherine Miller.
  (no statement of the outcome of the trial)

August Court 1786 Payments:
* Beale Babbs of Virginia, William Owens of Virginia, and Levy Davis
  witnesses for the State vs. Solomon Watson. Outcome: Condemned.
* John Stevenson a witness for the State vs. John Toms. The clerk noted: "Bill
  retd. [returned] Ignoramus".
* Elizabeth Matthews for the maintenance and burial of Elizabeth Stewart, a

poor woman.
* Bostian Derr for the maintenance and burial of Isaac Sheft, a poor man.
* Frederick Green, heir at law of Catherine Green, deceased. The balance of her account against the county not levied.
* Adam Loy for 1 old wolf's head, killed May 1786.
* Thomas Crampton for 1 old wolf's head killed Feb 24, 1786.
* Jacob Wellor of Jno., for 1 old wolf's head, killed Feb 7, 1786.
* Philip Wellor for 1 old wolf's head killed Oct 31, 1785. [after "Wellor" there are 3 dashes before "1" is written, not clear if Philip Wellor is also "of Jno."]
* Jacob Souder for the maintenance and burial of Conrad Young, a poor person.
* Abner Ritchie, Cryer, paid.
* William Beatty, Coroner, paid.
* Richard Potts, Esq., Prosecutor.
* Wm. Luckett for attending election.
* John Shellman paid.
* Adam Fisher crossed out.
* Henry Brim, Constable, for preventing the tumultuous meetings of Negroes.
* John Buckias, Constable, for attending court.
* Henry Stophel a witness for the State vs. Christian Karns. (no outcome of trial stated)
* Wm. Beatty, Esq., Coroner, paid.
* Upton Sheredine, Esq., for inserting an advertisement in the Baltimore newspapers about the court house.
* Thomas Beatty, Jun., for wood furnished to the gaol.
* Thomas Beatty, Sheriff, paid.
* Henry McCleary paid.
* Wm. M. Beall, Esq. paid.
* Jacob Young, Esq. paid.
* Yost Blickenstaff for 6 young wolves' heads killed May 12, 1786. Assigned to T. Beatty, Sheriff.
* George Scott, Esq. paid.
* William Ritchie paid.
* Jacob Young, Esq. paid for 2 days attendance of the scales and weights at the inspection.
* George Murdock, Esq. paid.
* Richard Potts submitted his account for the support of the poor for the following year.
* Col. Richd. Smith, Inspector, paid.

August Court 1786: Payment to those who served as jurors of inquest on the body of an unknown person:

Capt. Edward Dyer, Jacob Lease, John Silver, James Silver, James Newport, Christian Alinger, Charles Button, Christian Averts, George Wentz, William Umbaugh, George Evert, Samuel Fleming, and Henry Ramsbergh. [compare list of jurors to those in the Coroner's Inquest]

August Court 1786: Payments to those who served as jurors of inquest on the body of Negro Jack:
Col. Joseph Wood, Levi Bentley, Benjamin Barnhart, Zachariah Albaugh, David Cumming, Luke Bernard, Joseph Melton, Jacob Cookerly, Anglebert Hartsoke, Charles Clance, John Ream, and Balser Ream. [compare list of jurors to those in the Coroner's Inquest]

August Court 1786: Payments to those who served as jurors of inquest on the body of an infant:
Samuel Cock, Alexander Ogle, Philip Crist, John Hefner, Henry Jackson, Jacob Ketters, Joseph Shane, Jacob Layman, Henry Sellers, Henry Pitesell, Michael Crist, George Myers and Frederick Hoffman. [compare list of jurors to those in the Coroner's Inquest]

August Court 1786: Payments to those who served as jurors of inquest on the body of Josiah Miller:
Abednego Hyatt, Thomas Reynolds, Abner Bentley, John Shoemaker, William Stokes, John M. Keeny, Adam Strine, Conrad Mort, Martin Erhart, Adam Bush, Jacob Fox, and John Shockey. [compare list of jurors to those in the Coroner's Inquest]

August Court 1786: Payments to those who served as jurors of inquest on the body of Aaron Singleton:
Maj. Henry Darnall, John Darnall, Ignatius Davis, Joseph Smith, John Buckey, Balser Craymer, George Craymer, James P. Farthing, John Richardson, Henry Brandenbergh, Thomas Dawson, Francis Gilbert, and Adam Craymer. [compare list of jurors to those in the Coroner's Inquest]

August Court 1786: Payments to those who served as jurors of inquest on the body of Susanna Wilson:
Jacob Young (held inquest), Col. Richard Smith, Capt. Michael Bayer, George Bear, Jonathan Morris, Lilburn Williams, George Burckhartt, John Gebhart, Henry Kernhart, Isaac Mantz, George Ketzendanner, Jacob Steiner, Lawrence Hyme, Capt. Joseph Smith, Jacob Shisler, Christian Crise, Jacob Baltzell, Samuel Miller, Daniel Lear, George Kramer, Michael Karsner, Jacob Torff, and Frederick Reel. [compare list of jurors to those in the Coroner's Inquest]

Justices' Attendance in County Court:
Upton Sheredine, Esq.: Nov 1786, Mar 1787, Aug 1787
William Beatty, Esq.: Nov 1786, Mar 1787, Aug 1787
Jacob Young, Esq.: Nov 1786, Mar 1787, Aug 1787
James Johnson, Esq.: Nov 1786, Mar 1787, Aug 1787
William M. Beall, Esq.: Nov 1786, Mar 1787, Aug 1787
William Luckett, Esq.: Nov 1786, Mar 1787, Aug 1787
John Ross Key, Esq.: Nov 1786, Mar 1787, Aug 1787
George Scott, Esq.: Nov 1786, Mar 1787, Aug 1787
William Magruder, Esq.: Mar 1787, Aug 1787
Charles Warfield, Esq.: Nov 1786, Mar 1787, Aug 1787
Henry Darnall, Esq.: Nov 1786, Mar 1787, Aug 1787
George Murdock, Esq.: Nov 1786, Mar 1787, Aug 1787
John Gwinn, Esq.: Nov 1786, Mar 1787, Aug 1787

Judges' Attendance in Orphans Court: [probably November Court 1786]
Upton Sheredine, Esq., 3 days
William Beatty, Esq., 5 days
William M. Beall, Esq., 5 days
George Scott, Esq., 6 days

September 12, 1786: The tax collector was authorized to collect, from those who owned property in Frederick County, two shillings and six pence for each hundred pounds of property owned. Signed: Upton Sheredine, Wm. Beatty, Jacob Young, W. M. Beale, George Scott, Chas. Warfield, and Geo. Murdock.

September 1786 ? "By Balance due from Dr. Fisher late Sheriff as pd. account: recorded." [not clear if Fisher was the sheriff, or if Fisher paid the sheriff]

November Court 1786
Grand Jurors: Joshua Gist, Nicholas Tice, Thomas Sprigg, Henry Wood, Henry Warfield, Philip Smith, William Albaugh, William Thomas of Hugh, Charles Gartrill, Benjamin Musgrove, Benjamin Biggs, John Campbell, Thomas Darnall, Charles Beall, Edward Dyer, Michael Boyer, and Richard Smith.

Petit Jurors: Leonard Smith, Abraham Lemaster, Ignatius Davis, John Jacobs, Joseph Smith, Nicholas Hall, Christopher Burckhartt, William Purdy, Nathan Maynard, Guy Elder, Arnold Elder, William Elder, Nicholas Dawson, Daniel Hook, Conrad Duttero, Thomas Patterson, William Shields, Thomas Fleming, Robert Fleming, Philip Nollert, Michael Troutman, Elijah Beatty, Jacob Steiner,

Junr., Francis Thomas, George Bare, John Ramsburgh, Roger Brooke, Joseph Taney, Frederick Dern, John Keeny and John Laney.

March Court 1787
Grand Jurors: Basil Beall, Henry Koontz, William Crum, George Bare, Thomas Sprigg, Michael McGuire, Michael Null, Abraham Poorman, Charles Angell, William Albaugh, Ignatius David, Henry Maynard, Amos Davis, Henry Wood, Abraham Crapster, William Shields, Robert Fleming and John Shellman.

Petit Jurors:
James Beatty, Richard Simpson, Thomas Fleming, William Beckwith Head, John Crapster, John Ramsbergh, Philip Nollert, Philip Rodenpeeler, James Stevenson, William Brown, Nathan Maynard, Samuel Linton, Nicholas Tice, Samuel S. Thomas, Jacob Bayer, Junr., Michael Bayer, Adam Good, Benjamin Biggs, Christopher Burckhartt, John Rogers, Joseph Smith, John Jacobs, John Cumpton, Abraham Lemaster, Edward Boteler, Elie Dorsey of Elie, Henry Coleman, William Duvall, Nicholas Dawson and Adam Creager.

August Court 1787:
Grand Jurors: John McPherson, Henry Koontz, George Bare, Samuel Linton, William Albaugh, Thomas Harris, Philip McElfresh, John Crabbs, Daniel Boyle, John McKillup, Benjamin Biggs, George Noble Wheeler, John Stoner, William Dern, Samuel Cock, William Purdy, and Ralph Hilleary.

Petit Jurors: Richard Shekell, Ignatius Davis, Thomas Fleming, Philip Rodenpeeler, Thomas Burgee, William Brashears, Jeremiah Steuart, Hugh Flannigan, Peter Shover, Robert Fleming, Luke Mudd, Samuel S. Thomas, Nathan Maynard, Nicholas Dawson, William Beckwith Head, Peter Troutman, Joseph Taney, Thomas Dawson, Abraham Lemaster, Joseph Hughes, Junr., John Smith, Charles Beall, John Compton, Jacob Steiner, Junr., Jacob Gumbare, Francis Thomas, John Neill, John Beatty, John Ramsbergh, Lilburn Williams, Michael Boyer, Samuel Cock, Peter Engle, John Jacobs, James Shields, James Wells, Joseph Smith, and Benjamin Ogle.

August Court 1787: Payment to those who served as jurors of inquest on the body of Negro Jacob:
Garah Harding, Nicholas Dawson, John Jacobs, William Jacobs, John Johnson, Joseph Jacobs, William Marhsall, Jacob Boyer, Junr., Edward Bennit, Richard Freeman, William War, Levi Hughes and possibly John Duncan. Duncan's name was squeezed in between this case and the next case of Negro Mary. Duncan served as the constable of the inquest for whichever case he served. [compare list

of jurors to those in the Coroner's Inquest]

August Court 1787: Payment to those who served as jurors of inquest on the body of Negro Mary:
Jeremiah Covill, Jacob Lease, John Ward, Jonathan Covill, William Stevens, William Wood, William Cox, John Kirby, William James, Edward Barnes, Meshech Barnes, Christian Moseter, John Barnes, Plumer Ijams and possibly John Duncan. Duncan's name was squeezed in between this case and the previous case of Negro Jacob. Duncan served as the constable of the inquest for whichever case he served. [compare list of jurors to those in the Coroner's Inquest]

August Court 1787: Payment to those who served as jurors of inquest on the body of Mary Able:
Jacob Young, Esq., William Thomas, Benjamin Ogle, Abraham Faw, George Burckhartt, Nicholas Tice, John Adlum, John Beatty, Nicholas White, John Jacob Schley, John McPherson, John Gamber, Junr., Thomas Price, Jonathan Morris, Michael Raymer, and Jacob Boyer, Jun. [compare list of jurors to those in the Coroner's Inquest]

August Court 1787: Payment to those who served as jurors of inquest on the body of Cath. Harbaugh:
Jacob Herbaugh, Senr., John Weller, Jacob Weller, John Kemp, Lawrence Creager, John Wilyard, Philip Wilyard, Peter Wilyard, Daniel Smith, Martin Miksell, Ludwick Herbaugh, and Christian Smith. [compare list of jurors to those in the Coroner's Inquest]

August Court 1787: Payment to those who served as jurors of inquest on the body of Lawr. Lehay:
Maj. Abraham Haff, John Mills, Senr., William Lease, Casper Keller, Robert Haff, Conrad Pool, Charles King, James Hooper, Adam Snook, Nathaniel Henry, George Hyler, Samuel Stallions, John Miller, and George Adams. [compare list of jurors and name of deceased to that in the Coroner's Inquest]

August Court 1787: Payment to those who served as jurors of inquest on the body of an infant:
Richard Smith, Thomas Darnall, William Thomas, Thomas Sprigg, Mark Brayfield, Thomas Grover, Balser Cramer, Peter Kemp, Joseph Lock, Joseph Beall, William Tannehill, John Dawson, William Dawson, and Thomas Mitchell. [compare list of jurors to those in the Coroner's Inquest]

August Court 1787: Payment to those who served as jurors of inquest on the body of Ann Nell:
Joseph McCaleb, John Crouse, Jacob Rudecill, Jonathan Cochran, William Cary, Jacob Myer, Valentine Null, Elie Bentley, George Kelley, George Trucks, Adam Good, John Trucks, John Slick, Jacob Little, John McCaleb, John Hughes, Joseph Little, and Nicholas Fringer. [compare list of jurors to those in the Coroner's Inquest]

More March Court 1787 Payments:
* James Wells, Abraham Lane, and John Gwinn of Westminster, witnesses for the State vs. David Fisher. [just Gwinn noted as being from Westminster]
* Henry Warfield a witness for the State vs. Henry Landis.
* William Murphy and William Cawell a witness for the State vs. Benj. Kick.
* Sarah Scaggs a witness for the State vs. Mary Welsh.

More August Court 1787 Payments
* Jacob Snider, Adam Fink, Sarah Vanhorn, Barbara Store, Elizabeth Titlo, George Store, and Henry Brim witnesses for the state vs. John Able.
* Jacob Young, Esq. for attending the gaol for the release of insolvent debtors.
* Richard Potts, Esq. for fees paid.
* Henry Brim for services as constable.
* John Buckias for services as constable.
* John Gwinn, Esq. for services as coroner.
* William Beatty, Esq. for services as coroner.
* George Scott, Esq. for attending the gaol for the release of insolvent debtors.
* Mary Hedges for finding necessaries and burying Wm. Ayres, a poor man.
* George Adams for maintaining John Franklin, an orphan child.
* Wm. M. Beall, Esq. for attending the releasement of prisoners.
* Wm. Ritchie for fees.
* Jacob Young, Esq. for examining the weights.
* Richard Smith, late inspector at the Frederick warehouse. [apparently paid for performing inspections]
* William Thomas for balance of his account as inspector at the Frederick warehouse.
* George Murdock paid.
* Daniel Smith for attending the Barr of Court.
* John Shellman for keeping public standard court.
* Henry McClarey paid.
* Abner Ritchie paid.
* William James Turner for attending Negro quarters.
* William Thomas of William for attending Negro quarters.

* Mathias Smith for 6 young wolves' heads.
* Mathias Young for 1 old wolf's head.
* Martin Miksell for 9 young wolves' heads.
* Thomas Beatty, Sheriff, paid.

Justices' Allowances:
U. Sheredine, Esq.: Nov 1787, Mar 1788, Aug 1788
W. Beatty, Esq.: Nov 1787, Mar 1788, Aug 1788
J. Young, Esq.: Nov 1787, Mar 1788, Aug 1788
J. Johnson, Esq.: Mar 1788, Aug 1788
W. M. Beall, Esq.: Nov 1787, Mar 1788, Aug 1788
Wm. Luckitt, Esq.: Nov 1787, Mar 1788, Aug 1788
Jno. R. Key, Esq.: Nov 1787, Mar 1788, Aug 1788
Geo. Scott, Esq.: Nov 1787, Mar 1788, Aug 1788
Wm. Magruder, Esq.: Nov 1787, Mar 1788, Aug 1788
C. Warfield, Esq.: Nov 1787, Mar 1788, Aug 1788
H. Darnall, Esq.: Nov 1787, Mar 1788, Aug 1788
G. Murdock, Esq.: Nov 1787, Mar 1788, Aug 1788
Jno. Gwinn, Esq.: Nov 1787, Mar 1788, Aug 1788

Judges' Orphans Court Allowances: [probably November Court 1787]
Upton Sheredine, Esq., 5 days
Wm. Beatty, Esq., 8 days
Wm. M. Beall, Esq., 6 days
Geo. Scott, Esq., 8 days
Henry Darnall, Esq., 3 days

Probably November Court 1787: Col. Chas. Warfield paid 2 days worth of allowance which was previously omitted by the court.

October 8, 1787: Thomas Beatty, Esq., present sheriff, sent a copy of a document to the Governor and Council.

September 21, 1787: The tax collector was authorized to collect from "the inhabitants of, or property within" five shillings per hundred pounds of property owned in Frederick County. Signed: Upton Sheredine, Wm. Beatty, W. M. Beall, Chas. Warfield, and Geo. Murdock.

November Court 1787
Grand Jurors: Nicholas Tice the foreman, William Thomas of Hugh, Thomas Fleming, Frederick Holtzman, William Emmit, Henry Williams, Robert Fleming,

118

John Ferguson, Isaac Wilson, Jacob Bayer, Junr., Charles Gartrill, Benjamin Ogle, John Campbell, Edward Dyer, George Noble Wheeler, John Jacob Schley and Henry Wood.

Petit Jurors: George Bair, Robert Dean, Mathias Shreup, John Crapster, Edward Butler, Abraham Lemaster, John Compton, Leonard Smith, William Brown, Christian Smith, Thomas Barr, Nicholas Hall, Charles Beall, John Ramsbergh, Leonard Lontz, "Nathaniel Henry assigned Wm. Dern", Mathias Bartgis, Samuel S. Thomas, Charles Balsell, John Norris, Solomon Bentley, William Duvall, Thomas Burgee, William Dern, John Jacobs, Thomas Sprigg, Thomas Dawson, Nicholas Dawson, Jacob Gombare, Daniel Hook and Christopher Burckhartt.

### March Court 1788
Grand Jurors: Basil Beall, James Ogle, Michael McGuire, Junr., George Bair, Nicholas Dawson, William Tabler, Guy Elder, Robert Fleming, John Hays, Thomas Sprigg, Thomas Patterson, Benjamin Musgrove, Charles Balsell, Nicholas Tice, John Campbell, William Thomas of Hugh, and Joseph Hughes.

Petit Jurors: John Ramsbergh, Michael Boyer, Philip Smith, Daniel Boyle, Jacob Koontz, Samuel S. Thomas, Richard Coale, John Devilbiss, Adam Creager, Andrew Adams, Samuel Cock, Nathan Maynard, Edward Boteler, Michael Null, Jon McKaleb, Henry Brown, George Noble Wheeler, Thomas Fleming, John Compton, Joseph Smith, Henry Kemp, Benjamin Duvall, Henry Wood, Barny McSherry, John Crapster, Elisha Beall, William Duvall, Abraham Haff, Jacob Crist, Thomas Burgee, Daniel Hook, James S. Hook, Richard Shekell, and Daniel Smith.

### August Court 1788
Grand Jurors: Nicholas Tice, Henry Maynard, Daniel Dorsey, Abraham Crabster, Robert Fleming, William Shields, John Chisholm, Higginson Belt, Tobias Rudecill, Michael Null, Michael McGuire, Junr., William Albaugh, William Dern, Bernard Linganfelter, Raphael Brooke, John Witherow, John Shellman, and Thomas Darnall.

Petit Jurors: Ralph Hilleary, William Purdy, Evan Dorsey, Samuel Linton, Nicholas Dawson, Henry Kemp, Leonard Smith, Thomas Fleming, John Smith, George Bare, Andrew Hawne, Andrew Adams, Richard Shekell, James Hughes, Henry Leatherman, Benjamin Musgrove, Jacob Gumbare, Michael Late, Samuel Cock, Richard Jenings, Benjamin Price, George Schley, Amos Davis, William Duvall, Thomas Conner, Conrad Duttero, Hugh Flanigan, John Compton, Daniel Hook, Robert Dean, John Ramsbergh, Samuel S. Thomas, Isaac Mantz,

John Beatty, Daniel Smith, and Ely Dorsey.

Court Payments 1788: [apparently March and/or August]
* John McPherson for account filed.
* George Murdock for account filed.
* Henry McCleary for a coffin.
* Yate Plummer for 1 old wolf's head.
* Ralph Hilleary for 1 young wolf's head.
* Elisha Griffith for 1 young wolf's head.
* Philip Horton for 4 young wolves' heads.
* Peter Smith for 7 young wolves' heads.
* Mary Turner for her support.
* William Waugh for expenses incurred in burying Joseph Grayham, a poor person.
* Lenox Martin, Esq. crossed out.
* Michael Howard for nursing and attending Elizabeth Steel and child, and "funeral expenses of the former court."
* Leonard Smith, Coroner for holding an inquest on the body of an infant, on the body of Abraham Harvey a servant, and on the body of Philip Shaaf.

1788: Payments to those who served as jurors of inquest on the body of a child: Benedict James, Elias Williard, Peter Gaver, George Pom, Adam Knouff, Jacob Dunkel, George Cost, Philip Fink, Valentine Mesker, Jacob Shane, Aaron Fardin, and John Shilling. [compare list of jurors to those in the Coroner's Inquest]

1788: Payments to those who served as jurors of inquest on the body of Philip Shaaf: Hermanus Conrad, Peter Covrich, Conrad Yesterday, William B. Lamar, Daniel Weaver, John Long, George Blessing, John Blessing, Frederick Kershner, Ludwick Yesterday, and Francis Yesterday. [compare list of jurors to those in the Coroner's Inquest]

1788: Payments to those who served as jurors of inquest on the body of Abraham Harvey: Jeremiah Belt, Joseph West, John Hillery, Benedict Johnson, Benjamin Smith, Isaac Williams, David Snow, Conrad Ricker, Frederick Heater, Elimeleck Gast, Henry Fallen, and Patrick Goreman. [compare list of jurors to those in the Coroner's Inquest]

More Court Payments 1788: [apparently March and/or August]
* Stephen Winchester and Thomas Roberts, witnesses for the State vs. Mary
    Kitten. Case discharged.
* Henry Brim a witness for the State vs. Geo. Miller. No outcome stated.
* Aaron James a witness for the State vs. Jos. Day. No outcome stated.
* John Knox, Jane Knox, Frederick Chriesman, and John Roberts, witnesses for
    the State vs. Thos. Wilkason. No outcome stated.
* Thomas Stanley a witness for the State vs. Michl. Kile. "Left off."
* John Buckias, Constable.
* Henry Brim, Constable.
* Eleanor Williams for nursing a poor child.
* Henry Zealor paid.
* John Shellman as Standard Keeper.
* Lenox Martin, Esq. for acting as prosecutor.
* Martin Waltz paid.
* Wm. M. Beall, Esq. for attending the gaol.
* Jacob Young, Esq. for attending at the elections and at the gaol.
* Margaret, Ex. [apparently Margaret Fisher] of Adam Fisher.
* Richard Potts, Esq. for acting as prosecutor.
* Abner Ritchie paid.
* William Ritchie paid.
* Henry Cronise, Constable.
* William Beatty, Esq. for acting as Coroner.
* Col. Joseph Wood for keeping the old bridge over Pipe Creek in repair.
* John Alsop paid.
* George Murdock, Esq. for office rent.
* William Thomas of Hugh, Inspector.
* For the bridge at Geo. Snider's.
* Abner Ritchie, paid.
* Thos. Beatty, Sheriff and Collector.

1788: Payments to those who served as jurors of inquest on the body of Joseph
Graham:
Jacob Young, Esq., John Beatty, Jonathan Morris, William Thomas of Hugh,
William Ritchie, Benjamin Ogle, Jacob Rhore, Jacob Shisler, Philip Rhore, John
D. Cary, Henry Garnhart, David Mooris, James Clark (town), and Abner Ritchie.
[compare list of jurors to those in the Coroner's Inquest]

1788: Payments to those who served as jurors of inquest on the body of Negro
Clarissa:
Jacob Young, Esq., Edward Anderson, Henry Brother, Henry Garnhart,

George Schley, William Cook, Jacob Steiner, Christian Becker, Michael Balsell, John Buckias, Samuel Stallings, and George Bare. [compare list of jurors to those in the Coroner's Inquest]

1788: Payments to those who served as jurors of inquest on the body of Edward Bear:
Henry Darnall, Esq., Wm. M. Hall, Balser Cramer, George Cramer, John Richardson, John Bucky, George Bucky, John Brayfield, Edward Crabb, Walter Hagan, Edward Rose, Rudolph Everhart, Christopher Brim, John McClain, Charles Pebel, Charles Kregg, John Meder, John Ragon, John Davis, Charles P. Taylor, Thomas Mount, Christopher Tripell, Henry Alleidt, Joseph Waggoner, and Anthony Frietz. [compare list of jurors to those in the Coroner's Inquest]

Justice's Allowance:
Upton Sheredine, Esq.: Nov 1788, Mar 1789, Aug 1789
William Beatty, Esq.: Nov 1788, Mar 1789, Aug 1789
Jacob Young, Esq.: Nov 1788, Mar 1789, Aug 1789
James Johnson, Esq.: Nov 1788, Mar 1789, Aug 1789
Wm. M. Beall, Esq.: Nov 1788, Mar 1789, Aug 1789
William Luckett, Esq.: Nov 1788, Mar 1789, Aug 1789
John R. Key, Esq.: Nov 1788, Mar 1789, Aug 1789
Fielder Gaunt, Esq.: Nov 1788
George Scott, Esq.: Nov 1788, Mar 1789, Aug 1789
William Magruder, Esq.: Nov 1788, Mar 1789, Aug 1789
Charles Warfield, Esq.: Mar 1789, Aug 1789
Henry Darnall, Esq.: Nov 1788, Mar 1789, Aug 1789
George Murdock, Esq.: Nov 1788, Mar 1789, Aug 1789
John Gwinn, Esq.: Nov 1788, Mar 1789, Aug 1789

Judges of Orphan Court Allowance: (probably November 1788)
Upton Sheredine, Esq. 4 days
William Beatty, Esq. 7 days
Wm. M. Beall, Esq. 5 days
George Scott, Esq. 6 days
Henry Darnall, Esq. 6 days

September 18, 1788: The tax collector was authorized to collect from "the inhabitants of, or property within" two shillings and nine pence per hundred pounds of property owned in Frederick County. Signed: Upton Sheredine, Wm. Beatty, Jacob Young, W. M. Beall, George Scott, and Geo. Murdock.

November Court 1788:
Grand Jurors: Basil Beall, James Ogle, James Samuel Hook, John Hammond, John Maynard, George Noble Wheeler, Michael Boyer, George Bare, William Brown, Amos Smith, William Biggs, John Shelman, Nicholas Tice, William Thomas of Hugh, Benjamin Price, John Thomas of Francis, Henry Koontz, Senr., and Philip Smith.

Petit Jurors: Nathan Harris, Joseph Wood (Linganore), Henry Poole, Edward Anderson, Christopher Burckhartt, Robert Fleming, Luke Mudd, Samuel S. Thomas, Hugh Flanigan, Benjamin Ogle, Andrew Adams, Michael Late, James Phillips, William Purdy, Thomas Conner, Ralph Hilleary, Nicholas Hall, John Ramsbergh, Jacob Steiner, Junr., Basil Simpson, Charles Balsell, William Albaugh, John Mefford, John Jacobs, Levi Hughes, James Wood, Zephaniah Harding, Edward Boteler, Samuel Blair, and George Schnertzel.

Court Payments November 1788:
* Michael Noland and John Bagent, witnesses for the State vs. Thos. Murphy. Sentenced to labor.
* John Zimmerman and Peter Bell, witnesses for the State vs. Michael Weaver. Discharged by court.
* Thomas Fleming, William Beckwith Head, James Stevenson, William Brown, and Adam Good, petit jurors for March Court 1787, 1 day of payment omitted.
* John Whiteneck a witness for the State vs. Henry Cook. Outcome: "No prest. found."

March Court 1789
Grand Jurors: John Chisholm, Philip Smith, William Albaugh, Nicholas Tice, John Shelman, Conrad Doll, Henry Coon, Charles Shell, Nicholas Sinn, Michael McGuire, Frederick Holtzman, Thomas Fleming, Michael Boyer, Matthias Shreup, Samuel Phillips, Joshua Gist, Abraham Crabster, and Henry Maynard.

Petit Jurors: Conrad Duttero, Benjamin Musgrove, Azel Waters, Charles Balsell, Ludwick Wampler, Andrew Hawn, Andrew Shriver, John Ferguson, Peter Morser, William Duvall, Isaac Wilson, Christopher Burckhartt, Michael Troutman, Philip Rodenpeeler, James Phillips, Daniel Hook, Amos Davis, Elisha Beall, Samuel S. Thomas, Jacob Steiner, Junr., Nicholas Dawson, Joseph Smith, Henry Koontz, John Eckiss, William Beckwith Head, William Shields, Robert Fleming, Charles Robinson, William Brown, and George Smith.

March Court 1789 Payments:
* Samuel Smedley a witness for the State vs. James Clifton Coleman. Discharged by court.
* Matthias Young and Daniel Eichenbroad, witnesses for the State vs. John Mitchell. Case not taken.
* Amos Smith a witness for the State vs. Geo. Adams. Discharged.

August Court 1789
Grand Jurors: Basil Beall, Frederick Heisly, Henry McClary, Andrew Low, Ignatius Davis, Adam Cregar, Jeremiah Browning, Stephen Winchester, David Fisher, Henry Gollman, Michael Null, William Shields, James Moorison, Conrad Duttero, Adam Markley, Frederick Holtzman, William Murdock Hall, and Elisha Beall.

Petit Jurors: Abraham Lemaster, Peter Troutman, Jacob Miller, Senr., John McKaleb, James Pevry, George Ovelman, Henry Brawner, William Rupert, James Stevenson, John Mefford, John Bouden, Valentine Null, William Dern, Charles Schell, Thomas Fleming, John Gombare, Isaac Mantz, Jacob Gombare, Nicholas Dawson, John Jacobs, Philip Smith, William Duvall, Baltser Kramer, James Murphy, John Yengland, Jacob Woolf, Peter Beam, George Bare, Senior, John Ramsbergh, Benjamin Beckwith, Joseph Smith, and Jacob Crist.

August Court 1789 Payments:
* Mathias Young, Daniel Eighenbroad and Jacob Weller of Jno., witnesses for the State vs. John Mitchel. "Stet. by ord. Ct."
* Jacob Weller of John, a witness for the State vs. Jno. Mitchell, from November 1788.
* Yate Plummer for 2 old wolves' heads.
* William Albaugh for 1 old wolf's head.
* Jacob Weller of Jno. for 6 young wolves' heads.
* James Smith for account filed.
* Henry Cronise for suppressing Negroes and attending the Barr as Constable.
* Joseph Sim for timber.
* John Whiteneck for accounts filed.
* Crossed out Gilbert Falconer, written in Archd. Campbell, Constable for accounts filed.
* John Buckias, Constable.
* Henry McClary for account filed.
* Andrew McManos for account filed.
* Crossed out "Building a bridge over Bennet's Creek at John Bealls plantation."
* George Scott for account filed.

124

* Michael Houser for account filed.
* Mrs. Harrison for account filed.
* George Murdock for account filed.
* Abner Ritchie, Cryer.
* Margaret Fischer, Ex. of Adam Fischer.
* William Ritchie, Clerk.
* Matthias Bartgis, Printer.
* Martin Waltz for account filed.
* Jacob Young for account filed.
* William M. Beall for account filed.
* Jacob Young for account filed.
* William Owings, Prosecutor.
* Peter Mantz, Esq., Sheriff.
* Lenox Martin, Prosecutor.
* Thomas Beatty late sheriff.
* Thomas Taylor, Junr. for account filed.
* William Ritchie for cash paid to the printer.

Judges of the Orphan's Court August 1789
Upton Sherdine, Esq. 3 days
Wm. Beatty, Esq. 4 days
Wm. M. Beall, Esq. 6 days
George Scott, Esq. 4 days
Henry Darnall, Esq. 5 days

August Court 1789: Payments to jurors of inquest on the body of John Stull:
William Beatty, Coroner, held the inquest, Joseph Hobbs, Robert Gassaway,
Azel Waters, Andrew Adams, Joseph Ogle, Henry Wickham, Joseph Brown,
John Cammel, Samuel Baker, John Crise, John Hummer, and Charles Dorsey.
[compare list of jurors to those in the Coroner's Inquest]

August Court 1789: Payments to jurors of inquest on the body of Barba Red:
Leonard Smith, Coroner, held inquest, Joseph West, Thos. H. West, Benjamin
West, George Vickroy, George Poor, Michael Riddlemoser, John Niswanger,
Conrad Richer, Conrad Harmon, Frederick Uhl, Samson Smith, and John Croft.
[compare list of jurors to those in the Coroner's Inquest]

August Court 1789: Payments to jurors of inquest on the body of John
Zimmerman:
William Beatty, Coroner, held inquest, Ludwick Kemp, Alexander Wilson,
Michael Trisler, George Toup, George Zimmerman, Godfrey Leatherman

crossed out, Godfrey Prier written in, Michael Schatz, Stephen Bruner, Philip Shatz, David Shatz, Jacob Kideshoe, and John Baysole. [compare list of jurors to those in the Coroner's Inquest]

August Court 1789: Payments to jurors of inquest on the body of John Ryan: John Gwinn held inquest, Ralph Crabb, Frederick Yingling, Samuel Pevry, Joseph Little, Lawrence Erbaugh, Bernard McSherry, Henry Oharra, Jacob Shearman, Jonathan Hawn, Wendle Erbaugh, Felix Frogenfelter, George Trucks, Christopher Erb, Michael McGuire, Peter Baum, John Baker, Philip Slossmith, and Jacob Yingling. [compare list of jurors to those in the Coroner's Inquest]

August 1789 Petit Jurors summoned at adjourned court:
Henry McClary, Benjamin Ogle, Charles Gartrell, Nicholas Tice, Jacob Steiner, Junr., Peter Kephart, John Shellman, Andrew Lowe, John Neill, and Jacob Schnider.

September 15, 1789: The tax collector was authorized to collect from "the inhabitants of, or property within" three shillings and four pence per hundred pounds of property owned in Frederick County. Signed: Wm. Beatty, Jacob Young, W. M. Beall, George Scott, and Geo. Murdock.

November Court 1789
Grand Jurors: John Chisholm, William Albaugh, Azel Waters, Andrew Low, Thomas Conner, John Neill, William Thomas of Hugh, John Jacob Schley, Michael Boyer, Thomas Fleming, William Shields, Henry Williams, Jacob Ridgely, Ephraim Howard, Henry Wood, Conrad Doll and Stephen Shelmordine.

Petit Jurors: Basil Beall, Nicholas Tice, Henry McCleary, Frederick Heisly, John Ramsbergh, George Bare, Jeremiah Browning, Philip Smith, Stephen Winchester, John Richardson (Taney Town?), William Murdock Hall, Jacob Steiner, Junr., Frederick Holtzman, Joseph Wilson, Michael Row, Robert Fleming, Elisha Beall, Joseph McKaleb, William Duvall, Roger Brooke, Adam Markley, Junr., Conrad Dutterow, William Biggs, Senr., John Harmon Yost, Ralph Hilleary, Frederick Sholl, and Joseph Smith.

November Court 1789 Payments:
* Joseph Sagar, Samuel Price, Henry Isenagel, and Judy Gay, witnesses for the State vs. John Cain. Discharged by court.
* John Riggs and Samuel Lilly, witnesses for the State vs. Hildebrand. Outcome: Discharged.
* William Croney a witness for the State vs. Welsh. No case outcome stated.

March Court 1790

Grand Jurors: Col. Thomas Price, John Trux, Thomas Darnall, William Murdock Hall, John Compton, Henry McCleary, Michael Boyer, Ephraim Ridge, Michael Row, William Rupert, Adam Cregar, Charles Gartrill, Basil Wood, Henry Landis, Henry Warfield, Benjamin Musgrove, and William Lamar.

Petit Jurors: Joshua Howard, Richard Simpson, Junr., Solomon Bentley, Peter Beam, Andrew Hawn, Caleb Griffith, Nicholas Hall, Ralph Hilleary, Joseph Smith, Gariah Harding, Isaac Mantz, Jacob Steiner, Junr., Jeremiah Belt, John Crabster, Jeremiah Browning, Daniel Smith, Peter Shover, John Hilleary, Edward Anderson, William Crum of Abram., Hugh Reynolds, Anthony Livers, Stephen Shelmordine, William Beckwith Head, John Richardson of Pipe Creek, Elisha Beall, Frederick Heisly and Joseph Wilson.

March Court 1790 Payments:
* Philip Naile and Thomas Wilt witnesses for the State vs. Michl. Quinner. No outcome stated.
* Frederick Naile, John Stonecipher, and Michael Angel witnesses for the State vs. John Quinner. Outcome: Discharged.
* Thomas Hobbs, Basil Dorsey, and William Dorsey, witnesses for the State vs. William Morgan. Outcome: Discharged.
* Thomas Cheneworth, Elizabeth Cheneworth and Rebecca Cheneworth, witnesses for the State vs. M. Miler. Outcome: "Conv.'d to Wheelbarrow".

August Court 1790

Grand Jurors: John McPherson, John Adlum, Francis Mantz, Abraham Crabster, Charles Baltzell, William Lamar, Thomas Sprigg, Michael Null, Andrew Low, Michael Boyer, Thomas Samuel Pole, William Shields, Philip Smith, James Wells, John Crabster, and George Bare, Senr.

Petit Jurors: James Beatty, Ignatius Davis, Henry Wood, Azel Waters, George Obleman, Elie Bentley, John Neill, Joab Waters, William Duvall, William Murdock Hall, John Johnson, John Jacobs, John Grahame, Benedict Jamestone, William Beckwith Head, Samuel Skinner Thomas, John Bouden, Henry Coon, George Bare, Junr., Benjamin Ogle, David Mantz, Peter Shover, Nicholas Tice, William Dern, Peter Barrick, John Ramsbergh, Henry Matthews, Jacob Steiner, Junr., and John McGill.

August Court 1790 Payments:
* Henry Feaster and John Alexander, witnesses for the State vs.

Jacob Stottlemier. Aquitted.
* Frederick Naile a witness for the State vs. Jno. Quinner. Outcome: "Stk. off."

August 1790: Payments to jurors of inquest on the body of John Rodam Thomas Richards:
Leonard Smith, Coroner, held inquest, Benedict Jameson, George Shover, crossed out John Jacobs, written in Jacob Jacobs, William Atthomas, Peter Sickenfoose, John Calbfleish, Joseph Cullen, Jacob Tabeler, Jacob Krabs, William Oldham, Samuel Douglas, and John Niswanger.

August 1790: Payments to jurors of inquest on the body of Richard Cornoford:
Leonard Smith, Coroner, held inquest, Christian Yesterday, James Hook, Thomas H. West, Benjamin West, Elias Delashmutt, William Tabler, Henry Hershberger, Philip Nicolus, Dennis McGoine, John Caines, Christian Ovrey, and Ignatius Yates.

August 1790: Payments to jurors of inquest on the body of Negro Grace, property of Basil Dorsey:
Ephraim Howard, Coroner, held inquest, William Dorsey, David McKaleb, John Waggoner, George Ovelman, James Steel, Joseph Miller, Richard Coale, John Gun, Joseph James, John McKaleb, Henry Hoofman, John Dagen, and Brice Pool.

August 1790: Payments to jurors of inquest on the body of Joseph White:
William Beatty, Coroner, held inquest, Roland Dean, Michael Boyer, John Ritchie, Jacob Houseman, Frederick Holtzman, Jacob Holtzman, Thomas Knox, Michael Hawn, George Beckinbaugh, Leonard Geyer, Jacob Troxall, and Michael Moser.

August Court 1790: Paid Rinehart Motter for his assistance until August Court next.

August Court 1790: Payments to jurors of inquest on the body of a stranger:
Henry Darnall held inquest, Ignatius Davis, Joseph Hill, Junr., Robert Briscoe, Balser Cramer, George Cramer, Thomas Stanley, Ralph Hilleary, Leonard Jamison, John Christian Messing, Simon Cristburgh, William Murdock Hall, and John Bucky.


August Court 1790 Payments:
* James Beatty, Constable.

128

* John Shellman for keeping standard.
* John Whiteneck, Constable.
* William Luckett paid.
* Col. William Beatty paid.
* Philip Nail paid.
* Martin Fletcher, Paul Rinacre, Daniel Aradd ?, George Hawne, and Michael Kibler witnesses for the State vs. Thos. Webster. Outcome: Aquitted. March Court 1786?
* Henry McCleery for work at the gaol.
* Henry Zealer for smith's work at the gaol.
* Samuel Price a witness for the State vs. John Cain. Outcome: Discharged.
* Mathias Bartgis paid.
* Jacob Walter paid.
* Abner Ritchie, Cryer, paid.
* William Ritchie, Clerk, paid.
* Philip Smith of Wm. paid.
* William Davis paid.
* John Buckias paid.
* Peter Mantz, Esq., Sheriff.
* Henry Shell, Constable.
* Thomas Bradly paid.
* Barbara Davy paid for her support. Had a note from Upton Sheredine.
* James McGrath a witness for the State vs. Nicho. Welsh.
* William M. Beall, Esq. paid.
* Jacob Young, Esq. paid.
* Henry McCleary for sundry necessary repairs to courthouse.
* John Devilbiss for account filed.
* George Scott, Esq. for account filed.
* Gilbert Falconer, Constable.
* Geo. Murdock, Esq. paid.
* Joseph Wood for repairs to the bridge he built over Pipe Creek.
* Geo. Murdock, Esq. for one days work and also for the bridge over Bennet's Creek.
* George Scott, Esq. for the bridge over Bennet's Creek.

Judges of Orphan Court:
Upton Sheredine, Esq. 3 days
William Beatty, Esq. 6 days
Wm. M. Beall, Esq. 6 days
George Scott, Esq. 2 days
Henry Darnall, Esq. 4 days

August 31, 1790: The tax collector was authorized to collect from "the inhabitants of, or property within" three shillings and six pence per hundred pounds of property owned in Frederick County. Signed: Upton Sheredine, Wm. Beatty, Jacob Young, W. M. Beall, and Geo. Murdock.

September 1, 1790: A copy of the above tax decree was made and delivered to Mr. John Ritchie, Collector.

November Court 1790
Grand Jurors: Joseph West, Joseph McKaleb, George Creager, John Philips, William Biggs, Samuel Philips, Frederick Heisly, John Neill, John Stoner, William Shields, Henry Williams, James Beatty, Basil Wood, Conrad Dudderar, Anthony Sim, John Devilbiss, and Lawrence Brengle.

Petit Jurors: Thomas Sprigg, Henry Nichodemus, Henry Myers, Hugh Reed, Stephen Shelmordine, David Gist, Henry Stevenson, James Poulson, Jeremiah Browning, Jacob Bayer, Junr., Frederick Sholl, Charles Schell, James Ogle, James Simmons, William Crum, Patrick McGill, Daniel Smith, John Witherow, Hugh Reynolds, Peter Shover, John Hoffman, Peter Stilly, Matthias Bucky, Elisha Beall, William Dern, John Richardson, George Bare, Junr., John Gomber, Junr., William House, Samuel S. Thomas, and Ignatius Davis.

Petit Jurors at adjourned November Court 1790:
Henry Coon, Andrew Low, Frederick Sholl, Henry Koontz, Senr., Charles Schell, Jacob Steiner, Junr., Frederick Heisly, Isaac Mantz, Jacob Bayer, Junr., John Jacob Schley, and John Neill.

November Court 1790 Payments:
* Julianna Gensler a witness for the State vs. Timothy Connelly. Outcome: "Conv.'d Wheelbarrow."
* Edward Jenkins, George Carns, William Collins, John E. Norris, and Nathan Bell, witnesses for the State vs. Robert Hammet. Outcome: Discharged.
* Jacob Luther a witness for the State vs. Susanna Warring. Outcome: "Stk. off"
* John Zimmerman and Devalt Peale witnesses for the State vs. Adam Hoover. Outcome: Acquitted.
* Philip Naile, Frederick Naile, John Stonesifor, George Bumgardner, James Giving, Peter Slider, Jacob Quinner, Daniel Quinner and Michael Angel, witnesses for the State vs. Michl. and Jno. Quinner. Outcome: Convicted.

130

## CONVICTED SLAVES

This information was written in the back of the book which contained the Levy
    List.

"Negro Slaves convicted and adjudged to serve and labor on the Public Roads in
Baltimore County. By the Justices of Frederick County Court under the Acts of
Assembly entitled "An Act for the more effectual Punishment of Criminals" ...
the different Counties are to receive monies arising by their labor. Passed
November Session 1789."

November Court 1792: Negro Rachel convicted of house burning. To serve one
year. Owner: Frederick Birely. Sold by order of Criminal Baltimore County
Court. Money received by R. Butler, Sheriff.

March Court 1793: Negro Poll convicted of poisoning Mrs. Crabbs and others.
To serve seven years. Owner: Ralph Crabbs. Time of servitude expires April 4,
1800.

November Court 1794: Negro Jack convicted of stealing a pair of pantaloons. To
serve two years. Owner: Basil Dorsey, Senr. Time of servitude expires
November 22, 1796. Certificate filed May Term 1798; Jack ran away from the
overseer of the public road and never returned.

November Court 1794: Negro Plato convicted of assault and attempted rape of
Elizabeth Hill. To serve 14 years. Owner: Ignatius Jamison. Time of servitude
expires November 29, 1808.

March Court 1795: Negro Joe convicted of assault and stabbling with the intent
to kill John James. To serve one year. Owner Basil Dorsey, Junr. Time of
servitude expires March 26, 1796. Sold by the sheriff of Baltimore County.
Money received by Abner Ritchie, Esq., Sheriff April 27, 1798.

March Court 1796: Negro Zelph, convicted of burning her master's barn. To
serve two years. Owner Revd. Thomas John Clagett. Time of servitude to expire
April 8, 1798. Certificate filed of her having died in child bed before the
expiration of her term.

March Court 1798: Negro Lydia convicted of burning her master's barn. To
serve ten years. Owner: Shadrack Hedges. Time of servitude to expire April 7,
1808.

November Court 1801: Negro David convicted of assault and attempt to ravish [rape]. To serve five years. Owner: Joseph Gwinn. Time of servitude to expire November 23, 1806.

August Court 1802: Negro Moses convicted of burglary. To serve two years. Owner: John Grahame. Time of servitude to expire August 5, 1804.

August Court 1802: Negro Will convicted of robbery. To serve three years. Owner: Hugh Reynolds. Time of servitude to expire August 6, 1805.

The following information was written in the back of the book which contained the Levy List:
Sums of money levied for building and repairing bridges:
August Court 1782: Little Pipe Creek by Geo. Boners. Israels Creek by James Beattys.
August Court 1788: Town Bridge by Geo. Snyders

Ballinger
 John 54
Ballsell
 Jacob 43
Balsell
 Charles 118, 122
 Jacob 54
 Michael 121
Balser
 John 98
Balsor
 Jno. 107
 John 97
Baltimore County 130
Baltimore County Line
 102
Baltimore Road 101
Balto. Town 105
Baltzel
 Henry 54
Baltzell
 Charles 126
 Jacob 75, 76, 78,
  82, 90, 112
 Michael 78, 91
Bankard
 Peter 104
Banker
 Jacob 48
Barber
 Jno. 6
 John 31, 54
Bare
 George 54, 90, 105,
  106, 109, 110,
  114, 118,
  121-123, 125,
  126, 129
 Jacob 17
Bargue
 John 87

Barker's 103
Barlow
 Thomas 54, 87
Barnard
 Luke 35, 89
Barnell
 Hugh 8
Barnes
 Edward 91, 115
 Jacob 48
 John 91, 115
 Meshech 115
 Richard 43, 48
Barnet
 Hugh 31
 Luke 26
Barnhart
 Benjamin 77, 79,
  89, 112
Barr
 Thomas 118
 Thos. 87
Barrick
 John 54, 74, 101,
  102
 Peter 101, 126
 William 20, 74
 Wm. 21
Barrickman
 Peter 54
Bartgis
 Mathias 109, 118,
  128
 Matthias 80, 124
Bartgiss
 Matthias 86
Barton
 Benjamin 30
 Henry 72
Basil
 Walter 54

Bassett
 Thomas 43
 Thos. 48
Bateman
 John 24, 54
Batts
 Humprey 2
Baughman
 Andrew 73
Baum
 Peter 96, 125
Baxter
 James 6
 John 40
Bayard
 Samuel 54
Bayer
 Adam 105, 106,
  109
 Capt. Michael 90,
  105, 112
 Casper 75
 Jacob 80, 81, 86,
  91, 93, 105,
  106, 109, 114,
  118, 129
 Michael 86, 109,
  114
Bayerley's Mill 103
Bayley
 Alexander 48
Baylie
 John 54
Bayly
 Mountjoy 105
Baysole
 John 96, 125
Beading
 Edward 54
Beagler
 David 43

Michael 55
Bireley
  Frederick 82
Birely
  Frederick 130
  George 86
Biser
  Daniel 55
Bishop
  Jacob 43
  John 48
Biusey
  Samuel 48
Black
  ---m 43
  Adam 87
  William 48
Blackmore
  Charles 40
Bladen
  J. 19
Blair
  Brice 49
  John 55
  Samuel 122
  William 37-39
Bland
  Elias 17
Blessing
  Geo. 96
  George 83, 119
  John 119
Blickenstaff
  Elizabeth 77
  Yost 107, 111
Bob
  John 43
Bockman
  Andrew 74
Boggass
  Samuel 97, 98

Bohman
  Andrew 73
Boltz
  Conrad 83
Bond
  George 55
Boner
  Geo. 101
  George 77, 86, 98, 107
Boners
  Geo. 131
Bonham
  Mercy 97, 98
Bonnet
  Peter 5
Bonton
  Thomas 55
Boochler
  John 74
Boogher
  John 74
Booker
  Andrew 43
  Jno. 80
  Peter 43
Boon 39
Boone
  Abraham 82
  Humphrey 15
  John 43
  Saml. 73
Bordley
  Stephen 18
Bost
  Valentine 87
Bostian
  Andrew 55
Boteler
  Alexander 55
  Edward 106, 114,

  118, 122
  Henry 98
Bouden
  John 123, 126
Bowell
  William 27, 29
Bower
  Christian 98
Bowie
  Allen 49
Bowles
  George 5
  Thomas 55
Bowlon
  John 55
  Zech. 55
Bowman
  Baltis 55
  Baltsor 55
  John 49
  Sam. 40
Bowser
  David 49
Boyd
  Abram 49
  Andreas 83
  Andrew 81
  Jno. 26
  William 43
Boydsell
  Henry 55
Boyer
  Catherine 98
  Jacob 78, 84, 114, 115
  Michael 113, 114, 118, 122, 125-127
Boyle
  Daniel 114, 118
Boys

Valentine 55, 100
Brunner
  John 27
  Peter 104
  Stephen 78
  Val. 102
  Valentine 73
Brunor
  Valentine 97
Bryan
  Phillemon 40
  Rich. 40
Bucey
  Joshua 32, 34, 35
Buchanan
  John 74
  William 49, 55
Buchannan
  Dr. John 85
Buchgar
  Jacob 74
  John 74
Buckerduke
  John 49
Buckey
  George 95
  John 90, 95, 97, 98, 112
  Matthias 84
Buckhanan
  John 17
Buckias
  John 55, 91, 111, 116, 120, 121, 123, 128
Buckie
  John 55
Bucky
  George 121
  John 98, 121, 127
  Matthias 129

Bucy
  John 26
Budge
  Creek 55
Bullen
  John 15
Bumgardner
  Everhart 44
  George 129
  John 75
  Peter 2
  Richard 44
Bundrick
  Nicholas 6, 7, 12, 16, 18, 21
  Nick. 6
Bunkle
  Yost 44
Burcham
  Elizabeth 44, 49
Burchfield
  Robert 1
Burckhart
  Christopher 99
Burckhartt
  Christopher 106, 113, 114, 118, 122
  George 98, 105, 112, 115
  Nathaniel 108
  Peter 105
Burdus
  R. 12
Burgee
  Thomas 55, 114, 118
Burges
  James 7
  William 99
Burgess

  James 30
Burghart
  Peter 55
Burket
  Nathaniel 87
Burkett
  Matheas 44
Burkhard
  Capt. Geo. 90
Burkhart
  George 92
  Henry 99
  Jehew 49
  Peter 77
Burkhartt
  George 81
Burkitt
  George 97
Burnes
  George 44
  William 44
Burnt House Woods
  Hundred 61, 81
Burnt Housewood
  Hundred 59
Burris
  Adam 41
Burrows
  James 42
Burshers
  Thomas 24
Burton
  Jacob 109
  John 106, 109
  Joshuay 82
  William 55
  Wm. 26
Bush
  Adam 112
Bush Creek Forge 54

Andrew 41
Cotterall
Andrew 5
Cottrel
John 56
Cotuldy
Coonrod 71
Cotuldyin
Coonrod 71
Covel
Jeremiah 56
Covell
Jeremiah 91
Jonathan 91
Nehemiah 56
Cover
Daniel 99
Jacob 98
Covill
Jeremiah 115
Jonathan 115
Covrich
Peter 119
Cower
Henry 5
Cowman
John 44
Cox
Christian 56
Dav. 6
David 12
Ezekle 56
John 56
Paul 27
William 91, 115
Crab
Edward 95
Crabb
Capt. Henry Wright
26
Edward 121

Henry Wright 34,
44, 49
Mrs. 49
Ralph 125
Richard 56
Crabbs
Christian 84
George 84
Henry Wright 23
John 114
Mrs. 130
Ralph 96, 130
W. 34
Crabell
David 56
Crabster
Abraham 118, 122,
126
John 126
Cramer
Adam 90
Balser 90, 95, 115,
121, 127
George 90, 95, 121,
127
Cramphin
Henry 20
John 8, 16, 20
Thomas 29
Cramptin
Ann 4
Henry 28
John 13, 28
Crampton
Thomas 111
Cramtin
J. John 16
Crane
John 102
Craps
John 88

Crapster
Abraham 99, 114
John 114, 118
Jon 85
Craptree
James 40
Crasey
Jacob 49
Crawford
David 56
John 44
Craycraft
Joseph 56
Craymer
Adam 112
Balser 112
George 112
Creable
John 79
Creagebaum
Conrad 75
Creager
Adam 56, 110, 114,
118
George 98, 129
Laurence 92
Lawrence 115
Michael 44, 101
Valentine 79, 81
Creager's 101
Creagers Town 76
Creasy
Jacob 44
Creegar
Christian 56
Mary 56
Creeger
Christian 56
Creely
Mary 75
Cregar

Adam 123, 126
Creger
  Michael 49
  Peter 56
Cresap
  Col. Thomas 3, 8
  Thomas 2,4, 8, 10,
     30-32, 35, 40
  Thos. 30
Crider
  Peter 56
Criesman
  George 57
Crigger
  Jacob 73
Crine
  Henry 103
Criner
  Henry 103
Crise
  --- 44
  Christian 112
  John 124
  Stephen 49
Crist
  Christian 90
  Jacob 103, 106,
     110, 118, 123
  Michael 88, 109,
     112
  Philip 112
Cristburgh
  Simon 127
Croft
  John 124
Croghan
  George 2, 31
Cromwell
  Joseph 80
  Richard 57
Croney

William 125
Crongelton
  Joseph 21
Cronise
  Henry 120, 123
  Jno. 80
  John 72
Cronkelton
  Bridget 72
Crook
  Jacob 57
Cross
  James 49
Crosthwarte
  John 35
Crouch
  Charles 57
  James 30
Crouise
  Henry 99
Crouse
  Frederick 49
  John 93, 116
  Michael 57
Crowell
  Henry 100
Crowley
  Devault 57
Croxall
  C. 14
Croyley
  Francis 106
Crum
  Abram 126
  Balser 93
  William 57, 109,
     114, 126, 129
Crumbecker
  Jacob 57
Crumpton
  John 42

Cruse
  Paul 57
Crusey
  Aron 49
Cryder
  John 57
Cuirtain
  John 49
Cullen
  Joseph 127
Culler
  Jacob 71, 81
Cumber
  Christian 57
Cumberlidge
  Joseph 49
Cumming
  David 89, 112
  W. 12
  William 3, 6, 8,
     10-12, 16, 22,
     23, 44, 57
  Wm. 29, 30, 31
Cummings
  William 12, 13
Cumpton
  Aquilla 8
  James 6
  John 110, 114
Curch
  George 57
Currans
  William 84
Curry
  Nathaniel 3, 9, 16,
     20
  Nathl. 3
Curtz
  George 74
Custard
  George 77

Durbin
  John 49
  Samuel 49
  Thomas 109
  William 106
Durckel
  Jacob 96
Duttero
  Balser 104
  Conrad 97, 109,
    113, 118, 122,
    123
Dutterow
  Conrad 125
  George 57
Dutton
  Conrod 57
Duttro
  Balser 76
Duvall
  Alexander 57
  Benjamin 58, 118
  Capt. William 58
  Lewis 57, 58, 89
  Saml. 25
  Samuel 2, 3, 6, 29,
    31
  William 58, 106,
    114, 118, 122,
    123, 125, 126
Dycus
  Philip 58
Dyer
  --- 49
  Capt. Edward 89,
    112
  Christian 44
  Edward 113, 118
Eador
  Abraham 88, 108
Eagle

  Harmon 58
Earbaugh
  Balser 98
Earhart
  Martin 89
Eason
  John 58
Eastburn
  Benjamin 105, 106
Easter
  Adam 50
  George 44, 58
Easterday
  Christian 98
Easton
  John 58
Eastub
  William 44
Eastup
  William 105, 106
Eaton
  John 22
Eaverhart
  Christian 58
Ebernathy
  Wm. 103
Ebert
  Valentine 83
Eck
  John 58
Eckiss
  John 122
Eckus
  John 106
Edden
  Christopher 58
Edelen
  Charles 95
Edes
  Robert 58
Edmonson

  Thos. 26
Edmonston
  James 16
  Ninian 44, 50
  Rachel 50
Edwards
  Mark 25
  Mathew 4, 31
  Matthew 6, 11, 30
Eichelberger
  Leonard 98
Eichenbroad
  Daniel 123
Eighenbroad
  Daniel 123
Eikler
  Ulerich 50
Eison
  Frederick 58
Ekler
  Ulerick 44
Elder
  Aloysius 58
  Arnold 113
  Charles 103
  Guy 76, 97, 98,
    113, 118
  Thomas 76
  William 103, 105,
    113
Elerburten
  William 58
Ellett
  Mark 58
Ellis
  James 12
  John 41
  Saml. 41
  Samuel 58
  Solomon 41
  Zach. 41

Samuel 58
Farquhar
 Allen 58
 Moses 58
 William 58
Farrell
 Kennedy 3, 8, 17,
  24
Farthing
 James P. 112
 James Turtle 90
Fasant
 Samuel 110
Faud
 Barnet 58
Faulkner
 Elisha 99
Faw
 Abraham 72, 73,
  78, 80, 92,
  105, 106, 115
Feaster
 Henry 106, 107,
  109, 126
Fee
 William 7
Ferguson
 John 58, 106, 110,
  118, 122
Ferree
 Solomon 101
Ferrenee
 Wm. 107
Ferro
 Henry 102
Fetherly
 John 58
Fickle
 Mathias 58
Fife
 Abraham 74

James 41
Fight
 Henry 44
Finck
 Philip 96
Fine
 Peter 44, 50, 101
 Philip 98
Finffrock
 George 58
Fink
 Adam 116
 Philip 119
Firestone
 Matthias 58
Fischer
 Adam 58, 124
 David 99
 Margaret 124
Fisher
 Adam 58, 74, 111,
  120
 David 116, 123
 Doctor 109
 Dr. 113
 Dr. Adam 71
 Jacob 75
 Margaret 120
 Martin 58
Fishing Creek 64, 79,
  102, 104
Fister
 Henry 58
Fitzgerald
 Michael 88, 108
Fivecoat
 George 58
Flanagan
 Lackey 79
Flanigan
 Hugh 118, 122

Flannigan
 Hugh 106, 114
Fleatzer
 Jacob 98
Fleck
 Lucas 105, 106, 109
Fleming
 Robert 106, 113,
  114, 117, 118,
  122, 125
 Samuel 105, 106,
  112
 Thomas 109, 113,
  114, 117, 118,
  122, 123, 125
Flemming
 James 58
 Saml. 102
 Samuel 89
 Thomas 76, 81, 105
Fletchal
 John 41
Fletchall
 John 25, 58
 Thomas 5
 Thos. 24
Fletchell
 Thomas 3
Fletcher
 Martin 58, 60, 98,
  128
 Thomas 4
Flickinger
 Peter 94
Flint
 John 44, 50
Flintham
 William 6, 11, 19,
  21, 30
Flinthem
 William 58

Walter 121
Hagar
  Jonathan 7, 29, 50
Hagarty
  Thomas 98
Hager
  Jonathan 3, 59
Hagon
  Edward 76
  Monica 76
  Susannah 76
  Walter 95
Hains
  Michael 75
Hale
  James 102
Haley
  John 98
Hall
  Benjamin 59
  Edward 59
  Elijah 59
  Henry 45
  John Stephen 98
  Leonard 26
  Mary 4
  Michael 59
  Nicholas 113, 118,
    122, 126
  William 50
  William Murdock
    95, 106, 123,
    125-127
  Wm. M. 121
Halligan
  Patrick 2
Hallon
  Batholomew 17
Halt
  Ralph 59
Hamel

John 59
Hamen
  Andrew 77
Hamilton
  Francis 59
  George 18, 89
  Gowen 26
  Ninian 20
Hammer
  John 16
Hammet
  Robert 129
Hammitt
  Robert 80
Hammond
  Charles 32, 50
  George 110
  John 59, 99, 106,
    110, 122
  Nathan 50, 99
  Phillip 9
  Vachel 99
Hamon
  Ormond 91
Hampton Furnace 102
Hanes
  Martin 98
Hanker
  William 60
Hann
  Henry 109
Hanson
  John 11
  Samuel 60
Harbaugh
  Cath. 115
  Catharine 92
  Christian 60
  Francis 60
  George 93, 94
  Jacob 92

John 92
  Ludwick 92
Harbert
  William 19, 60
Harbin
  James 41
Harbine
  Edward Willers 50
Harbough
  Jacob 60
Hardee
  Isaac 21
Harden
  Grove 25, 26
  Samuel 4
Hardesty
  Samuel 60
Hardey
  William 50
Hardin
  Grove 26
  John 60
Harding
  Charles 50, 60
  Elias 90, 96
  Garah 114
  Garey 106, 110
  Gariah 126
  Gary 60, 91, 92
  John 29
  William 90
  Zephaniah 122
  Zepiniah 90
Hardister
  Francis 60
Hardman
  Joseph 4, 24, 28, 45
Hardy
  Sam 41
Hargate
  George Peter 60

158

John 118
William 60
Wm. 26
Hayse
  Jeremiah 60
Haysson
  Jeremiah 26
Hazelton
  George 89
Head
  Biggar 50, 76, 98
  Bigger 9
  Richard 79, 81
  William 60, 79, 81
  William Becket 81
  William Beckwith
    114, 122, 126
  William Edward 60
Headerck
  George 76
Hearnden
  James 10
Heartsooch
  Jno. 103
Heartsook
  John 79
Heater
  Frederick 119
Heath
  Thomas 25
Heaver
  John 78
Heavly
  Michael 60
Hebner
  Johannes 73
Heck
  Balser 98
  Balsor 97
Hedding
  John 24

Hedges
  Charles 81
  George 116
  Jacob 60
  Joseph 60
  Peter 73
  Shadrack 130
Heeter
  Frederick 94
Heffner
  George 106
  John 88
  Michael 106
Hefner
  John 112
Heisly
  Frederick 123, 125,
    126, 129
Helm
  Joseph 60
Hembleton
  Gowen 41
Hempel
  Frederick 73
Henderson
  Archd. 35
  Archibald 34
Hendricks
  Andrew 40
Hendrickson
  Hendrick 60
Henley
  Joseph 8
Hennongirth
  John 60
Henry
  Capt. Nathaniel 92
  Fortnoy 60
  Nathaniel 115, 118
Henwood
  John 41

Hepburn
  John 6, 8, 12, 27,
    28
Herbaugh
  Christ. 103
  Jacob 115
  Ludwick 115
Hergert
  Abraham 60
Herman
  Jacob 105
Hermon
  Marks 60
Hern
  Margaret 45
Herr 74
Herring
  John 60
Herschman
  Mathious 60
Hershberger
  Bernard 60
  Henry 127
Hervin
  Joshua 60
Hess
  Jacob 60
Heugh
  And. 36
  Andrew 13, 35-39
Hevring
  Casper 99
Heyler
  Michael 60
Hickey
  Cornelius 58, 60
  Edmund 60
Hickman
  Arthur 40
  David 41, 60
  Henry 41

Joshua 40, 41
Margaret 60
Solomon 41
Stephen 41
William 41
Willm. 41
Hickrey
  Geo. 97
Higdon
  John 99
Higgins
  John 60
Hildebrand 125
  Martin 50
  Nicholas 97, 98
Hilderbrand
  Martin 45
Hildrebrand
  Christian 102
Hill
  Abm. 60
  Elizabeth 130
  George 92
  Isaac 60
  James 60
  Joseph 7, 30, 101,
    127
  Richard 60, 104
Hilleary
  John 126
  Ralff Crabb 60
  Ralph 106, 110,
    114, 118, 119,
    122, 125-127
  Thomas 24
  Thos. 50
Hillery
  John 94, 101, 119
Hime
  Andrew 60
  Samuel 90

Hinds
  John 72
  Patrick 45
Hine's Tavern 105
Hines
  Anthony 95
  Christopher 73
  Daniel 72
  Henry 72
  Herbert 86
  Philip 97, 99
Hinkle
  Ballsor 60
  Boltzer 60
  John 60
Hinton
  John 101
  Richard 60
  Thomas 60
  William Robert 30
  William Robt. 31
Hisler
  John 50
Hissler
  Michael 86
Hisson
  Peter 50
Hisung
  Adam 60
Hizor
  Frederick 110
Hobbs
  Eli 83
  Ephraim 61
  John 61
  Joseph 61, 63, 87,
    94, 104, 108,
    124
  Leonard 61
Hobbs' Tavern 69
Hobbs

  Leond. 103
  Nicholas 61, 87,
    108
  Sam. 98
  Sarah 66
  Thomas 126
  Widow 60
  William 56, 69, 97,
    98
  Wm. 103
Hobs
  Josua 61
Hockensmith
  Conrod 85
  George 85
  Jacob 85, 99
Hockersmith
  George 97, 98
Hockersmith's Mill 102
Hodgekiss
  Edward 98
Hodgkins
  Edward 97
Hodgkis
  Michael 2
Hodgkiss
  Michael 11
Hoff
  Christopher 82
Hoffman
  Francis 82
  Frederick 88, 112
  Jacob 82, 83, 86
  John 80, 99, 129
Hoggins
  Peter 41
Holland
  Capewell 61
  Capt. 13
  Thomas 13
Holliday

James 74
Holligan
  Pattrick 1
Holmead
  Anthony 39, 61
Holmes
  Hanor 50
Holtshoble
  Fredrick 61
Holtz
  Benedict 61, 76
  Jacob 61, 76
Holtzman
  Frederick 76, 117,
    122, 123, 125,
    127
  Henry 61, 76
  Jacob 98, 127
  John 99
Hoofman
  Henry 127
Hook
  Daniel 106, 110,
    113, 118, 122
  James 103, 104,
    106, 127
  James S. 118
  James Samuel 106,
    110, 122
  Snowden 103
Hooper
  James 72, 92, 115
Hoover
  Adam 61, 74, 129
  Henry 61
  Jacob 61
  John 82
Hopkins
  Benjamin 19
  John 2, 21, 27
  Matthew 14, 24, 27

Matthus 4
Horner
  Richard 61
  Robert 23
  Thomas 61, 76
Horse
  Conrad 76
Horton
  Philip 119
Houbert
  Peter 61
Houck
  John 84
  Peter 102
Houcks
  Jacob 78, 98
  Matthias 82
Houkmson
  Chas. 41
House
  Andrew 5, 61
  George 27, 61
  Jacob 98
  John 28
  William 3, 82, 86,
    129
Houseman
  Jacob 127
Houser
  Isaac 61
  Michael 124
Houstie
  Isaac 61
Houx
  Jacob 98
Howard
  Benjamin 24
  Ephraim 109, 125,
    127
  Gideon 1
  Henry 74

Jno. 1
John 24, 45, 50
Joshua 105, 126
Mathew 6
Michael 119
Philip 20
Phillip 1
Samuel 50
Thos. 26
Howe
  George 61
Hower
  McDaniel 80
Hoy
  Paul 61
Hubberd
  Philip 110
Huff
  George 77
Huffman
  Henry 61
  John 78
  Rudolph 61
Hufford
  Philip 101
Huffstadler
  Ulerick 50
Hufman
  Barbara 17, 21
  John 21
Hughes
  James 99, 110, 118
  Jno. 26
  John 50, 93, 116
  Joseph 114, 118
  Levi 92, 114, 122
Hughs
  Gabriel 31
  James 61
  John 61
Hull

Abram 50
Human
    Jacob 61
Humbart
    Jacob 102
Humbert
    Michael 61
Humer
    John 94
Hummer
    Jacob 61
    John 61, 124
Hunt
    Eleazor 2
    Thomas 2, 11, 29
Hunter
    George 103
Hunting Creek 104
Hurley
    David 50
Hutchcraft
    Thos. 50
Hutchins
    Christopher 79
Hutchzel
    George 73
    Magdalene 73
Hutin
    Frederick 83
Hutton
    John 107
Hutzell
    George 73
Hyat
    Seth 21
Hyatt
    Abednego 112
    Elisha 61
    Obednigo 89
Hyde
    Samuel 50

Hyer
    John 45
Hyler
    George 115
Hyme
    Andrew 61
    David 97, 98
    Lawr. 104
    Lawrence 112
Hymes
    David 61
Hynes
    Rudy 61
Iams
    Plummer 91
Ice
    Frederick 18
Ijams
    Plumer 115
Inch
    Jacob 61
Ingle
    Peter 61
Ingleman
    William 50
Ingram
    William 61
Inman
    Edward 61
Ipe
    Joseph 83
Ipes
    Joseph 83
Ireland
    Alexander 61
Iseminger
    Adam 97
Isenagel
    Henry 125
Isominger
    Adam 98

Israel
    Basil 109
Israel's Creek 101, 103
Israels Creek 54, 55,
    101, 131
Israels Creek Hundred
    69
Ivans
    John 86
J----
    Johannes 78
Jack
    Jeremiah 18, 61
Jackson
    Henry 88, 112
    John 61
    Mary 4
Jacob
    Morda. 23
    Mordecai 16
Jacobs
    Adam 83
    Elizabeth 61
    Jacob 127
    Jno. 30
    John 17-19, 31, 61,
        91, 106, 107,
        109, 110, 113,
        114, 118, 122,
        123, 126, 127
    Joseph 61, 91, 92,
        114
    William 91, 114
James
    Aaron 120
    Benedict 119
    Grifey 61
    John 130
    Joseph 127
    William 91, 115
Jameson

Kune
   Richard 28
Lacefield
   William 1
Ladd
   William 21
Lagaser
   Jacob 62
Laighie
   Laurence 92
Lakea
   Laurence 92
Lakey
   William 15, 24, 28
Lamar
   Alexander 9, 10
   James 51
   Robert 34, 62
   Robt. 26
   Saml. 26
   Thos. 26
   William 126
   William B. 119, 96
Lamb
   Henry 62
   Price 87
   William 62
Lambky
   William 99
Lamburgh
   Henry 80
Lamon
   Jacob 88
Lancaster
   Jno. 23
   Joseph 23
   Thomas 28
Land
   John 2
Landis
   Henry 75, 97, 116,

126
Lane
   Abraham 116
   John 105
Laney
   John 62, 97, 106,
     114
   Mathew 62
   Peter 5
   Teter 5
Lanor
   John 98
Lanos
   John 98
Lantz
   Leonard 81, 84
   William 82, 86
Larain
   John 62
Larkin
   Jno. 7, 11, 30
   John 105
Larkins
   John 45
Larsh
   Valentine 45, 51
Late
   Michael 74, 118,
     122
Laurance
   Geo. William 51
   George William 62
Laurence
   Richard 87
Law
   Patrick 51
Lawrance
   Mary 62
Layman
   Jacob 112
   John 51

Laysur
   Thomas 62
Lazenby
   Henry 51, 62
Leace
   Philip 62
Leakey
   William 1, 22
Lear
   Daniel 112
   Jacob 62
Lease
   George 99
   Jacob 88, 89, 91,
     101, 112, 115
   Philip 78, 79
   William 115
Leaser
   Jacob 108
Leatherman
   Frederick 51
   Godfrey 62, 124
   Henry 62, 118
   Nicholas 62, 102
Lebegh
   Peter 62
Lecroy
   John 5, 10
   L. 10
   Lu. 6
   Lucas 9, 10
   Lukus 5
Lee
   Aaron 62
   James 15
   Philip Ludwell 51
   Robert 62
Leece
   Jacob 62
Leepley
   Peter 97

Leeply
  Peter 98
Lees
  Conrod 87
Leese
  William 92
Legh Furnace 67
Lehay
  Lawr. 115
Lemar
  Alexander 13
  James 45
  Jno. 26
  Robert 62
  Thomas 23
  Thos. 25, 26
Lemaster
  Abraham 62, 105,
    106, 109, 110,
    113, 114, 118,
    123
Lemman
  Jacob 74
Lemmon
  Adam 81
  Geo. 51
Lenham
  Aaron 62
Lenthicum
  Zachariah 62
Letherman
  Henry 62
Letton
  Michael 62
Levens
  Henry 62
Leverit
  Henry 95
Levingstone
  Andrew 62
Levy

David 62, 98
Lewellen
  Samuel 51
Lewellin
  Saml. 45
Lewis
  Charles 45
  Evan 51
  Jonathan 62
Leyster
  John 98
Lick
  Peter 81
Liday
  Henry 62
Lighty
  Adam 62
Lilley
  Richard 109
Lilly
  Samuel 105, 125
Lin--
  Zachariah 101
Lindsey
  John 62
Linganfelter
  Bernard 62, 118
Linganore 64, 69, 109,
  122
Linganore & Sams
  Creek 61
Linganore Chappell
  100
Linganore Ford 100,
  105
Linganore Hundred 67
Lingenfelter
  Valentine 101
Lingo
  James 62
Link

Adam 81
Andrew 62
John 74
Linn
  David 7, 13
  Philip 62
Linnic
  Richard 106
Linthicom
  Joseph 62
Linton
  Samuel 63, 80, 105,
    106, 110, 114,
    118
Lipps
  John 106
Little
  Jacob 93, 116
  Joseph 93, 96, 99,
    116, 125
Little Creek 63
Little Pipe Creek 55,
  56, 58, 59,
  101, 131
Litton
  Caleb 26
  Michael 63
Litzinger
  Philip 45
Livers
  Anthony 126
  Ignatius 98
Livingston
  John 63
Livinston
  Andrew 63
Lochman
  Jacob 106
Lochn
  Danl. 90
Lock

William 91
Marshall
  James 63, 102
  Philip 63
  William 63
Marshall's Branch 102
Marshall's Ford 101
Mart
  Matthias 63
Martin
  Charles 51
  Edmd. 40
  Edmond 45, 51
  Jacob 99
  James 45
  John 51
  John Elias 38
  Lenox 119, 120, 124
  Nehemiah 40
  Thos. 42
Mason
  John 51, 63
  Philip 40
  Robert 75
Massing
  Dr. John Christian 90
Master
  Leigh 51
Mathens
  Chidley 4
Mathewes
  Patrick 30
Mathews
  Geo. 51
  Patrick 28
Matter
  Valentine 63
Matthews
  Chidley 23

Conrad 95
Elizabeth 110
George 45, 101
Henry 126
James 26
Patrick 8
Philip 95
Matthews Lot 24
Matthias
  Joseph 75
Mauduiet
  William 19
Maxwell
  George 14, 21
May
  Jacob 51, 63
  Rowland 45, 51
  William 4, 51
Mayes
  Andrew 51
Maynard
  Henry 110, 114, 118, 122
  Jno. 103
  John 122
  Nathan 63, 83, 87, 108, 109, 113, 114, 118
  Thomas 7, 109
McAlister
  Alexd. 104
  John 82, 84, 85, 87, 109
McAlister's Mill 101
McAllister
  Jno. 108, 109
  John 74
McAtee
  Samuel 63
McAvicker
  Archibald 99

McBride
  James 63
McCaleb
  John 116
  Joseph 116
McCardel
  James 80
McCarte
  Adam 40
McCay
  James 63
  William 80
McClain
  James 63
  John 63, 121
McClann
  William 16
McClarey
  Henry 116
McClary
  Henry 123, 125
  William 45, 51
McCleary
  Henry 105, 107, 111, 119, 125, 126, 128
McCleery
  Henry 128
McClellan
  William 63
McCormack
  Daniel 95
McCoy
  Daniel 63
  James 63
McCrachan
  William 45
McCray
  William 45, 51
McCubbin
  Moses 45

Mummye
  Jacob 84
Munday
  Henry 1, 21, 24,
    31-33
Mundel
  Robert 35
Mundell
  Robt. 36
Munfoord
  William 1, 13
Mung
  Godferett 25
Murdock
  G. 117
  Geo. 107-109, 113,
    117, 121, 125,
    128, 129
  George 109, 111,
    113, 116,
    119-121, 124
  Revd. George 29
  William 82
Murphey
  Philip 51
Murphy
  Charles 64
  James 25, 123
  Philip 46
  Thos. 122
  William 116
Murray
  Joseph 107
Museater
  Christian 91
Musgrove
  Benj. 104
  Benjamin 97, 98,
    110, 113, 118,
    122, 126
  Henry 64

John 64
  Samuel 64
Musser
  Peter 64
Myer
  A-- 104
  Jacob 116
  Jo 105
Myers
  Bostian 106
  Christ. 104
  Christian 51
  George 88, 112
  Henry 64, 129
  Jacob 64, 93
  Joseph 64
Myre
  Conrod 64
Nabors
  Nathan 64
Nail
  Philip 128
Naile
  Frederick 126, 127,
    129
  Philip 97, 126, 129
Nairey
  Andrew 81
Narrison
  Thomas 64
Naughtinger
  Rudy 64
Nave
  Peter 96
Nead
  George 64
Neaff
  Jacob 64
Neal
  Charles 11, 30
  Wm. 41

Neale
  George 46
  Raphael 46
Neall
  Ralph 51
Nearson
  Benjamin 46
Neat
  George 46
Need
  George 64
  Mathias 46
Needham
  Jno. 14, 15, 17
  John 33, 34
  Sarah 51
  William 51
  Wm. 26
Neel 17
  Doctr. Charles 64
Negro
  Bosen 80
  Clarissa 91, 120
  David 131
  Fortune 74
  Grace 127
  Hiaro 91
  Jack 89, 112, 130
  Jacob 87, 91, 108,
    114, 115
  Joe 130
  July 77
  Lydia 130
  Mary 91, 114, 115
  Moses 131
  Paul 79
  Plato 130
  Poll 130
  Rachel 130
  Sam 86
  Steven 91

174

Tom 92
Unnamed 80
Will 131
Zelph 130
Neighbours
Nathan 64
Neill
John 114, 125, 126, 129
Nell
Ann 93, 116
Philip 93
Nellson
Arthur 64
Nelson
Arthur 64, 104
New
Christian 46, 51
Newport
James 88, 89, 108, 112
Newsbaume
Margaret 51
Nichodemas
Henry 100
Nichodemus
Henry 129
Philip 99
Nicholas
Jacob 1
Nicholls
Benjamin 64
Jacob 46
James 64
John 5, 51
Samuel 46
Thomas 24, 46, 64
Nichols
Beckett 64
John 40, 46
Nicholson

Ble. 18
William 64
Nickols
John 64
Nickring
Benjamin 46
Nicolus
Philip 127
Nisbet
Charles 42
Niswan
John 97
Niswanger
John 83, 124, 127
Nixon
Jonathan 64
Noble
Thomas 46
Thos. 51
Nobs
John 42
Noland
Michael 122
Paul 10
Pierce 11
Samuel 64
Thomas 64, 109
Noller
Philip 110
Phillip 73
Nollert
Philip 110, 113, 114
Norres
William 16
Norris
Benj. 75
Benjamin 64
Eliz. 26
John 3, 118
John E. 129

Joseph 64
Nathaniel 109
Thomas 35-37
Thos. 36, 37
William 3, 35, 46
William Seir 65
Norriss
Benjamin 65
Northcraft
Richard 65
Norwood
Richard 65
Nubinger
Andrew 46
Null
Jacob 46
Michael 65, 87, 105, 106, 109, 110, 114, 118, 123, 126
Valentine 93, 116, 123
O'Brian
Perry 88
Tevry 108
O'Hara
Henry 96
O--tts
Conrad 6
Oats
George 76
Peter 76
Obian
Perry 88
Obleman
George 126
Ockerman
Jacob 104
Ocks
Adam 65
Odaniel

John 65
Oden
David John 65
Odonnell
Neale 27
Offut
Sarah 25
Will. 25
Offutt
Easter 23
James 65
Mrs. Sarah 65
Nathaniel 46, 65
Sarah 26
Thomas 65
Thos. 26
William 19
Ogdon
Nehemiah 28
Ogle
Alex 88
Alexander 65, 73,
112
Alexd. 102
Benjamin 65, 86,
92, 95, 99,
105, 109, 114,
115, 118, 120,
122, 125, 126
James 102, 118,
122, 129
Joseph 65, 94, 105,
106, 124
Major Joseph 46
Thomas 65, 81, 98
Thos. 51, 107
William 99
Ogle's Ford 102
Ogle's Mill 102
Ogles on Owens Creek
56

Ogulion
Neal 9, 10, 18
Ogullion
Duncan 24
Neal 1, 5, 9, 18
Oharra
Henry 125
Ohaven
Christopher 65
Oime
John 38
Old
Henry 65
Oldham
William 127
Oliver
John 51
Olliver
Levin 65
Oneal
William 65
Ontz
Ruperd 82
Orbison
Thomas 46
Orme
Jeremiah 65
Moses 65
Orndorff
Christian 65
Henry 65
Peter 99
Osborn
Wm. 42
Oseburn
Thomas 25
Ott
George 105
William 86
Otto
Mathias 65

Oulenbaugh
Adam 65
Ovalman
Henry 86
Jacob 86
Ovelman
George 123, 127
Ovrey
Christian 127
Owen
Edward 23, 26
Jno. 21
John 42, 65
John Jas. 51
Joshua 46, 51
Lawrance 25, 26,
35
Lawrence 23, 25
Rebeckah 98
Robert 65, 97, 98
Robt. 82
Sarah 65
Spicer 42
Thomas 31
Owens
Lawrance 31
Rachel 65
William 110
Owens Creek 56
Owings
Christopher 99
Rachel 65
Richard 65
Samuel 46, 65
William 124
Owins
Rachel 65
O'Donnall
Michael 65
O'Neill
Laurence 51

Abner 95, 107, 111,
116, 120, 124,
128, 130
John 127, 129
William 80, 95, 97,
105, 111, 120,
124, 128
Wm. 98, 100, 105,
107, 116
Rivert
William 46
Road
Jacob 66
Roads
Wm. 42
Roahr
Rudolph 98
Roar
Rudolph 97
Roarer
Samuel 66
Robason
William 66
Robbins
Daniel 52
John 52
Roberson
William 73
Robert
Stephen 46
Roberts
Hugh 17
John 29, 85, 98,
120
Robert 82
Thomas 120
William 52, 66
Robertson
John 85
Robinson
Charles 122

Enoch 5, 10
Geo. 23
James 42, 66
John 103
Joseph 7
Mary 11
Sarah 7
Robonet
Joseph 2
Rock Creek 58, 69
Rock Creek Church 70
Rode
Christian 66
Jacob 66
Rodebeler
Philip 66
Roden
Thomas Newman 6,
31
Rodenbiller
Phillip 66
Rodenpeeler
Philip 107, 114,
122
Rodenpeelor
Philip 105
Rodenpeler
Philip 67
Roderick
Lodowick 67
Roderock
Andrew 67
Rodger
George 67
Rogers
Alexander 67
John 98, 114
Patrick 82
Rohr
Jacob 95
Philip 95

Rollins
Arron 67
Rolls
John 31
Rombarah
Lawrance 46
Roof
Anthony 52
Michael 67
Rose
Edward 95, 121
Rosenplatt
John Harmon 52
Ross
David 11
Doctor David 46
Doctr. David 52
John 1
William 10
Rossell
Jacob 67
Rouse's Ford 102, 103
Row
John 20, 46
Michael 125, 126
Rowe
Aron 82
John 19
Rudecill
Jacob 116
Tobias 98, 118
Rudey
Daniel 67
Rudisill
Jacob 93
Michael 73
Rudoff
Gilbert 80
Rudolph
Gilbert 67
Rue

Staup
George 68
Steel
Elizabeth 119
James 71, 127
Steiner
Jacob 90, 91,
112-114, 121,
122, 125, 126,
129
Stemple
Frederick 97-99
Jacob 104
Stenson
Samuel 87
William 87
Stephenson 17
Daniel 17, 20
Dinel 68
James 47
Sterrett
James 68
Steuart
George 15
Jeremiah 114
Thomas 68
Stevens
Jemima 30
William 91, 115
Willm. 30
Stevenson
Henry 87, 129
James 114, 122,
123
John 68, 110
Richard 68
Thomas 81
Steward
Jeremiah 97
Stewart
Elizabeth 110

William 47
Stickle
Simon 53
Stidley
Jacob 75
Stigar
Andrew 53
Andw. 48
Stilley
Peter 107
Stilly
Peter 129
Stimmell
Jacob 68
Stinnel
Peter 72
Stitely
Jacob 68
Stoddert
Thomas 47
Thos. 53
Stoh
Antoin 83
Stokes
Jerh. 41
William 89, 112
Stolae
Henry 47
Stole
Henry 53
Stone
Adam 68
Henry 47
John 105, 106
Stonecipher
John 126
Stoner
Bened. 101
Catharine 75
Henry 68
John 53, 73-75, 88,

114, 129
Stonesifor
John 129
Stophel
Henry 111
Store
Barbara 116
George 116
Storm
Leonard 98, 109
Leond. 97
Stottlemire
David 68
Stottlemyer
George 68
Stouder
John 104
Stouder's Ford 104
Stouffer
Yelles 94
Stout
John 105
Straffer
Joyham 68
Strawbridge
Robert 26
Street
Francis 42
Strever
Joachim 73
Youcham 84
Stricker
George 68
Michael 68
Strider
Killeon 68
Striker
Michael 68
Strine
Adam 89, 112
Stripe

Jacob 75, 81
Stroope
  William 47, 53
Stuart
  Adam 39
  Dan 42
  George 32
Stuck
  Anthony 72
Stull
  Christophel 75
  Christopher 68, 105
  John 94, 124
Stullman
  John Hance 53
Sugar Loaf 66
Sugar Loaf Mountain
  56
Sugarlands 69
Sumer
  Valentine 68
Sumers
  Valentine 68
Summer
  Valentine 68
Summers
  Felty 68
Sunfrang
  Jacob 47
Swainy
  Edward 68
Swam
  John 42
Swan
  Andrew 68
Swaney
  Edward 47, 53
Swearingan
  Joseph 97
Swearingem
  Charles 68

Van 68
Swearingen
  Joseph 68, 105, 106
  Samuel 68
  Thomas 98
  Van 6, 12, 68, 73,
  103
Swearingen's Tavern
  103
Sweet
  Timothy 40
Swigen
  David 77
Swilley
  Peter 102
Swinford
  Mary 68
Swinson
  John 39
Switezer
  Lawrence 99
Swope
  Benedict 47
Symmer
  Alexander 53
  Andrew 53
Symmers
  Alexander 47
  Andrew 47
Tabeler
  Jacob 127
Tabler
  Melchor 68, 82
  Wilhelm 82
  William 118, 127
Talbart
  Philip 80
Talber
  Peter 82
Talbert
  Henry 42

Thos. 53
Talbott
  William 68
Talbutt
  Robert 97, 98
Tallbert
  Thomas 47
Tanehill
  John 68
Taney
  Joseph 109, 110,
  114
  Ralph 47
Taney Town 103, 104,
  125
Tannehill
  Andrew 14
  Ninian 68
  William 115
  Wm. 23
Tanner
  David 82
  Leon 78
Tannihill
  William 90, 93
Tannyhill
  Andrew 7, 26
Taregksinger
  Samuel 83
Tasker 19
Tavers
  Nicholas 5
Tawney
  Ralph 49
Tawnihill
  Ninian 68
Tayler
  George 47
Taylor
  Charles P. 121
  Charles Philpot 95

Robert 68
Torff
    Jacob 90, 112
Totheral
    Edward 47
Touchstone
    Caleb 7, 30, 47, 53
    Henry 3, 17, 27
    Richard 3, 7, 11,
        17, 30
Toup
    George 96, 124
Town Creek 102
Townsley
    James 85
Tracey
    Alexander 53
    William 68
Trafford
    Edward 18
Trammel
    John 68
Trammell
    Sampson 47
Trammel's Island 57
Tranceway
    Widow 47
Tressler
    Michael 96
Trine
    Philip 68
Tripell
    Christopher 121
Tripple
    Christopher 95
Trisell
    Jacob 22
Trisler
    Goodheart 53
    Michael 124
Trit

Paul 99
Trotter
    John 40
Troup
    Adam 68
    Adom 69
Trout
    Jacob 47, 69, 71,
        73, 80, 109
Trout's Ford 102
Troutman
    Michael 69, 105,
        106, 109, 113,
        122
    Peter 79, 81, 104,
        109, 110, 114,
        123
Troxall
    Jacob 127
    John 82
    Peter 82
Troxell
    Christian 69
Trucks
    George 77, 93, 96,
        105, 116, 125
    John 69, 77, 93,
        116
Trucks' 103
Trueman
    Henry 16
Trundel
    Ann 69
Trundell
    Josiah 69
Trundle
    John 47, 53, 69
Trunnel
    Thomas 69
Trussels
    Goodheart 69

Trux
    George 106, 110
    John 126
Tryor
    Frederick 47
Tucker
    John 69
    Jonathan 69
    William 69
Tulaghpan
    Samuel 53
Tullice
    Henrich 82
Tulse
    James 11
    John 10
Turner
    Charles 69
    Edmond 47
    Mary 119
    Robert 104
    William 69
    William James 116
    Wm. 102
Turst
    Casper 69
Tutaror
    Michael 69
Tutchstone
    Richard 19
Twigg
    Robt. 53
Tyeshoe
    Elizabeth 11
Tyeshue
    Boston 4
Tyshoe
    Sebastian 27
Tyshowe
    Basthin 27
Udia

194

35
Webbster
John 53
Webster
John 47
Thos. 128
Weddel
Peter 69
Weddle
Jacob 69
Weekly
James 83
Weentz
George 70
Welch
Benjamin 53
John 81
Thomas 70
William 53
Welder
Samuel 40
Weller
Jacob 70, 77, 92,
115, 123
Jno. 123
John 77, 92, 115,
123
Welles
Anne 1
Wellor
Jacob 111
Jno. 111
Philip 111
Wells
Alexander 4, 47, 53
James 110, 114,
116, 126
Nathan 2
Samuel 6
Thomas 47, 70
Welsh 125

Infant 93
Mary 93, 116
Nicho. 128
William 8, 30
Welty
John 98
Wentz
George 89, 112
Werner
George 106
John 99, 106
Wertenburgh
Bernard 53
West
Benjamin 29, 97,
124, 127
John 29, 42, 70
Jos. 94, 97
Joseph 70, 109,
119, 124, 129
Stephen 38, 39, 47
Thomas 94
Thomas H. 127
Thomas W. 97
Thos. H. 124
William 29, 47, 53,
70
Westenhaver
Christopher 70
Margaret 76
Westminster Town
Hundred 75
What
Thomas 70
Wheat
Wm. 26
Wheatcroft
Edward 99
Wheeler
George Noble 70,
114, 118, 122

Wheet
William 25
White
Abraham 74
David 70
Henry 98
James 70
John 11, 53, 70
Joseph 70, 127
Leonard 70
Nicholas 83, 93,
105, 115
Robert 26
Whiteneck
John 99, 122, 123,
128
Whitmon
Abram 53
Whitmore
George 70
John 70
Whitsell
Martin 24
Whitting
Thomas 72
Wickham
Col. Nathaniel 34
Henry 94, 124
John 77
Nathan 32
Nathaniel 14, 17,
21, 22, 25-27,
31-35, 47
Widow Barker's 103
Widow Berrier's 104
Widow Tranceway 47
Wiesinger
Peter 53
Wigart
Andrew 70
Wilburn

196

Peter 70
Winter
George 70
Winters
George 75, 85
James 40
Lockland 2
Wise
Francis 48
Jacob 53
Wisner
Ignatious 70
Mary 70
Witers
John 82
Witherow
John 118, 129
Witmore
Benjamin 70
Witterick
George 70
Wivell
Jane 48, 53
Wolf
Paul 70
Wolford
Conrad 70
Wolken
Peter 78
Woltzin
Matthias 83
Wood
Basil 105, 126, 129
Charles 1, 8, 31, 70
Col. Joseph 112,
120
Henry 110, 113,
114, 118, 125,
126
James 122
John 70

Jonathan 105, 109
Jos. 36, 37
Joseph 1, 9, 15,
34-39, 70, 75,
89, 105, 108,
109, 122, 128
Richard 70, 79
Robert 70
Thomas 70
William 70, 91, 115
Woods
Col. 89, 101, 103
Joseph 54
Robert 104
Woods' Mill 101, 103,
104
Woodward
Francis 70
Wooford
Jno. 26
Woolf
Jacob 123
John 48
Paul 64, 70
Woolfkill
Conrad 70
Woolfs
Paul 63
Woolf's Tavern 64
Wooten
T. Sprigg 39
Wootton
Thomas Sprigg 39
Worner
George 70
Worthington
John 48
Wotton
Thomas Sprigg 70
Wray
Rebecca 4

Wright
Amos 70
George 83
Jesse 99
John 97
Joseph 103
Wyat
Edward 2
Wyatt
Edward 2, 16
Wybright
Jacob 26
Wyvill
William 19
Yates
Ignatius 127
Yeater
Peter 53
Yengland
John 123
Yengling
John 99
Yesterday
Christian 70, 97,
98, 101, 104,
127
Conrad 96, 119
Francis 96, 119
Ludwick 96, 119
Yingling
Frederick 96, 125
Jacob 96, 125
Yoot
Harman 70
York Road 101, 103
Yost
Harmon 73
John Harmon 125
Ludowick 64
Young 19, 106
J. 117

582875

Made in the USA